EMERGING ISSUES IN
ECONOMIC DEVELOPMENT

EMERGING ISSUES IN ECONOMIC DEVELOPMENT

A CONTEMPORARY THEORETICAL PERSPECTIVE

Essays in honour of
Dipankar Dasgupta and Amitava Bose

edited by
SUGATA MARJIT
AND
MEENAKSHI RAJEEV

OXFORD
UNIVERSITY PRESS

OXFORD
UNIVERSITY PRESS

Oxford University Press is a department of the University of Oxford.
It furthers the University's objective of excellence in research, scholarship,
and education by publishing worldwide. Oxford is a registered trademark of
Oxford University Press in the UK and in certain other countries

Published in India by
Oxford University Press
YMCA Library Building, 1 Jai Singh Road, New Delhi 110001, India

© Oxford University Press 2014

The moral rights of the authors have been asserted

First published in 2014

All rights reserved. No part of this publication may be reproduced, stored in
a retrieval system, or transmitted, in any form or by any means, without the
prior permission in writing of Oxford University Press, or as expressly permitted
by law, by licence, or under terms agreed with the appropriate reprographics
rights organization. Enquiries concerning reproduction outside the scope of the
above should be sent to the Rights Department, Oxford University Press, at the
address above

You must not circulate this work in any other form
and you must impose this same condition on any acquirer

ISBN-13: 978-0-19-809906-2
ISBN-10: 0-19-809906-1

Typeset in 11/13.2 Adobe Garamond Pro
by Excellent Laser Typesetters, Pitampura, Delhi 110 034
Printed in India by G.H. Prints Pvt. Ltd, New Delhi 110 020

Contents

Foreword *by Kazuo Nishimura* vii

Acknowledgements ix

Introduction xi
Sugata Marjit and Meenakshi Rajeev

SECTION I CORRUPTION, INFORMATION, AND TRANSPARENCY

1. When Is Competitive Behaviour a Best Response? 3
   Anjan Mukherji

2. Many Facets of Corruption 21
   Mukul Majumdar and Seung Han Yoo

SECTION II GROWTH, POVERTY, AND MARKETS

3. Inefficiency and the Golden Rule: Phelps–Koopmans Revisited 43
   Tapan Mitra and Debraj Ray

4. A Multidimensional Poverty Index 57
   Asis Kumar Banerjee

5. Transaction Costs and Optimal Market Structure 81
   Meenakshi Rajeev

6. The Determination of Profits 106
   Romar Correa

SECTION III   INFORMAL CREDIT AND MICRO-FINANCE

7   Vertical Linkage between Formal and Informal Credit
    Markets: Corruption and Credit Subsidy Policy   117
    Sarbajit Chaudhuri and Krishnendu Ghosh Dastidar

8   Sequential Lending: Dynamic Institutions
    and Micro-finance   135
    Prabal Roy Chowdhury

SECTION IV   DEMOCRACY AND DEVELOPMENT

9   Democracy, Development, and the Informal Sector   153
    Abhirup Sarkar

10 Efficient and Equilibrium Federation Structures
    with Externalities   167
    Gordon Myers and Abhijit Sengupta

SECTION V   BARGAINING, TECHNOLOGY TRANSFER, AND DETERRENCE

11 Markets with Bilateral Bargaining and
    Incomplete Information   193
    Kalyan Chatterjee and Bhaskar Dutta

12 Technology Transfer as a Means to Combat
    Global Warming   218
    *Vivekananda Mukherjee, Dirk T.G. Rübbelke, and
    Tilak Sanyal*

13 Early Withdrawal of Patented Drugs as an
    Entry-deterring Device   248
    Sugata Marjit, Tarun Kabiraj, and Arijita Dutta

14 Entry Deterrence in Banking: The Role of Cost
    Asymmetry and Adverse Selection   265
    Indrajit Mallick, Sugata Marjit, and Hamid Beladi

About the Editors and Contributors   281
Index   287

Foreword

Emerging nations, worldwide, are going through significant changes as a result of economic reforms and transition to market-driven economy. While the implications of some of these changes are yet to be fully comprehended by the politicians and the academicians alike, no doubt such changes raise a set of challenges for the state as well as for the discipline. For example, while one expects competition, withdrawal of the state, and adoption of a market-driven economy to lead to more transparency and less corruption, corruption-related issues continue to disturb many developing economies, including India. Theoretically, then questions such as 'why corruption persists in a competitive world', become relevant. Similarly, in the process of reform, many of the developing economies are experiencing high-income growth, yet poverty and inequality refuse to recede from some of these countries. In a related area, modelling of the informal market, especially informality in the credit market, becomes a challenging task for the theoreticians. Thus, the various facets of economic theory have a direct bearing on the understanding of critical development issues.

In this backdrop it is rewarding to find a volume that is in honour of Dipankar Dasgupta and Amitava Bose, both respected and distinguished economists from the University of Rochester. This excellent collection of theoretical works on economic development is a valuable resource for graduate and upper-level undergraduate students.

Kazuo Nishimura
Professor
Institute of Economic Research, Kyoto University

Acknowledgements

We are grateful to the Reserve Bank of India (RBI) for its endowment at the Centre for Studies in Social Sciences, Calcutta, and Institute for Social and Economic Change, Bangalore, which provided the financial support to carry forward this work. We also thank our respective institutes for the support we have received in this duration. However, the views expressed in this book are strictly our own and are not attributable to the RBI.

Introduction

Sugata Marjit and Meenakshi Rajeev

Developing countries all around the globe have been trying to adopt market-driven institutional systems. As the pace of economic reforms gains momentum, it is becoming increasingly evident that age-old theoretical concerns are still as credible as ever. Policies meant to raise levels of income quite often sink in the quagmire of corruption. As the growth rate picks up in countries such as India and China, a sustained threat of inflation haunts such a process. There was a time when economists were concerned as well as excited about managing scarce foreign exchange resources. In contrast, managing the plentiful inflow of foreign exchange has now become a critical policy issue. Once micro-finance was hailed as the saviour of the poor; now new issues related to incentive mechanisms affecting the projects are subjected to close scrutiny. Informality in economic theory was simply a non-existent term. However, recent theoretical work on informal economic arrangements, including the informal credit system, has engaged the attention of a substantial number of researchers. Literature on industrial organization is getting enriched with innovative models of entry deterrence in the healthcare business and strategic interactions related to environment-friendly technology. Conceptual issues continue to surprise us not only in terms of their pure theoretical form but also in terms of practice such as in banking and finance.

These are different aspects of economic theory which have a direct bearing on the ongoing process of development. Some of these concerns are traditional, but are brought to the context with new twists and turns, while some others are related to more recent developments in the field. A clear understanding of these issues is absolutely essential if one attempts to extend the frontier of current knowledge. The gap between emerging empirical concerns of development and the existing and updated theoretical understanding needs to be bridged, and this is the precise purpose of this volume. We are trying to bring together some of the leading theorists on a single platform for a rigorous discussion on these issues. It is hoped that this volume, written in honour of two of India's most outstanding teachers of economic theory, Dipankar Dasgupta and Amitava Bose, will be both illuminating and purposeful.

About Dipankar Dasgupta and Amitava Bose

Professors Dipankar Dasgupta and Amitava Bose have been a major force in motivating a large number of young students to take up economics as their career discipline. In particular, they have been instrumental in generating and sustaining the interest of these young scholars in the field of economic theory. They acted as mentors for young teachers and researchers guiding them in interpreting complex arguments as both of them were groomed in the highest order of training in economic theory. They spent most of their working life in Kolkata, but students, teachers, and researchers all around the globe have benefited from them. This is the reason why the current volume could readily get so many illustrious contributors. While Professors Dasgupta and Bose have different styles of engagement with the academic world, both are outstanding theoreticians. This volume is a token of appreciation for their commitment to serious scholarship.

Dipankar Dasgupta completed his PhD in Economics from the University of Rochester in 1972. His thesis, titled 'On Optimal Economic Growth', was supervised by the noted economists J.W. Friedman and L.W. McKenzie. He began his academic career as an

Assistant Lecturer in the Department of Economics at the University of Rochester and then at the University of York, Canada, before returning permanently to India to join the Indian Statistical Institute, Calcutta. He remained affiliated to this institute for more than three decades, until he retired as a full professor in 2006. He has also taught and researched in the capacities of professor and visiting scholar at many prominent universities in Japan, Hong Kong, and India.

Professor Dasgupta has authored three books on macroeconomics: *The Macroeconomy: A Text Book View* (1997), *Growth Theory: Solow and His Modern Exponents* (2005), and *Modern Growth Theory* (2010). All the books, published by Oxford University Press, have received high accolades from the academic fraternity. His articles have been published in various national and international journals of high repute as also in various edited volumes. A dedicated scholar and acclaimed by his students as an inspiring teacher of economics, he is also a brilliant expositor of the subject.

On the personal front, Professor Dasgupta has an avid interest in the arts, music, literature, and languages. He enjoys singing semi-classical Bengali songs, writes creatively in both English and Bengali, maintains an active blog, and is proficient in Japanese. He also writes for the print media and is often consulted by the electronic media on socio-economic matters.

Amitava Bose received his MA degree from the Delhi School of Economics, University of Delhi, and a PhD in Economics in 1974 from the University of Rochester, under the supervision of noted economist J.W. Friedman. In his PhD thesis, titled 'Pareto Optimal Consumption Loans With or Without Production', Bose completely characterized Pareto-optimality for both the pure exchange and the production models. After having completing his PhD, Bose returned to Calcutta and joined Indian Institute of Management Calcutta (IIMC). He has been associated with this institute since then, first as an Assistant Professor and then as a full Professor before becoming the Director of IIMC in 1997. He has also remained affiliated to various other institutes of repute in India and abroad. Currently he is the Chairman of the Board of Governors of the Centre for Studies in Social Sciences, Calcutta.

His articles have been published in various reputed international and national journals as well as in several edited volumes. His paper

'Short Period Equilibrium in a Less Developed Economy', which appeared in a volume edited by Professor Mihir Rakshit, is a great contribution to the literature. Bose has also co-edited two volumes for Oxford University Press India. He is considered a brilliant teacher by his students. As a recognition of his contribution to the field of economic research, Bose was awarded the Panchanan Chakraborty Memorial Award by the Bengal Economic Association in 1995. On the personal front, Bose likes to call himself a 'laid-back but, private person, fond of the arts', who loves to be surrounded by family and friends.

Overview of the Volume

The book is divided into five sections highlighting five different themes, with each section containing chapters devoted to that theme.

The first section, dealing with the issue of corruption, contains two chapters—one by Anjan Mukherji and the other by Mukul Majumdar and Seung Han Yoo. While the former deals with the intrinsic problems of maintaining a competitive equilibrium, with non-enforceable contracts binding the agents to choose a competitive response, the latter deals with influence peddling.

The idea of Mukherji's chapter is clearly brought out by the following statement:

> It should thus be noted that even if the market forces or the Invisible Hand manages to equilibrate markets, unless the regulators do their jobs of enforcing the controls properly, competitive transactions will not occur since agents can hope to be better off by doing something else provided they can get away with it. Thus competitive behaviour is not incentive compatible, in general. What will take place are transactions which involve various 'shady' practices (as compared to the competitive transactions) and consequently the existence of 'scams' of various types would be observed.

Competitive strategy may not be the best response for agents in an environment where supernormal profits can be made by hurting others. Mukherji looks at the problem of corruption essentially as an arbitrage opportunity in the presence of institutional distortions.

While competitive equilibrium or competition per se is always in the background of policymaking as the first best choice, the chapter shows that with a slight twist in the institutional assumption, the competitive outcome may become strategically untenable. Scams or financial scandals are always consequences of a process which fails to punish non-competitive responses. Generically, this is a very interesting result. That scams are inherent in a competitive system and one needs a very careful institutional design to thwart such possibilities, is elegantly borne out by the chapter.

The chapter by Majumdar and Yoo focuses on 'revolving doors' that open up the possibility that a public servant may be negligent in enforcing the rule of law for possible future personal gains. A game-theoretic model of interaction between a track of bureaucrats and multiple firms is presented to highlight the issue and its important implications. The unique point of the chapter is its reiteration of the idea that senior public servants may engage in distributing favours to firms during their tenures because of promises of post-retirement assignments to them. It is important to understand the downside of such arrangements, such as the appointment of a former US Secretary of Treasury as a top man in a private bank. In countries where corruption is rampant and clandestine, alliances of this genre are the order of the day. The conventional view that such post-retirement possibilities have to be severely restricted is gaining increasing acceptance. Bringing in such considerations in a formal model of corruption, the authors make a substantial contribution to the existing literature. However, the authors argue that such restrictions may not have the desired effect, and increasing penalty rates is the only way out. Another interesting discussion in the chapter pertains to policies of single window clearance and rotation of bureaucrats. Both of these popular policies might not usher in greater efficiency. The idea of rotation is related to the concept of transfer of bureaucrats in the existing literature (Marjit et al. 2000). It is also argued that bureaucrats who are fully informed regarding the type of agents may actually work against the objective of the principal, and therefore lack of information sometimes is desirable.

Section II has four chapters on growth, poverty, and markets, that are dealt with a theoretical perspective. While the chapter by Tapan Mitra and Debraj Ray demonstrates that over accumulation of capital may not necessarily indicate an inefficient allocation of resources over time, Asis Banerjee provides us with a new multi-dimensional poverty index (MPI), satisfying certain desirable properties. Meenakshi Rajeev deals with the issue of coexistence of multiple forms of markets in a developing economy. While Rajeev's chapter deals with commodity markets, the chapter by Romar Correa concentrates on financial markets. Correa emphasizes the need to distinguish activities of financial institutions that support production from investment-related activities through money markets.

The Phelps–Koopmans theorem is one of the more well-known results on intertemporal effciency. Mitra and Ray examine the validity of this theorem in the context of a class of non-convex production functions. Given the fact that empirical reality often reveals non-convexity while substantial literature in this area tends to ignore this possibility, the motivation behind the chapter is quite clear. The authors claim that the failure of the Phelps–Koopmans theorem with non-convex technologies is quite robust. The chapter's main contribution is in showing that if the net output function has any increasing segment between the golden rule and maximum sustainable capital stock, the Phelps–Koopmans theorem necessarily fails to hold. That is, in such cases, it is always possible to find an efficient program in which capital stocks ultimately lie above (and stay bounded away from) the golden rule.

Multi-dimensional poverty measures have attracted a lot of research as a single attribute of poverty is too narrow an element for policymakers to work with. The endeavour therefore is to construct indices that have more than one or multiple components. There are several approaches available in literature. Banerjee, in his chapter in this volume, introduces a new condition, which surprisingly no earlier work has dealt with. The condition introduced here, Prioritization of Attributes under Comonotonicity (PAC), roughly states that if the poverty matrix is comonotonic, attribute measures move together, and, if the individuals are more deprived w.r.t. attribute i than w.r.t. attribute j, a reduction of individuals' deprivation levels to some target level w.r.t. i should be considered to be more beneficial (in terms of reduction of MPI) than the reduction of the individuals' deprivations w.r.t. j to the same target level. This means that if the poor are more deprived in terms of access to education than in terms of health, increasing such access in education by 10 per cent will be better than increasing such access in health by 10 per cent and the rate of poverty or deprivation must go down more in the first case. The index proposed in the chapter is shown to be a multi-dimensional generalization of the widely used uni-dimensional index by Foster, Greer, and Thorbecke. Existing literature on MPIs does not seem to contain an example of an index satisfying a number of axioms discussed in the chapter.

Apart from the new index that Banerjee suggests, the new condition (PAC) is of remarkable significance in so far as allocation of resources towards targeted poverty reduction is concerned. Public resources are always scarce and one needs to be extra careful in terms of their best possible use. Any such policy leading to a decline in the poverty index, as proposed in this chapter, should mean that the relative importance of attributes is naturally factored in. This is an interesting idea that requires further pursuance.

The third chapter by Rajeev examines the conditions under which different market forms can prevail in a developing economy. The chapter considers a competitive equilibrium setup where the agents are trying to attain their consumption goods, starting from their production goods, through a decentralized exchange process. In a dynamic game-theoretic framework, the chapter highlights the role of the social institution of markets in facilitating exchange. Beginning with a setup of pair-wise commodity markets, the chapter demonstrates how, depending on the level of transaction costs associated with a market setup (synonymously, trading posts), an appropriate trading strategy emerges and makes some markets non-functioning in equilibrium. In literature, many authors have considered a pure random search for a complementary trading partner to execute trade. Such trading arrangements, no doubt, are more time consuming. However, even though a market setup can help buyers and sellers to quickly identify each other, in developing countries, one often observes pure random search in the form of hawkers trying to sell their fares by calling out or approaching people individually. In this context, it can be shown that a pure random search for a complementary trading partner can coexist with a market setup in equilibrium.

While, on the one hand, a random search to explore trading possibilities prevails in the presence of pair-wise markets (trading posts), on the other hand, there are markets where many commodities are traded simultaneously (à la supermarket) and are preferred over pair-wise trading posts (as in specialized local shops). Rajeev's chapter identifies the constraints under which a multi-commodity market may be preferred over a limited commodity market in a steady state Nash equilibrium. In other words, it considers important conditions under which a multi-commodity so-called supermarket may drive away a limited-commodity local shop. This exercise assumes significance in the face of the recent debate in India about allowing foreign direct investment (FDI) in the retail sector, which can have a distributional impact on income.

The fourth chapter in this section by Romar Correa deals with the problem of accounting for profits in a capitalist economy. The chapter shows aggregate profits as a part of the solution of a difference equation in the central bank's funding of economic activity which, in turn, can get affected by capital gains on long-term government bonds. The recent financial crises which originated in the US motivated the author to deliberate on this issue. The dilemma that has been highlighted in the chapter is how to distinguish between profits generated in the financial circulation from profits earned on the production of goods and services. The author argues that it is necessary to emphasize the distinction between banks supporting production and inventory accumulation and long-term investments backed by financial institutions through money market funds.

Concentrating on the same financial-market-related issues, Section III deals with an important institutional mechanism for enhancing growth and poverty alleviation—the credit institution—which has its own distinguishing features in a developing economy. Even though the Indian banking sector has grown enormously, the poor in India still do not get the desired access to the formal banking network. Given this background, providing financial services using the model of group lending with joint liability is perceived as an effective approach to ending financial exclusion of the poor and the weaker sections of society. However, such an institution will be successful only if borrowers take up well-thought-out income-generating projects, which would help them make timely repayments. Roy Chowdhury's chapter deals with this critical issue of repayment and examines how sequential lending schemes may be used for proper monitoring. The other chapter in this section, contributed by Chaudhuri and Dastidar, is also concerned with the general problem of accessibility to credit by the poor. Further, given the fact that corruption is an issue of immense significance for India today, expectedly, a number of chapters in this volume are concerned with this aspect some way or the other; and this chapter touches on the issue as well.

The first chapter by Chaudhuri and Dastidar models corruptive activities on the part of a bank official in making credit accessible to a certain section of borrowers who may relend such funds in the informal credit market. The problem is posed in a game-theoretic framework consisting of three stages: the dominant moneylender (visualized as a Stackelberg leader) first decides the informal interest rate (to be paid by the final borrowers); then the bank officials determine the level of a bribe; and finally the smaller borrowers (perceived as followers) determine the level of borrowing from banks for relending purposes. Given this setting, it has been established that under reasonable parametric restrictions, a credit subsidy policy, which ensures an increase in the supply of institutional credit, is likely to lower the informal sector interest rate by enhancing competition in the system. The chapter subsequently throws up an interesting result: it shows that change in the formal sector interest rate will have no effect on the informal sector's rate of interest. However, it is argued that anti-corruption measures, introduced through an increase in penalty for taking a bribe, unambiguously lower the interest rate in the informal credit market, and thereby make credit available to the poor at a lower interest rate. Finally, the effects of alternative policies on the incomes of different economic agents are also examined in the chapter.

Micro-finance is a financial intermediation built around the premise that the poor are creditworthy. A study of the functioning of micro-finance institutions assumes considerable importance in the context of countries such as India, especially after suicides committed by borrowers in states such as Andhra Pradesh (see Rajeev 2011) due to their inability to repay their loans. No doubt, self monitoring and joint liability lending under micro-finance have been successful to a large extent in tackling the non-repayment problem faced by lending institutions while lending to the poor. The chapter by Roy Chowdhury rightly discusses the type of projects that may be taken up with borrowed funds that will be productive and also empower the borrower to make timely repayments. Generally, a profit-maximizing lending agency may not lend to a borrower opting for a non-profitable or less-productive project. Consequently, the subset of poor borrowers with lower productivity projects may find it difficult to access the credit market even through micro-finance institutions (Aniket 2011). However, if the loans are made sequential, with some members receiving the loans earlier than the others, and subsequent borrowers receiving their loans only if the earlier borrowers have been successful in their repayments, then a different paradigm will emerge. The chapter shows that a sequential lending scheme leads to positive assortative matching whereby good borrowers group with good borrowers and bad borrowers group with bad borrowers and derive conditions under which a micro-finance institution finds it feasible to lend to the group.

While an economic institution—financial or otherwise—can influence growth and its distributional outcomes, political forces are equally critical for economic growth and development. The next section titled 'Democracy and Development' concentrates on development issues from a political perspective. There are two chapters in this section. The first chapter by Sarkar theoretically accepts a federal structure of governance, but asks whether a democratically elected government within a federal structure always acts for the benefit of citizens. The theoretical formulation by Sarkar demonstrates that it is to the advantage of the ruling government to keep a large section of the population in a less-privileged informal sector in order to be able to extend political patronage in exchange for votes. The second chapter by Myers and Sengupta deals with the issues of sustainability and efficiency of the federal form of governance system.

Most federations in the world today have a democratic form of governance. India, which is termed as a 'holding together federation' (Stepan 1999), is one of the largest democracies. One important question that arises in this context is whether a democracy can be really helpful in achieving economic development. There is substantial literature that examines the relation between democracy and economic performance. Liberal thinkers often emphasize that economic freedom, as offered by a free market, and political freedom, as granted by a democracy, are mutually reinforcing. But there are other scholars who are not so convinced. For example, Barro (1994) finds that the overall effect of democracy on growth is weakly negative and it can be non-linear. More precisely, a higher level of democracy enhances growth at low levels of political freedom but the opposite holds true when a moderate level of political freedom has already been achieved. Bardhan (1993) clearly states that there is no conclusive evidence to state whether democracy fosters or hinders economic growth. The chapter by Abhirup Sarkar deals with this issue from a different standpoint; it illustrates yet another channel through which a democratic country without well-defined property rights can affect economic efficiency. In a developing country, due to lack of well-defined property rights coupled with inadequate legal protection, a considerable proportion of the population will have to depend on political favours. In a democracy, with universal franchise, the ruling party may wish to keep this section of the population dependent on political favours for a life time, which can subsequently hinder economic development. It also illustrates the role of informal institutions in determining political incentives and economic performance in a less-developed country in terms of a model of electoral competition.

In a country like India, where a large proportion of the people depends on informal employment, applicability of the model by Sarkar can be easily perceived. As Sarkar writes:

> In the absence of a secured formal sector job, they are compelled to sell their votes, the only endowment they have apart from labour, for economic survival. The ruling party takes advantage of this dependence to secure votes in exchange of political favours. This, in turn, creates an incentive for the ruling government to maintain a large informal sector. As a result, universal franchise might prove inefficient for less developed countries.

The theoretical model developed in the chapter considers infrastructure as a crucial variable, the level of which is decided by the ruling government, which, in turn, determines capital inflow to a region on which hinges formal sector employment. One important result that has been derived from the model is that even if the ruling government and the voters in the formal sector have a preference for infrastructural investment, as long as the ruling government also cares for re-elections, there is a possibility of sub-optimal investment in infrastructure.

Sarkar's argument is also related to the strategic policy of a poor, welfare state to nurture informal or unorganized sector as a substitute for social security. Violation of property rights is tolerated and public space is leniently doled out so that the poor can also make a living. While in Sarkar's chapter, informality guarantees votes for re-elections, in a related paper Marjit et al. (2006) theorize the existence of such a sector as an implicit social subsidy and transfer.

In one of the recent papers, Gupta and Panagariya (2011), by analysing the voting pattern of the 2009 Lok Sabha elections in India, show that better growth performance at the level of states helps an incumbent to get re-elected. However, we can counter this view by citing the experience of states like Karnataka under the Congress regime (during 1999–2004) or Maharashtra, where economic performance did not help the party in power electorally. Economic performance, as perceived by a voter, may actually be different from the concept of growth defined by economics. Thus, there may be a need to examine other factors such as law and order conditions and the extent of unorganized activities to understand voters' preferences. Future research can concentrate in these areas.

Apart from the issues highlighted by Sarkar there may be other problems of a federal structure of governance system. Historically, it has been seen in the case of many countries that there had been considerable coordination problems among the states or colonies that constitute a country today. These problems were due to the existence of different types of national defence setups, different tariff regulations, currency in circulation, etc., across federating territories. Needless to say, in order to form a federation, the constituent states need to enter into a binding covenant to coordinate their actions, which is indeed a difficult process, and pre-play communications are a necessary pre-requisite for forming a federation. The chapter by Myers and Sengupta on federation structures develops a framework to arrive at an equilibrium model of forming a federation. One of the major objectives of the chapter, which uses the concept of coalition proof Nash equilibrium, is to arrive at conditions under which a grand federal structure constituting of all states can be founded as an equilibrium structure. More specifically, the chapter establishes that a grand federation structure can be supported as a coalition-proof equilibrium, though such a formation need not be efficient. Further, the framework developed by Myers and Sengupta can be utilized to probe certain pertinent issues. For example, if the population of each member country needs to give permission to introduce certain changes in the existing constitution, what additional restrictions become necessary for the sustainability of a grand federation with a structural equilibrium?

The last section titled 'Bargaining, Technology Transfer, and Deterrence' provides a micro-perspective on how certain strategies or actions taken by different decision-making agents or parties can impact sector-specific outcomes, especially by deterring healthy competition and, in turn, affect overall growth and development. Among the four important chapters in this section, the first one by Kalyan Chatterjee and Bhaskar Dutta discusses bargaining with incomplete information amongst multiple buyers and sellers and examines the equilibrium outcomes under varying conditions. Another chapter in this section, contributed by Indrajit Mallick, Sugata Marjit, and Hamid Beladi, also focuses on information by considering an asymmetric information situation in the context of the banking industry and theoretically demonstrates how such asymmetric information regarding costs involved in running a bank may in turn deter entry into the industry. The third chapter, by Marjit, Kabiraj, and Dutta, deals with the entry deterrence problem for the pharmaceutical industry. This chapter shows that a drug company enjoying patent rights over a product may even withdraw the product from the market ahead of expiry of its patent rights, in order to deter subsequent entry of other firms in the market that may produce generic substitutes, possibly using a more efficient technology. The chapter by Mukherjee, Rübbelke, and Sanyal also concentrates on technology issues but in the context of environment and its protection. By introducing the possibility of trade between an advanced nation and other developing nations, the chapter discusses conditions, for both autarky and free-trade situations, under which transfer of more environmentally sound technology can successfully stabilize global emission levels.

The first chapter in this section by Kalyan Chatterjee and Bhaskar Dutta studies the relationship between bargaining and competition with incomplete information. They consider a model with two uninformed and identical buyers and two sellers. One of the sellers knows the reservation price, which can be either low or high. The other seller's reservation price is commonly known to be in between the low and high values of the privately informed seller. Buyers move in sequence and make offers, with the second buyer observing the offer made by the first buyer. The sellers respond simultaneously. They show that there are two types of (perfect Bayesian) equilibria. In the first equilibrium, the buyer who moves second does better, but in the second equilibrium, both buyers' expected payoffs are equalized, and the price received by the seller with the known reservation value is determined entirely by the equilibrium of the two-player game between a single buyer and an informed seller. The authors also discuss extensions of the model to multiple buyers and sellers, and to cases where both sellers are privately informed.

Chatterjee and Dutta's chapter has wide applicability in any kind of negotiation involving multiple buyers and sellers. For example, this becomes quite evident in cases where more than one country confronts procurement decisions from multiple firms. In bidding for a project, the strategic decision to move first becomes critical and this chapter bares the essentials behind such decision making.

The chapter by Mukherjee, Rübbelke, and Sanyal also deals with the procurement-related issues—in particular, with respect to technology. The chapter concentrates on technology transfer as a means of combating global warming and deals with the issue of involving developing nations in the endeavour of protecting the environment against climate change. The model considered in the chapter incorporates an immobile polluting intermediate good in the production technology, where two nations—one developed and the other developing—are exploring potential trade benefits between them. Both the countries have the technology to abate pollution, but the developed North has a better technology than the South and there exists the possibility of technology transfer from the North to the South. It is assumed that the North has a comparative advantage in the production of relatively less pollution-intensive good 2, while the South has a comparative advantage in the production of the relatively more pollution-intensive good 1. This pattern of comparative advantage determines the pattern of production specialization by the countries in the trading equilibrium.

Since the main responsibility for combating global warming is largely assigned to industrialized countries, the chapter assumes that it is the North that is committed to stabilizing the global emission levels while the South faces no abatement obligations. The necessary conditions have been visualized in this framework, both under autarky and free trade, for which the transfer of technology successfully stabilizes global emission levels. Subsequently, conditions are also derived under which the South is willing to accept technology transfers. In the case of free trade, all possible configurations of complete and incomplete specializations of production of goods are taken into account to identify the success of pollution control.

It is further argued in the chapter that technology transfer induces the South to increase the output of commodity 1 and to reduce the output of commodity 2. In this case it gains some utility from increased consumption of commodity 1 but also loses some utility due to reduction in its consumption of commodity 2. The South accepts the technology transfer only when its overall gain in utility is positive. This is not the case when the output elasticity of commodity 1 is very low, showing that overall utility, the subsequent level of production, and the resulting level of pollution, depends critically on output elasticity.

An OECD report (1994), dealing with the issue of export of clean technology from an OECD country to a developing nation, talks about the government's assistance in terms of loans with preferential terms or grants to developing countries. The model developed in this chapter may be further extended to deal with such important research issues.

The next chapter by Marjit, Kabiraj, and Dutta, titled 'Early Withdrawal of Patented Drugs as an Entry-deterring Device', deals with the issues of innovation, patenting, and subsequent withdrawal of patented products from the market as a strategic move. The chapter concentrates on the lifeline industry, which is pharmaceuticals. The model in the chapter has been developed while keeping in mind changes in the GATT-based patent system faced by developing countries like India that mandates a uniform patent protection law for all products including pharmaceuticals, genetically engineered organisms, and plants and animal varieties for 20 years.

Changes in the policy environment have sparked considerable debate, and pharmaceutical associations such as the India Drug Manufacturing Association (IDMA) and scholars such as Chaudhuri (2005) and Watal (1997) have argued that the policy change will be detrimental to the further development of the Indian generic industry which has always followed the strategy of imitation for its growth. This chapter constructs a dynamic model to highlight another potential problem for existing smaller firms in the market or a new entrant, which is caused by early withdrawal of a drug from the market by a large firm. The model is based on certain empirical findings from a survey conducted by Dutta. It establishes that it may be optimal for a firm having patent rights to withdraw a drug from the market before expiry of the patent period. Early withdrawal of the patented drug increases entry costs of potential entrants with generic substitutes. When a drug is out of circulation, a new entrant has to spend more to persuade doctors to prescribe an out-of-circulation drug. But early termination also comes with a cost as the incumbent firm has to forego a certain amount of profits that it could have otherwise earned. This trade-off, in turn, determines the optimal termination period which is dependent on certain parameters of the model, including the length of the patent period, cost of introduction, and promotion of the new drug.

The last chapter in this section also discusses the issue of entry deterrence on the basis of asymmetric information. When it comes to the role of information, resulting moral hazard, and adverse selection problem, the banking sector assumes prime importance. The chapter by Mallick, Marjit, and Beladi considers the issue of entry barriers in an industrial organization's framework, taking into account information asymmetry and adverse selection problems to understand why the banking sector is fragmented even in developed countries. What prevents the entry of new banks into the sector? Existing literature tries to explain this phenomenon as a function of increasing returns or limit pricing. The chapter argues that since the banking industry is knowledge intensive, cost differentials among banks can be significant. Costs in this sector have two major components: interest cost of funds and cost of management of a bank. When cost asymmetry is pronounced and the cost structure of a bank is private information, the model constructed in the chapter becomes relevant for developing a benchmark model of entry deterrence in the banking industry. In other words, cost differentials and asymmetric information regarding costs among the firms can be a plausible reason for deterrence of entry. In particular, the chapter shows that adverse selection between banks and borrowers is not necessary for entry deterrence, and develops an alternative externality generating model in terms of cost asymmetry. Subsequently by assuming the presence of a classical adverse selection problem, the chapter shows that a differential adverse selection may not be sufficient to deter entry in this model.

References

Bardhan, P. 1993. 'Symposium on Democracy and Development', *Economic Perspective*, 7(3): 45–9.
Barro, Robert J. 1994. 'Democracy and Growth'. Working Paper No. 4909. National Bureau of Economic Research, pp. 4–48. Cambridge, Massachusetts.
Chaudhuri, S. 2005. *The WTO and India's Pharmaceutical Industry*. New Delhi: Oxford University Press.
Gupta, Poonam, and Arvind Panagariya. 2011. 'India: Election Outcomes and Economic Performance', Working Paper No. 2011-4, Columbia Programme of Indian Economic Policies, SIPA and ISERP.
Kumar, Aniket. 2011. 'Queuing for Credit: Increasing the Reach of Microfinance Through Sequential Group Lending', Pre-print available at: https://editorialexpress.com/cgi-bin, accessed on 14 April 2013.
Marjit, Sugata, Meenakshi Rajeev, and D. Mukherjee. 2000. 'Incomplete Information as a Deterrent to Crime', *European Journal of Political Economy*, 16(4): 763–73.
Marjit, S., V. Mukherjee, and M. Kolmar. 2006. 'Poverty, Taxation and Governance', *Journal of International Trade and Economic Development*, 15(3): 325–33.
OECD. 1994. 'Export Promotion and Environmental Technologies', OECD Environmental Monograph 87, GD(94)9. Paris: OECD.
Rajeev, Meenakshi. 2011. 'Money Lenders, Micro Finance and Poverty Alleviation', *Canada Watch*, (Fall Issue): 30–2.

Stepan, Alfred. 1999. 'Federalism and Democracy: Beyond US Model', *Journal of Democracy*, 10(4): 19–34.

Watal, Jayashree. 1997. 'Implementing the TRIPS Agreement Policy Options Open to India', *Economic and Political Weekly*, 32(39): 2461–8.

SECTION I

CORRUPTION, INFORMATION, AND TRANSPARENCY

1

When Is Competitive Behaviour a Best Response?[*]

Anjan Mukherji

This chapter is in support of a long period of friendship: of over 50 years with Dipankar Dasgupta and of about 40 years with Amitava Bose. With Dipankar, this friendship started from our undergraduate days at Presidency College. With Amitava, it started during our graduate student days in Rochester; he came a year later than myself. And if I recollect correctly, we three had the same dissertation

[*] Earlier versions of this chapter, reporting preliminary findings about the requirements for the establishment of a competitive equilibrium, have been presented at various places such as CESP at JNU, IGIDR, University of Mumbai, and University of Hyderabad. Discussions with Satish Jain over the years have helped and are acknowledged gratefully. Comments from Amal Sanyal and Tridib Sharma have been very helpful. The present version was prepared while the author was the Jawaharlal Nehru National Fellow at NIPFP and the facilities at the NIPFP are gratefully acknowledged. I am also indebted to Sugata Marjit and Meenakshi Rajeev for providing me with an opportunity to contribute to this volume.

committee. In fact, my going to Rochester was crucially dependent on Dipankar's going there and excelling. Our common teacher, Professor Dipak Banerjee, wrote to Rochester that he expected my performance to come up to Dipankar's. I recall that I was quite nervous when I heard this since I knew that Dipankar was doing exceedingly well. When I reached Rochester Airport, or, to give it its proper name, Monroe County Airport, Dipankar was there waiting to take me to his home and he helped me settle down although I had landed up at an inconvenient time since he was preparing for his qualifying examination. It was really an examination which turned out to be very taxing as I was to find out later.

With Amitava Bose, my introduction was first via a conversation with Lionel McKenzie; one day in 1970, around February or so, Professor McKenzie called me to his room and showed me two applications for admission to the graduate programme and asked me whether I knew the applicants. One was from Amitava Bose and the other was from Tapan Mitra. I had of course heard of their academic exploits and told McKenzie that they were very good students. Professor McKenzie had of course made up his mind to offer admissions to them and was running a last check. He said that he hoped they would come; their presence would enrich the programme he added.

Certainly I benefitted from their coming to Rochester: I would not have been there if Dipankar had not been there first and certainly writing my dissertation became much easier with Amitava around whenever I wanted to discuss something. We go back a very long time and I owe them a lot. I hope and pray that they have many happy years ahead.

The Basic Query

Consider a competitive equilibrium configuration, which is, a price system at which demand matches supply in each market. Now consider any decision maker in this setup and ask the question whether that person should transact whatever he or she was supposed to at the competitive equilibrium, if everyone else is behaving competitively. If the answer is yes then we really have nothing to worry about; if the answer is no then we need to ask what else do we need to impose to ensure that people carry out their competitive equilibrium transactions? This is the central point of enquiry in the present chapter.

Why is this at all of any interest? The framework of the competitive market is of course very important since for some time now, all over the world, this paradigm has been central to policymaking. There never has been such a commonality about the framework. Only recently, various people have woken up to the fact that this dependence on the efficacy of competitive markets is causing a lot of problems and people have begun mentioning that competitive markets need to be carefully monitored or regulated. Economists have always been aware that regulation was needed when externalities were involved but the unpleasant fact that such control may be necessary even if no such factors are present has not been realized in spite of assertions of the need for control to support economic activity[1] and, in addition, papers like the one by Akerlof (1970) being present for quite some time now. We shall see how these questions arise in standard general equilibrium frameworks.

We shall accordingly proceed as follows. First we will re-examine the arguments on why competitive equilibrium is at all a useful concept. We will then present an example and a general result. And finally we will draw together the implications of our exercise.

The Rationale for Interest in a Competitive Equilibrium

Given the strong belief that reliance on the market forces will be beneficial for us, we need to examine the theory behind this strong belief, if there is any. Accordingly, we address ourselves to these issues.[2]

Fundamental Theorems of Welfare Economics and the Equivalence Theorem

First of all what is it that competitive market forces are likely to achieve and why is that something to be desired? The market forces

---

[1] See the last section of this chapter for some references.
[2] Sen (1999: 112), 'The need for critical scrutiny of the standard preconceptions and political-economic attitudes have never been stronger'.

or the 'Invisible Hand'[3] is supposed to achieve a competitive equilibrium by which we mean a configuration where plans of all agents can in fact be carried out. But why is such a state 'desirable'?

There are two distinct routes to an appreciation of the properties of a competitive equilibrium. The first is through a consideration of what has been termed to be the 'Fundamental Theorems of Welfare Economics'.[4] These results relate the competitive equilibrium to an efficient state: one cannot better the lot of anyone without making someone else worse off; and second, given such a state, one can construct some prices such that with appropriate redistribution of initial resources, the given state may be achieved as a competitive equilibrium. These two results have been used by different sets of economists to further their own point of view; the First Theorem is invoked by those who believe in the efficacy of the market mechanism. The Second Theorem is of interest to those who believe in tinkering with the market mechanism to attain desirable optimal states. Both types of persons share their complete faith in the working of the market mechanism.

There are many reasons why these results may not hold. There may be externalities (that is, interdependence in consumption or production) of some kind or other and once these types of interdependence are present, the market always invariably does the wrong

---

[3] Which, according to most people, is supposed to be an Adam Smith creation. Since the term 'Invisible Hand' was thought to be coined by Adam Smith in the celebrated book *Wealth of Nations*, the role of the Invisible Hand in equilibrating markets is sometimes attributed to Adam Smith; but Smith mentions Invisible Hand once in *History of Astronomy*, for the first time. This book was completed around 1758 The next reference was in his book *The Theory of Moral Sentiments* (1759), and then again in the *Wealth of Nations* (1776). In addition, the reference in the *Wealth of Nations* was made not while discussing markets in Books I and II but only in Book IV where Smith was advocating support of domestic industry over foreign! So while we use the term Invisible Hand in our chapter, it should be noted that the failures or successes of this instrument to equilibrate markets should not be attributed to Adam Smith but rather to those who thought that he said so and followed this bit of fiction blindly.

[4] For a detailed examination of the Fundamental Theorems of Welfare Economics, see Arrow (1951).

thing. To explain, suppose that there is an externality in production, that is, the output of one firm affects the output of another. It may be shown that the good causing a negative externality will be produced in too great a quantity while a good causing a positive externality will not be produced in adequate quantities. These situations are referred to as cases of market failures. Our policymakers and analysts just do not have a feel for how widespread these cases are. And given the prevalence of these externalities, the failures are the rule rather than the exception. So markets will, 'on the balance', fail.

The second route to appreciate the properties of a competitive equilibrium lies in what has been called the 'Equivalence Theorem'.[5] Suppose we look at the problem of distribution through non-market means; where each individual or each possible group of individuals has the power to block some proposed allocation. That is, any group has the right to reconsider any proposed allocation and check whether it can propose for the members of the group an alternative allocation, which leaves no one worse off, and at least one member better off. Further, the group should be able to make the alternative allocation from its own resources. In such a situation, the group will be said to block the first allocation and the group will be said to form a blocking coalition. Solutions to the distribution problem are those allocations that cannot be blocked. Such allocations constitute the core. The Equivalence Theorem referred to earlier provides the equivalence of the core with the competitive equilibrium allocations under appropriate conditions. In some sense, therefore, a competitive equilibrium allocation is a fair allocation. It is these properties that make a competitive equilibrium desirable.

There is also, additionally, a more deep-seated belief that market forces will be able to attain such a competitive equilibrium. Of course, if this belief were not firmly in place, there would be little point in reposing faith in the market forces. However, the state of economic theory in this context leaves many unsatisfactory gaps.[6] That these issues have been of serious concern has also been noted by,

---

[5] This was a conjecture made by Edgeworth. The first demonstration of this result was in a paper by Debreu and Scarf (1963).

[6] I have attempted to clear up some of these gaps in my recent paper (Mukherji 2012: 125–38).

among others, Herbert Simon (2000). However, I do wish to point out the results of some experiments being conducted at Caltech by Plott (Anderson et al. 2003) and his associates. One of the reasons for considering the area to be a 'failure' was surely, because results in this area appeared to require rather stringent conditions and this is why economists generally considered the theoretical developments in this connection to be inadequate. The experiments however show that on the contrary, the theoretical predictions are quite accurate. My own recent results seem to indicate that attaining a competitive equilibrium depends crucially on the initial distribution of resources and further, it is always possible to redistribute resources, so that equilibrium prices remain undisturbed and become attainable. Since this is not our main line of enquiry in this chapter, we do not follow this up further.

Competitive Equilibrium and Nash Equilibrium

As the last section indicated, the relationship between a competitive equilibrium and the core is an important facet of competitive behaviour. The core is however a solution for co-operative games where players or decision makers have binding contracts. In the marketplace, such binding contracts may not be enforceable and hence may create problems for the existence of a competitive equilibrium. It is for this reason that we need to recall the links between a competitive equilibrium and a Nash equilibrium; the latter is the generally accepted solution for non-cooperative games, where there can be no binding contracts between the players.

Here too we shall be referring to exhaustive literature which exists in this connection. One of the approaches to showing the existence of competitive equilibrium attributed to Arrow and Debreu (1954) proceeds as follows. It considers an abstract non-cooperative game involving $m+1$ players; the m players are the economic decision makers, the households, with the payoff functions $U(x)$, the usual utility functions; their choice variables are consumption bundles x^i; while the additional player is the fictitious market manager (MM), who chooses prices P and whose payoff is $P.Z(.)$ where $Z(.)$ is the excess demand vector. What Arrow and Debreu showed was that this abstract game has a Nash equilibrium; and it is easy to see that such a Nash equilibrium will always be a competitive equilibrium. Remember, however, that in this 'game' there is an additional player (MM) who chooses prices according to some well-defined payoff. What we shall investigate involves removing this fictitious player and investigating whether trading at the competitive equilibrium prices is the best response and as we shall see, the answer will be generally in the negative.

There is another link between a Nash equilibrium and a competitive equilibrium and that is through the Nash implementation literature. Consider a social choice correspondence (SCC) which picks out a socially desirable set of alternatives from a given environment. For example, the Walras correspondence picks out from the Edgeworth Box, the set of competitive equilibrium allocations. The objective of this literature is to find out whether given a SCC and an environment, the outcomes of the SCC can be seen as the Nash equilibrium outcomes of some game. Thus, can competitive equilibrium allocations emerge as Nash equilibrium outcomes of some game? If the answer is yes then the particular SCC (the Walras correspondence, for example) is said to be Nash implementable. And we need to find out what the game looks like.[7] The Walras correspondence is Nash implementable; however the strategies that the agents need to have access to in the game that will implement a competitive equilibrium are quite different from the strategies available when markets are competitive.

To provide an appreciation of what exactly is required to obtain a competitive allocation as an outcome at a Nash equilibrium for a particular game, a reference to the paper by Saijo et al. (1996) is necessary. In particular, the table on page 970 is revealing. In case of two goods and two persons, the Walrasian correspondence may be implemented with agents quoting his or her own quantity; however even with two persons and three goods, just quoting quantities is not enough for this result to hold. In fact, what is required is that each person announce, a price vector and his or her own quantity. It is

---

[7] For a good account of the literature and the interconnections between some results, see Saijo et al. (1996).

evident that what is required is completely different from a competitive market; competitive allocations may have desirable properties, but it is unlikely that they will be achieved in the framework of competitive markets. Consequently, the question that we are investigating appears to be a difficult one to answer. What we proceed with next is considering an example where there are three persons and three goods; the easy theorems referred to earlier with two individuals and two goods are no longer applicable.

Incentive for Competitive Transactions

An Example

There are three individuals A, B, and C with utility functions and endowments involving three goods x, y, and z as:

A: $\min(x, y)$; $(1, 0, 0)$. B: $y.z$; $(0, 1, 0)$. C: $\min(z, x)$; $(0, 0, 1)$

Thus, although there are three goods each individual is interested in consuming only two goods, and further, each has a stock of only one commodity. We first compute the competitive equilibrium in this setup. The first step involves the computation of demand functions. For A, we have $x = y$ and hence from the budget constraint $p.x + q.y = p$ where p, q are the prices of goods x, y relative to good z, which we consider to be the numeraire. Thus, demand function for A is given by:

$$x = y = \frac{p}{p+q}.$$

For B, the budget constraint is given by $q.y + z = q$, hence the first order conditions imply that $z = q.y$ and hence the demand functions for B are given by:

$$y = \frac{1}{2}; \; z = \frac{q}{2}.$$

For the individual C, we have the budget constraint $p.x + z = 1$ and we must have $z = x$, so that the demand functions for C are given by:

$$x = z = \frac{1}{p+1}.$$

Thus, the excess demand function for good x denoted by Z_x is given by:

$$Z_x \equiv \text{Aggregate Demand} - \text{Aggregate Supply}$$

$$= \frac{p}{p+q} + \frac{1}{p+1} - 1 = \frac{p(1-q)}{(p+q)(p+1)};$$

similarly the excess demand for good y is given by:

$$Z_y = \frac{p}{p+q} + \frac{1}{2} - 1 = \frac{p-q}{2(p+q)}.$$

Thus, the unique interior equilibrium is given by $p^* = 1, q^* = 1$. We look at the trades, which take place at equilibrium, next. The arrows in Figure 1.1 show the direction of price movements in dis-equilibrium when the dynamics is specified by a classical tatonnement discussed earlier; global stability is more tedious to establish but local stability of the interior equilibrium, for a process where price adjustment is proportional to excess demand is given from the characteristic roots of the Jacobian, evaluated at $(1,1)$:

$$\begin{pmatrix} 0 & -1/16 \\ 1/16 & -1/16 \end{pmatrix};$$

the trace being negative and the determinant being positive, signifies local asymptotic stability. But this aspect is of secondary concern at the moment. We are interested in what transactions take place at equilibrium.

12 Emerging Issues in Economic Development

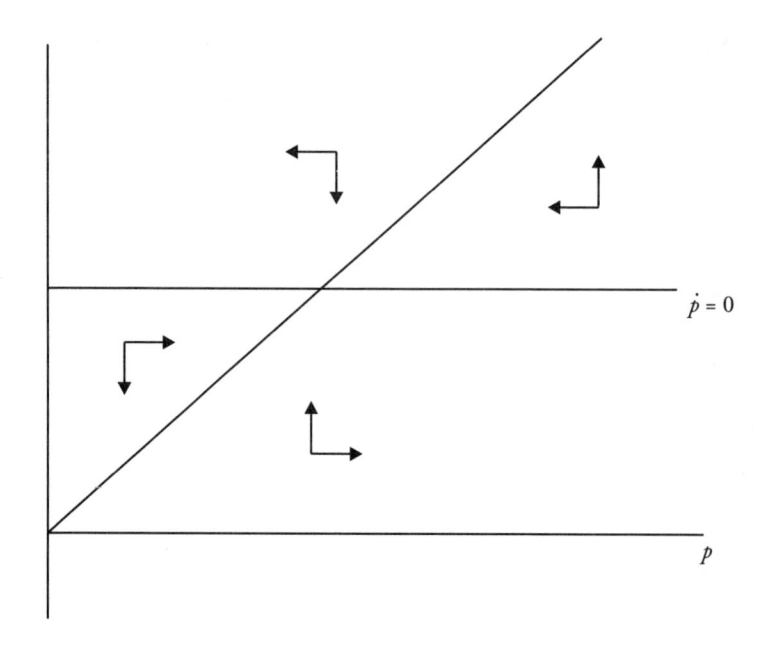

$\dot{p} = 0$

p

Figure 1.1 Competitive Equilibrium

Trades at Competitive Equilibrium and Possible Deviations

A gets 1/2 units of good z from C in exchange for 1/2 units of good x; which is then traded to B for 1/2 units of good y.

Suppose now at the competitive equilibrium, B does not surrender 1/2 units of good y and say, surrenders only $1/2 - \epsilon$ units of y, $\epsilon > 0$; then B ends up with the bundle 1/2 units of x and $1/2 + \epsilon$ units of y with utility $1/4 + 1/2.\epsilon$ which is more than 1/4 the utility enjoyed at the equilibrium and hence B will have an incentive to undersupply.

Consider then the probability of being undetected; let this be given by $\theta = f(\epsilon)$, with $f'(\epsilon) \leq 0$, $f(0) = 0$, say; if detected undersupplying, a penalty of say $\tau = 2\epsilon$ units of good y is imposed on B. Thus, B's expected utility is given by:

$$V(\epsilon) = \theta.\left[1/2\left(1/2+\epsilon\right)\right] + (1-\theta)\left[1/2\left(1/2-\epsilon\right)\right]$$
$$= 1/4 + 1/2\,\epsilon\left(2\theta-1\right)$$

Notice that:

$$V'(\epsilon) = 1/2(2\theta - 1) + \epsilon f'(\epsilon);$$

Hence, it follows that $V'(0) = -1/2$ and B will stick to the straight and narrow and behave competitively.

However, note that with the assumption on the function $f(\epsilon)$, we are in fact assuming the probability of being detected when $\epsilon = 0$ is 1; in case this is not so, as may be expected, then notice that $f(0)$ is the highest probability of being undetected and suppose that this is $\bar{\theta} > 0$; then for small deviations, the probability of being detected is of the order of $1 - \bar{\theta} < 1$; what happens then? Assume then that the penalty is some factor $\lambda > 1$ of the amount held back ϵ, (we had assumed $\lambda = 2$ earlier). Now:

$$V(\epsilon) = 1/4 + \left[\lambda.\theta - (\lambda - 1)\right]\epsilon/2;$$

and consequently, recalling that $\theta = f(\epsilon)$, we have:

$$V'(\epsilon) = \left[\lambda f(\epsilon) - (\lambda - 1)\right]/2 + \lambda f'(\epsilon).\epsilon/2.$$

Now:

$$V'(0) = \left[\lambda.\bar{\theta} - (\lambda - 1)\right]/2$$

which is negative only when:

$$\bar{\theta} < \frac{\lambda - 1}{\lambda}.$$

Thus, competitive behaviour is seemingly ensured only when the probability of being detected is high enough in comparison with the penalty rate.

Before passing on to other matters, it should be noted that neither A nor C have any incentive to renege on the competitive transactions. It is individual B who has an incentive to deviate and whose behaviour needs to be regulated.

A General Result

How general is the finding noted earlier? To answer this question we consider a standard exchange model; the arguments for a model involving production are not that different. We analyse the standard exchange model involving m individuals and n goods and that the total amounts of these goods is given by the components of $\bar{W} \in \Re^n_{++}$; each individual has a real-valued utility function $U^i : \Re^n_+ \to \Re$; further each U^i is assumed to be *strictly increasing, strictly quasi-concave, and continuously differentiable*. Sometimes, we shall specify a distribution of $\bar{W}$ among the individuals usually denoted by $w^i \in \Re^n_{++}$ such that $\sum_i w^i \leq \bar{W}$; let us denote the set of all such feasible allocations by the set W; if an allocation $\{w^i\}$ has been chosen from W, we can then proceed with defining demands $x^i(P)$ as the unique maximizer of U^i in the budget set provided by[8] $\{x: P^T.x \leq P^T.w^i\}$, where $P \in \Re^n_{++}, P = (p_1, \ldots, p_n)$ is the price vector; in case we have a numeraire, we shall consider good n to be the numeraire and write the price vector as $P = (p, 1)$; the vector of relative prices will then be written as $p \in \Re^{n-1}_{++}$.

Market demands are defined by $X(P) = \sum_i x^i(P)$; excess demand is then defined by $Z(P) = X(P) - \bar{W}$. Strictly speaking we should write $Z(P, \{w^i\})$, however, we usually omit the distribution of the resources and write $Z(P)$.

Excess demand functions are expected to satisfy:

1. $Z(P)$ is a continuous function and bounded below for all $P > 0$;
2. Homogeneity of degree zero in the prices, that is, $Z(\theta P) = Z(P) \forall \theta > 0, P > 0$.
3. Walras Law, that is, $P^T.Z(P) = 0 \forall P > 0$;

to these we add the following assumptions:

4. $Z(P)$ is continuously differentiable function of prices for all $P > 0$.

These conditions are standard and have been around for many years. The problem was that these assumptions did not allow

---

[8] We shall use the superscript T to denote matrix transposition.

the excess demand function to be restricted in any substantial manner.[9]

Finally, the equilibrium for the economy, with individual resources $\{w^i\} \in w$, is defined by P^* such that $Z(P^*) = 0$. Under the assumptions mentioned earlier, we know that an equilibrium exists and the set $E = \left\{ P \in \Re_{++}^n : Z(P) = 0, \text{ for some } \{w^i\} \in W \right\}$ is non-empty.

We shall say that given $\{w^i\} \in W$, P^* constitutes a zero-trade equilibrium if $\forall i, x^i(P^*) = w^i$. In this circumstance, $\{w^i\}$ is said to be a Pareto Optimal or efficient allocation in W; otherwise the initial distribution is said to be inefficient. Notice therefore that if the initial distribution of resources is inefficient, then at a competitive equilibrium, P^*, $x^i(P^*) \neq w^i$ for some i and some trade occurs. For such equilibria, we have the following result:

Proposition 1 Consider $\{w^i\} \in W$ such that at a competitive equilibrium P^*, $x^i(P^*) \neq w^i$ for some i *and some trade occurs. In such a situation, there will be at least one i who would benefit from undersupplying* (compared to the competitive transaction).

Proof: Given the nature of the competitive equilibrium there will be at least one i and a commodity j such that $x_j^i(P^*) < w_j^i$. For if no such pair i, j exists then $x_j^i(P^*) \geq w_j^i$ for all i, j and consequently given the condition of competitive equilibrium, the only possibility is that $x_j^i(P^*) = w_j^i$ for all i, j and we have a zero-trade equilibrium: a contradiction. Hence, for such an i, j the amount to be sold at a competitive equilibrium is the amount $t_j^i = w_j^i - x_j^i(P^*) > 0$. If the agent undersupplies, say $\epsilon > 0$ then the agent concerned is left with $x^i(P^*) + \epsilon.\delta^j$ where $\delta_k^j = 0 \forall k \neq j$ and $\delta_j^j = 1$; consequently given the nature of the utility function, it follows that $U^i\left[x^i(P^*)\right] < U^i\left[x^i(P^*) + \epsilon.\delta^j\right]$ and consequently i will always benefit from undersupplying.

Remark 1 Thus, the phenomenon exhibited by the example given in an earlier section is quite general whenever trades occur at a competitive equilibrium.

Remark 2 Note the crucial role played by the assumption that utility functions are strictly increasing; notice that the phenomenon

---

[9] See, for instance, Debreu (1974); Mantel (1974); and Sonnenschein (1972). However, the addition of a Boundary Condition and a Rank Condition at equilibria allowed us to obtain the results mentioned in Mukherji (2012).

described earlier will take place whenever the agent sells a good which is valued (marginal utility is positive). In fact, in this connection, see later what happens when the initial resources are redistributed.

Remark 3 It also follows that unless we impose fairly rigid controls, of the type discussed in the section 'Trades at competitive equilibrium and possible deviations', competitive transactions are unlikely to take place. In fact with multiple markets and many individuals, the penalties and probabilities of detection must be carefully balanced: surely a very difficult and maybe even an impossible task.

Remark 4 It should thus be noted that even if the market forces or the Invisible Hand manages to equilibrate markets, unless the regulators do their jobs of enforcing the controls properly, competitive transactions will not occur since agents can hope to be better off by doing something else provided they can get away with it. Thus, competitive behaviour is not incentive compatible, in general. What will take place are transactions, which involve various 'shady' practices (as compared to competitive transactions) and consequently the existence of 'scams' of various types will be observed.

We next turn to investigate whether there are any other means of restoring incentive compatibility of competitive transactions, that is, apart from introducing controls and market regulators.

Any Other Options for Restoring Competitive Behaviour?

What seems easy to state, actually opens up an entire Pandora's box: regulation of competitive markets actually creates further problems as a moment's reflection will clarify. Since regulators may lack proper incentives to carry out the task assigned to them, insisting on regulators may have unleashed a whole set of new and additional problems and competitive behaviour seems almost impossible to ensure in any meaningful way, even in the context of such a simple example as the one discussed in the section 'An Example.'

We shall restrict our discussion to this example. Consider however the following option of redistributing endowments so that A has $(0, 1, 0)$ and B has $(1, 0, 0)$ while C continues to hold $(0, 0, 1)$: notice that at the equilibrium, purchasing power has not changed, which implies that neither has demand; however, transactions have altered substantially.

With the changed endowments, routine calculations lead to the following excess demand functions:

$$Z_x = \frac{q-p^2}{(p+1)(p+q)} \text{ and } Z_y = \frac{p(p-q)}{2q(p+q)}$$

Hence, the situation is as depicted in Figure 1.2.

The phase diagram in Figure 1.2 shows that the new equilibrium, is the old equilibrium (1, 1); the phase diagram may be exploited to show that this equilibrium is globally asymptotically stable under the usual price adjustment process; the demands at the new equilibrium, however remains as before:

A: (1/2, 1/2, 0); B: (0, 1/2, 1/2); C: (1/2, 0, 1/2);

however the transactions are different now: B sells $1/2x$ to A to get $1/2y$ and sells $1/2x$ to C to get $1/2z$; notice that now B too has no incentive to go back on the competitive transactions. Thus a redistribution of endowments has succeeded where other measures such as

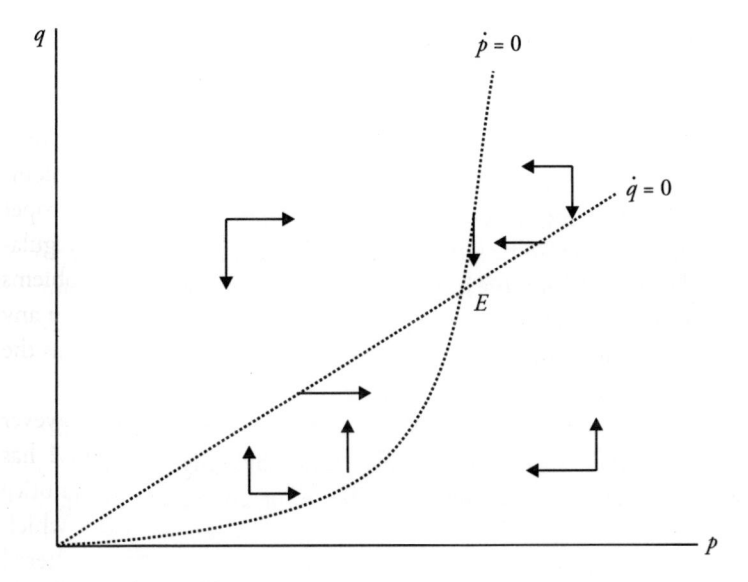

Figure 1.2 The Equilibrium

regulation would have led to many other associated problems: creating more problems for the establishment of competitive transactions.

* * *

The desirability of free competitive markets has a universal appeal; few realize the utmost importance of regulation or control. The necessity of an outside agency to keep watch and exert control over the functioning of the market was advocated by even Friedman (1962): '[The government's] major function must be to protect our freedom both from enemies outside our gates and from our fellow citizens: to preserve law and order, to enforce private contracts, to foster competitive markets'.

In fact this aspect was known to Indians much earlier as can be seen in the following passages from the *Arthashastra*: 'In the interests of the prosperity of the country, a king should be diligent (and) remove all obstructions to economic activity', and further 'The pursuit of the peoples welfare...the economic well-being of the society is dependent on the sceptre wielded by the King. The maintenance of law and order by the use of punishment is the science of government' (pp. 116 and 108, respectively). Putting these together, one might conclude that the prosperity of the country follows from the removal of obstructions to trade, and that further it is necessary to maintain law and order by the use of punishment to ensure economic prosperity. Our discussions in this chapter provide the basis for such conclusions. Neither Friedman nor Chanakya give us any argument to support why this should be so, although both seem to make these assertions as being self evident.

It is also taken to be self evident that people must adhere to some social norms.[10] But more importantly these norms should be enforced and this is crucially important otherwise the entire structure disintegrates. The problem lies with the necessity of enforcement: since the enforcers may not actually carry out the tasks assigned to them and hence some new problems may surface. We now need to enforce the enforcers to carry out their jobs...and obviously, we shall require a whole hierarchy of enforcers. This is of course not being very

---

[10] See, for instance Basu (1998: Section 1.3).

realistic and clearly, we need to think of alternatives since otherwise, dependence on market forces will lead to aberrations from the competitive outcome.

Finally, a word about the method used to restore the best response property of competitive behaviour in the example considered in this chapter. The example was especially constructed so that there was only one agent B who would deviate from competitive behaviour when others were on competitive behaviour. Moreover B has as initial resources a unit of good y which he values, whereas when we redistribute the resources so that B has a unit of good x, there is no reason for B to undersupply the good x, since B does not gain from doing so and consequently, since that is the only good he can undersupply, the problem disappears. If one looks at the situation what has happened is that by redistributing the resources we have made B behave. If one considers for a moment the nature of scams around us, they all involve illegal transactions involving large sums of money and these are desirable because people value money by itself because of the values that have been fostered in today's society. In fact, educational institutions are ranked not because of academic excellence but by the salaries that students from these institutions can command. If then there are possibilities of people making large sums of money without too high a risk of being brought to book (the sceptre wielded by the state is not strong enough) then what else can one expect but scams of various kinds? Thus, just as redistributing initial resources worked in the case of our example, by removing what B values from B's control, so too could a change in the value systems help. Of course, this will not be a quick fix but when anything deep rooted such as the value that people put on money needs to be changed then it can be only done through a long period of training in ethics and good moral behaviour. Notice that this is the only reasonable manner of retrieving competitive behaviour; any other way of doing so will involve regulations and enforcers and it is not clear why they will perform the job expected of them. This then is the somewhat unexpected conclusion that we may get competitive behaviour only if the value system supports such behaviour otherwise there is no reason to expect a competitive equilibrium to ever be attained.

References

Akerlof, G.A. 1970. 'The Market for Lemons: Quality Uncertainty and the Market Mechanism', *Quarterly Journal of Economics*, 488–500.

Anderson, C.M., C.R. Plott, K.I. Shimomura, and S. Granat. 2003. 'Global Instability in Experimental General Equilibrium: The Scarf Example', *Journal of Economic Theory*, 115(2): 209–49.

Arrow, K.J. 1951. 'An Extension of the Basic Theorems of Classical Welfare Economics', in J. Neyman (ed.), *The Proceedings of the Second Berkeley Symposium on Mathematical Statistics and Probability*, pp. 507–32. Berkeley: University of California Press.

Arrow, K.J. and G. Debreu. 1954. 'Existence of an Equilibrium for a Competitive Economy', *Econometrica*, 22: 265–90.

Basu, Kaushik. 1998. *Analytical Development Economics, The Less Developed Economy Revisited*, section 1.3. New Delhi: Oxford University Press.

Debreu, G. 1974. 'Excess Demand Functions', *Journal of Mathematical Economics*, 1: 15–21.

Debreu, G., and H. Scarf. 1963. 'A Limit Theorem on the Core of an Economy', *International Economic Review*, 4: 235–46.

Friedman, Milton. 1962. *Capitalism and Freedom*. Chicago: University of Chicago Press.

Mantel, R. 1974. 'On the Characterization of Aggregate Excess Demand', *Journal of Economic Theory*, 7: 348–53.

Mukherji, Anjan. 2012. 'The Second Fundamental Theorem of Positive Economics', *International Journal of Economic Theory*, 8: 125–38.

Rangarajan (ed.). *Arthashastra*, pp. 116 and 108. New Delhi: Penguin Books.

Saijo, T., Y. Tatamitani, and T. Yamato. 1996. 'Towards Natural Implementation', *International Economic Review*, 37: 949–80.

Sen, A. 1999. *Development as Freedom*. New Delhi: Oxford University Press.

Simon, H. 2000. 'Barriers and Bounds to Rationality', *Structural Change and Economic Dynamics*, 11: 1–2, 243–253.

Sonnenschein, H. 1972. 'Market Excess Demand Functions', *Econometrica*, 40: 549–63.

2

Many Facets of Corruption*

Mukul Majumdar and Seung Han Yoo

Interest in corruption (use of public office for personal gains) is certainly not of recent origin in India. Judging from the current political climate, it is a fair guess to speculate that in the years to come, corruption will be a major issue in assessing the quality of governance in Indian subcontinent (as well as other countries!). In the Arthashastra, a book the origin of which is lost in the mists of time ('those who question the ascription of the 4th century BC as the date of work place it not later than AD 150') (Rangarajan 1992: 20–1), Kautilya was invoking and contesting even *earlier* prescriptions on deterring corruption (see ibid.: 285–7). Among the prominent themes, Kautilya dwelled on the strength of the state treasury ('[A]ll state activities depend first on the Treasury. Therefore, a King shall devote his best attention to it…a King with a depleted treasury eats into the very vitality of the citizens and the country'

---

* This paper is dedicated, with affection and admiration, to Amitava Bose and Dipankar Dasgupta.

(ibid.: 253). Such deliberations led to many incisive comments on the collection of revenues, management of the treasury, and corruption. One finds repeated references to officials who deplete the treasury for personal gains: (a) how they succumb to the temptation to 'taste, at least a little bit of the King's wealth' (ibid.: 281); (b) how difficult it is to detect misappropriations and to challenge the tainted: 'Just as it is impossible to know when a fish moving in water is drinking it, so it is impossible to find out when government servants in charge of undertakings misappropriate money' and '[I]t is possible to know even the path of birds flying in the sky, but not the way of government servants who hide their (dishonest) income' (ibid.: 281, 283). He also made suggestions on creating proper incentives for honest officials. These are themes still under exploration (see Mauro (1995, 1997) on the cost of corruption, and Mookherjee and Png (1992, 1995) on the compensation for bureaucrats).

Over the years, corruption has cast its shadow over public debates in many countries in different stages (developing economies, transition economies, industrialized economies), and the perception of repeated abuse of public office and arrogant disregard for the spirit, if not the letter, of law has led to outrage in different contexts. The voluminous literature on many facets of corruption sheds light on the scale and nature of corruption in many countries and the policy measures needed to mitigate its harmful effects (see, in particular, the collection by Elliott (1997) and Rose-Ackerman (1999) for comprehensive lists of references). Klitgaard (1988), Andvig (1991), Ades and Di Tella (1996), Bardhan (1997), Lambsdorff (1999), and Aidt (2003) are also useful surveys. The annual reports from Transparency International [TI] available on its website also provide valuable insights.

To organize our thoughts, we follow the useful stylized framework proposed in Elliott (1997) which classifies individuals in a particular economy into three groups: 'citizens', 'non-elected officials' (bureaucrats/civil servants) and 'non-elected members of the judiciary' (magistrates often presiding over civil cases), and 'elected officials' (legislative/administrative/judicial branches). Three *types* of corruption are portrayed in this framework:

1. *Grand corruption* typically occurs at the highest levels of the government, usually involving all three groups;

2. *Influence peddling* describes corruption that arises out of the interaction between specific groups of citizens and elected or recently retired public officials, or bureaucrats going through 'revolving doors' (promise to promote legislation that protects or favours special groups in exchange for campaign contributions, arrangements to lure prominent politicians to help lobbying after the end of their terms, and using former bureaucrats to work in firms that they had regulated); and
3. *Petty corruption* occurs when private citizens (individuals/ owners of small–medium businesses) interact with lower-level non-elected officials on approval of privileges (passports, driving license, ration cards, import duties collected in ports/airports, and freight charges) or business requirements (registration of a firm confirming that it meets the laws/regulations on public safety on construction/housing, environmental laws on emissions and waste disposals, on payment of minimum wages, meeting safety standards for preparation or storage of food items) or government benefits (pensions, loans, jobs).

We emphasize that 'pettiness' refers to 'the size of each transaction and not to its total impact on government income or policy' (Scott 1972: 6).

In designing policy prescriptions, it is also useful to keep in mind the primary ingredients/environments of corruption as identified by Klitgaard (1988) in his well-known work:

1. *Government monopoly* in granting special privileges, in introducing new laws or amendment of old laws;
2. *Discretion* enjoyed by government bureaucrats on interpreting the scope of laws, relevance of precedents, proper procedures and documentations; and
3. *Lack of direct accountability* to the citizens, *lack of transparency*, and a *timeframe* for decision making, and *absence* of an appeal procedure (that can resolve a dispute at a reasonable cost to the victims of corrupt practices).

Grand corruption has far-reaching consequences, not simply as a drain on public treasury. It contributes to, if not creates, a culture in which a sense of despair grips the citizens, who see little choice beyond accepting it as a way of life. It is surely a deplorable betrayal of public trust and can paralyze the law enforcement branches of the government. If linked to the underworld, it may pose a challenge to the legitimacy of the state. Perhaps the first line of defence is an independent judicial system that is willing to challenge those who are enjoying 'absolute power'. In this chapter, we take a formal game theoretic approach, and to our knowledge there is no such analysis of grand corruption. Thus, our scope is limited to a review of two game-theoretic models, dealing with petty corruption and influencing peddling through revolving doors. The first is a simple model drawn from papers by Lambert-Mogiliansky, et al. (2007, 2008, 2009) (referred to in the chapter as the L-M-R model) and the second is reported from Majumdar and Yoo's paper (2012) (referred to in the chapter as the M-Y model). We present, in each case, a one-stage game in some detail. We also describe, avoiding complicated notations and demanding game-theoretic issues, some interesting implications when the games are repeated. In the rest of this section, we present an informal interpretation of these two 'models'.

The primary motivation behind the specifications in the L-M-R model is the extensive discussion of 'multiple approvals' or 'multiple verifications' that characterize the interactions between citizens and bureaucrats in the Indian subcontinent, the link between such systems and pervasive petty corruption, and the resultant effects on India's development efforts. Even after liberalization and reforms beginning in the early 1990s, the project approval processes have remained a source of irritation. The following sharp remarks from Roy (2003), who had served at the highest level of policymaking, stress on the 'multiple verifications' problem:

> As a member of the Task Force on Indirect Taxes, I highlighted that the administrative procedures associated with trade are probably the most primitive in the world. Even to just export, we require 257 signatures, 118 copies of the same document taking 22 hours to key-punch. This involves dealing with a multitude of Government of India agencies separately! This evokes hardly a protest from established exporters who have mastered the knack of going around the

system and having prompt clearance by paying bribes. But for new global players this is posing as a major irritant.[1]

The bureaucracy in the Indian subcontinent was inherited from British Raj. Its growth and importance became pronounced (and alarming) during the period of planning as the micro-management of both the real and financial sectors was expanded. However, adverse effects of 'competing bureaucracies' and the procedural labyrinth have been noted for other countries during the transition from the command to market systems (see Shleifer and Vishny 1993: 615–16).

In the next section the L-M-R model is interpreted as an interaction between an investor and bureaucrats. We recall Rose-Ackerman's (2010: 218) emphasis on the role of corruption in discouraging the flow of foreign direct investment to developing countries. Thus, the L-M-R model is of interest to a broad group of developing and transition economies.

The L-M-R model is a game with *incomplete* information. Here, an investor may apply to a 'track' of two or more bureaucrats (must submit the proper documents to two or more 'windows'). The investor has a project that has a specific (expected present) value that will be realized if the project is approved. This value is known to the investor, but *not to the bureaucrats,* but its *probability distribution is common knowledge.* The investor must apply to each bureaucrat in the track in a prescribed order (there is a constant cost per application), and her project is approved if and only if *every* bureaucrat in the track approves it. Each bureaucrat may demand a bribe (in a pay-it-or-forget-it manner) as a condition for approval. At any step in the track, the investor may refuse to pay the bribe, in which case the investor leaves the process, and the value of the project is not realized, although the investor loses the total amount of bribes paid up to that point. If the project is approved by the entire track, then

---

[1] The *Financial Express* reported on 21 November 2001: 'The Japanese envoy... gets upset over India's much talked about "single window" for Foreign Direct Investment. The joke is that India has forty "single windows" for one investor... It is not easy to work here.'

the investor receives the value of the project, minus the total amount of bribes paid. The payoff to a bureaucrat is the amount of the bribe received, if any. It is shown that in the one-stage game, there is *no* equilibrium in which the project is approved with positive probability. On the other hand, there is an equilibrium in which the investor refuses to apply to even the first bureaucrat in the track, no matter what the value of the project (within the support of its distribution) (see Rose-Ackerman's comments on the L-M-R model (2010: 232)).

We now turn to influence peddling. When an elected official favours a specific group in response to campaign contributions or other monetary favours, democracy gets degraded and a government of the people is reduced to a government by the few and for the few. The M-Y model's focus, however, is the well-documented case[2] of influence peddling through the 'revolving door': the possibility that a public servant (typically, a senior bureaucrat, call her a 'regulator') may be negligent in enforcing the rule of law or representing public interests for possible *future* personal gains (employment in a firm, compensation as a lobbyist), or 'post-government employment opportunities' (PGEO). Laws on outright restrictions and/or a 'cooling-off' period on such a passage from the public to the private sector have been enacted in many countries.[3] The M-Y model reviewed in the section 'Revolving doors' involves two regulators and two firms and attempts to capture two distinct elements involved in understanding revolving doors: *human capital transfer* and *collusion building*. Firms and regulators may seek to build collusion that allows a leniency in

---

[2] Almost 51 per cent of the 142 ex-commissioners took related private sector jobs (Eckert 1981). Adams (1982) shows that 1,455 former military and 186 civilian employees in the Department of Defence were hired by eight major defence companies during 1970–9, and 31 former employees of NASA were hired by these companies during 1974–9. According to the New York Times (18 June 2006), among the highest-level executives of the Department of Homeland Security in its beginning years, over two-thirds had moved through the revolving door. For more evidence and descriptions of revolving doors, see Che (1995) and Laffont and Tirole (1996: Chapter 11).

[3] In the United States, a 1962 Act (18 U.S.C. 207(a)) provided for a one-year cooling-off period Gely and Zardkoohi (2001). Most countries have similar post-government employment restrictions. According to a survey by Brezis and Weiss (1997), Canada uses a period of 1.5 or 2 years, the UK 2 years, France 5 years, Japan 2 years, and Israel 1 year.

the enforcement of current laws (when there is discretion in interpreting the laws or loopholes known to the specialists) and enhances the prospects for a future association. This is troublesome particularly when the future rewards come in the form of a side contract that is not easy to challenge, and an explicit illegal bribe is replaced by a credible understanding in collusion (see Martimort 1999).

We construct simple functions with some parameters which satisfy conditions in the M-Y model in which each regulator is either 'qualified' or 'unqualified', and the firm cannot observe the qualification level or skill of the official but knows the probability of qualification. We identify conditions under which, with PGEO in a one-stage game, an equilibrium exists and the incumbent regulator chooses a regulation rate greater than the high type's regulation rate without PGEO. The case with no PGEO is contrasted with the one where the bureaucrat has PGEO: it is shown that, in the latter case, the qualified bureaucrat regulates more stringently to signal his ability.

Investor and Bureaucrats

It is important to distinguish between two types of interventions by a bureaucrat when an investor plans an investment project. In order to get formal approval, each project typically has to conform to certain 'requirements' (for example, by satisfying some safety standards or meeting appropriate norms on financing). A bureaucrat *may reject a qualified project* if a demanded bribe is not paid. On the other hand, a bureaucrat may accept an unqualified project in exchange for receiving a corresponding bribe that he demands. Thus, the bribes demanded for the approval of qualified and unqualified projects may be different. We refer to the phenomenon of the approval of unqualified projects as 'capture', as distinct from the phenomenon of demanding a bribe for the approval of a qualified project, which we refer to as a 'hold-up' or 'pure extortion'. For simplicity of exposition, *we assume that all the projects are qualified and focus on 'hold-up.'* A more complete formal treatment of both types of interventions is given in Lambert-Mogiliansky et al. (2008).

The players in the one-stage game consists of a single investor (IV) and a single *track* of N bureaucrats (BUs), in which $N \geq 2$, arranged in a specific sequence. In order to get the project approved, IV must apply to and *obtain approval from each of the BUs in the prescribed order* (that is, BU_1 first, then BU_2, etc.). If the project is rejected by any one BU, the game ends and IV does not proceed further in the track.

Here is the complete description of the extensive form of the game. Let V denote the project's potential value, which is uniformly distributed on some closed interval which we may normalize to be [0, 1]. Yoo (2008) shows that the main results of Lambert-Mogiliansky et al. (2007, 2008) can be generalized: the assumption that the project value V is *uniformly distributed* can be dispensed with. The probability distribution of V (the 'prior') is common knowledge, but the realized value of V is known only to IV.

If and when IV applies to BU_n, she incurs a cost $c > 0$. (For convenience of exposition, this cost is assumed to be the same for all BUs: c is known to *all* the players). If IV applies to BU_n, let $b_n \geq 0$ denote the bribe demanded by him. The project is approved if and only if the bribe is paid. The bribe is demanded on a 'take-it-or-leave-it' basis, so that if the IV refuses to pay the bribe, the game ends. It is assumed that the BUs do not observe the bribes demanded by the other BUs.

Let $a_n = 1$ or 0 as IV does or does not apply to BU_n. If she does apply, she incurs the application cost $c > 0$ and *then* learns the magnitude b_n of the bribe demanded by BU_n. Let $p_n = 1$ or 0 as IV does or does not pay the bribe. Note that if $a_n = 0$ or $p_n = 0$, then the game is over. Thus, if $a_n = 0$, we have $p_n = 0$ and if $p_n = 0$, then $a_m = 0$ for all $m > n$.

Call the part of the game in which IV faces BU_n as the *n*th step ($n = 1,..., N$). The action taken by IV in step n is the pair (a_n, p_n). The action taken by BU_n in step n is, of course, b_n.

For $n \geq 1$, let H_n denote the history of the game through step n, that is, the sequence of actions taken by all players through step n. A strategy for IV is a sequence of functions, $\alpha = \{A_1, P_1,..., A_N, P_N\}$, which determines IV's actions according to:

$a_n = A_n (V, H_{n-1})$,

$p_n = P_n (V, H_{N-1}, a_n, b_n)$.

Since BU_n does not know the magnitudes of any previously demanded bribes, his strategy for the game is the magnitude of the bribe he demands:

$$b_n \geq 0.$$

To complete the description of the game, we must describe the players' payoff functions. The payoff for BU_n is the bribe he demands, if it is paid, that is:

$$U_n = p_n b_n.$$

The payoff for IV is the value of the project if the project is approved, less the sum of the application costs and bribes paid (whether or not the project is completely approved). Thus IV's payoff is:

$$U_0 = p_n V - \sum_{1 \leq n \leq N} (a_n c + p_n b_n).$$

Finally, assume:

$$0 \leq Nc < 1.$$

(otherwise, no project would be profitable.)

As usual, a Bayes–Nash *equilibrium* of the game is a profile of strategies such that no player can increase his or her expected payoff by unilaterally changing his or her strategy. A strategy is (weakly) undominated if there is no other strategy that yields the player as high a payoff for all strategy profiles of the other players, and a strictly higher payoff for some strategy profile of the other players. We shall confine ourselves to equilibria in undominated strategies and our goal is to characterize the equilibria.

Theorem 1 There is no equilibrium in which the project is approved with positive probability.

We sketch here a proof of the theorem by contradiction. First observe that for an equilibrium in undominated strategies, the bribes demanded by the BUs must be strictly positive. Hence, if IV ever applies to the *last* BU_n, he infers that IV *has already* incurred a positive cost (and this is true *even if* the application cost is zero). This inference influences the size of the bribe he demands. One can verify the following calculation:

Suppose that the IV has applied to BU_n, and BU_n infers that, for some M such that $0 \leq M \leq 1$, *the project's value*, V, satisfies $M \leq V \leq 1$. Then BU_n's optimal bribe is:

$$b_N = \max\left\{M, \frac{1}{2}\right\}.$$

Suppose that in an equilibrium, BU_n demands a bribe $b_n > 0$. Then IV will apply to BU_1 if and only if:

$$V \geq \sum_{n=1}^{N}(c + b_n) \equiv M,$$

But conditional on $V \geq M$, BU_n's optimal bribe is:

$$b_N^* = \max\left\{M, \frac{1}{2}\right\} \geq M = Nc + \sum_{n=1}^{N-1} b_n + b_N > b_N.$$

Hence, Prob{IV applies to BU_1} > 0 implies that b_N is *not* an optimal response to other players' strategies, contradicting the supposition that the original strategy profile was an equilibrium.

Remark 1 Observe that, for $N \geq 2$, the theorem is valid even when $c = 0$.

We shall now construct a family of strategy profiles for which *no IV applies to the first BU, and hence no project is ever approved*. A strategy profile in this family will be called a *null strategy profile* (NSP). We shall then show that there exists an NSP that is an equilibrium.

A particular NSP is characterized by N parameters, $b'_n, n = 1,\ldots, N$. The parameter b'_n represents the bribe that IV expects BU_n to demand and it is also the bribe that BU_n plans to demand. These parameters satisfy the conditions:

$$0 < b'_n < 1; \text{ for } n < N, \max\left\{1 - c, \frac{1}{2}\right\} < b'_N < 1.$$

IV's strategy is: for $1 \leq n \leq N$, IV applies to BU_n only if the value of her project is as large as the sum of the *expected* cost of completing the track, whereas she pays the *actual* bribe demanded only if the value of her project is as large as the sum of this actual bribe and the cost of completing the track if the remaining BUs demand their planned bribes.

The strategy of BU_n is: if IV applies to him, demand the bribe b_n.

As is common in game-theoretic analyses, we wish to confine attention to equilibria in which the strategies are, in some sense, 'credible', which involves examining the behaviour of the system 'off the equilibrium path'. To this end, for the purpose of the next theorem, we find it convenient to replace the requirement that strategies be undominated by a condition that we call *admissibility,* which is in some sense more demanding, but also somewhat more complex to state. First, *a strategy of BU_n is admissible* if the bribe demanded is strictly between zero and one. *A bribe profile is admissible* if each BU's strategy is admissible. *A strategy for IV is admissible* if it is a best response to *some* admissible bribe profile.

For a BU, we alter somewhat the definition of undominated strategy. An admissible strategy for BU_n is *quasi-undominated* if there is no other admissible strategy for him that yields him as high a payoff for all admissible strategy profiles of the other players, and a strictly higher payoff for some admissible strategy profile of the other players.

Finally, *an equilibrium strategy profile is admissible* if IV's strategy is admissible, and each BU's strategy is admissible and quasi-undominated.

Theorem 2 Suppose that for each n, $1/2 < b'_n < 1$; then the corresponding NSP is an admissible equilibrium, and for every value of V, *IV does not apply to* BU_1.

For proof of the theorem, see Lambert-Mogiliansky et al. (2007).

Remark 2 There may be other equilibria of the one-stage game in which the probability that IV's project is approved is also zero.

At the risk of belabouring the obvious, we emphasize that, *in an NSP equilibrium, each player has a zero payoff*. This property of an NSP equilibrium will be important in the 'repeated game', where the threat of reverting to an NSP will, under certain conditions, deter a BU from deviating from 'cooperative-like' behaviour.

Suppose that the one-stage game is repeated in a potentially infinite sequence of periods, with a succession of investors (one per period) with independent and identically distributed project values approaching the same track of BUs. The total payoff of a bureaucrat is the sum of expected discounted bribes he receives. To complete the description of such a repeated *supergame* one needs to specify *the information* each player has about the actions of other players. With this, and some technical assumptions, L-M-R proved that for *any* given profile of strictly positive bribes, if the BUs' common discount factor is sufficiently close to one, there is a positive probability that the investors will apply to the BUs, pay the bribes, and retain a positive surplus. Two types of policy prescriptions are also explored: (a) rotation of BUs; and (b) the possible social gain from a 'single window' policy. It should perhaps be noted that in the L-M-R framework, one cannot conclude that a single-window policy will unambiguously result in an increase in social efficiency. Under plausible conditions, a rotation policy will result in a decrease in social efficiency. The vast multiplicity of equilibria typically makes the results ambiguous.

Revolving Doors

Consider a game with two regulators and two identical firms. The one-stage game consists of *two periods*. At the beginning of period 1, the first regulator works for the government when he is 'young', and at the end of the period, he is approached by firms with wage offers.[4] Accepting one of the offers, he works for the relevant firm in period 2 when he is 'old'. At the beginning of period 2, the second regulator is born and works for the government when he is young. Hence, in period 1, the first regulator lives as a government official, and in period 2, the first regulator lives as an employee for one of the firms, and the second regulator as a government official. The two firms live for the entire stage.

Each regulator is either qualified ($q = H$) or unqualified ($q = L$). The firms cannot directly observe the qualifications level $q \in \{H, L\}$, but they know the likelihood that a regulator is qualified, which is

---

[4] If the former regulator works as a lobbyist outside of the firms, his wages can be interpreted as fees for a contract with him.

given by $Pr(q = H) = \theta \in (0, 1)$. A qualified regulator acquires regulatory expertise and (or) insider information gained from experience in government, whereas an unqualified regulator has no such advantage over other employees working for non-governmental sectors, and after the first regulator retires, the firms wish to hire the former regulator in order to utilize his or her experience in government.

While working for the government, each regulator chooses a 'regulation rate' for each firm, denoted by $(r_1, r_2) \in \mathbb{R}_+^2$. A regulation rate indicates the level of monitoring effort or performance in terms of intensity and/or frequency. The cost of the regulation is denoted by $e_q : \mathbb{R}_+ \to \mathbb{R}_+$ for $q \in \{H, L\}$. e_q captures the tradeoff between *expected* 'penalties' for being lenient in regulating a firm[5] and 'personal costs' from being stringent. $p : \mathbb{R}_+ \to \mathbb{R}_+$ denotes the former, and $c_q : \mathbb{R}_+ \to \mathbb{R}_+$ the latter. In other words, a unit increase in the regulation rate has both marginal benefits and costs. For each r, we let $p(r) = -r + \frac{1}{2}$, $c_H(r) = \frac{1}{2}r^2$ and $c_L(r) = r^2$, so $e_H(r) = -r + \frac{1}{2} + \frac{1}{2}r^2$ and $e_L(r) = -r + \frac{1}{2}r^2$. Then, the Spence-Mirrlees property is satisfied for each $r \geq 0, c_L'(r) > c_H'(r)$, which implies that the marginal cost of a qualified regulator is lower than that of an unqualified regulator.[6]

The two firms are in 'Bertrand competition', so they earn zero profits if they comply with regulations and laws. However, each firm can obtain a *positive* expected payoff $y_q : \mathbb{R}_+ \to \mathbb{R}_+$ by hiring a former regulator and either by *not* complying with regulations and laws or by exploiting *loopholes*. We let $y_H(r) = -ar + b$ and $y_L(r) = -2ar + b$ where $a > 0$ and $b > \theta + a$, such that y_q depends on whether the firm hires a *qualified former* regulator, that is, $y_H(r) > y_L(r)$, given the same regulation rate r by the *incumbent* regulator. If the firm hires a qualified former regulator, the firm's payoff is higher than otherwise. The higher the level of monitoring effort, the lower is the

---

[5] The expected penalty consists of the probability that each regulator will be caught by the government and the amount of the penalty.
[6] One can also check that for any $r' > r \geq 0$, $e_L(r') - e_H(r') > e_L(r) - e_H(r)$.

payoff involving explicit or implicit illegal activities, so y_q is assumed to be a strictly decreasing function on $r > 0$.

Without PGEO, neither regulator wishes to exert any effort on regulation different from the cost-minimizing regulation rate given each type. Denote $r_q := \arg\min_{r \in \mathbb{R}_+} e_q(r)$ for each q, and $r_H = 1 > r_L = \frac{1}{2}$. Hence, without PGEO, the high type's regulation rate is greater than the low type's regulation rate. Without PGEO, there is no incentive for either type of the regulators to deviate from r_q, but with PGEO, the firms can infer q through the regulation rates.

Without PGEO, both the first and second regulators choose r_q for $q \in \{H, L\}$.

Even with PGEO, the second regulator will behave just as he does without PGEO since in the one-stage game, the second regulator is the last in the time sequence. However, given PGEO, the first regulator wishes to signal his qualifications using the regulation rates for both firms.

The time line can be seen formally as:

Step 1: Nature chooses q for the first regulator.
Step 2: The first regulator chooses regulation rates for both firms (r_1, r_2).
Step 3: Given (r_1, r_2), the two firms make inferences about the first regulator's qualifications.
Step 4: After the first regulator retires, the two firms simultaneously make wage offers (w_1, w_2).
Step 5: The first regulator decides which firm to work for.
Step 6: Nature chooses q for the second regulator.
Step 7: The second regulator determines regulation rates for both firms.

Since Step 7 is the last stage, the second regulator does not have PGEO, so a qualified second regulator chooses r_H, and an unqualified one r_L.

A strategy of firm i is a mapping from $\mathbb{R}_+^2$ to $\mathbb{R}_+$ such that:

$$w_i = W_i(r_1, r_2).$$

Hence, if the type of the first regulator is *revealed*, the payoffs of firm i when he is qualified and when he is not, respectively, are:[7]

$$\theta_{yH}(r_H) + (1-\theta) yH(r_L) - w_i \text{ and } \theta_{yL}(r_H) + (1-\theta)_{yL}(r_L) - w_i.$$

A strategy of the first regulator is a mapping from $\{H, L\}$ to $\mathbb{R}^2_+$ such that:

$$(r_1, r_2) = [R_1(q), R_2(q)],$$

and the payoff of the first regulator is:

$$\delta \max \{w_1, w_2\} - [e(r_1) + e(r_2)],$$

where $\delta \in (0, 1)$ is the common discount factor for the one period.

A strategy profile in the one-stage game is a sequential equilibrium if for each step in the time line, the strategy of each player is the best response to the other players' strategies, and firms' beliefs about the first regulator's types are updated by Bayes' rule. We focus on a sequential equilibrium satisfying *the intuitive criterion*. The intuitive criterion typically eliminates pooling equilibria if the high type can attain a higher payoff by deviating from a pooling equilibrium (see Cho and Kreps (1987) for details). A *pooling* equilibrium is an equilibrium in which both types choose same actions, that is, $[R_1(H), R_2(H)] = [R_1(L), R_2(L)]$, whereas a *separating* equilibrium is one in which both types choose different actions, $[R_1(H), R_2(H)] \neq [R_1(L), R_2(L)]$, so their types are revealed in an equilibrium. In what follows, an equilibrium refers to a sequential equilibrium satisfying the intuitive criterion.

An unqualified regulator is one who has not acquired regulatory expertise, so we assume that the firms can hire many employees of the same quality as the unqualified regulator from elsewhere. A perfectly competitive labour market exists in which firms can hire such employees given $\bar{w}_L$. Hence, $\bar{w}_L$ is the wage that the unqualified regulator can obtain from PGEO in a *separating* equilibrium.

---

[7] Note again that r_H and r_L are the regulation rates of the second regulator.

Let $\theta y_L(r_H) + (1-\theta) y_L(r_L) - \bar{w}_L = 0$, that is, $\bar{w}_L = -(a+\theta) + b$ so that the payoff of a firm hiring the unqualified former regulator is zero from PGEO in a separating equilibrium. Denote

$$\bar{w}_H := \theta y_H(r_H) + (1-\theta) y_H(r_L) = -\frac{1}{2}(a+\theta) + b,$$ and we have $\bar{w}_H > \bar{w}_L$.

The two firms are identical and make wage offers simultaneously, so $\bar{w}_H$ is the wage that the qualified regulator can obtain in a separating equilibrium like is found in Bertrand competition cases. For a separating equilibrium, we introduce the individual rationality condition for the low type:

$$\delta \bar{w}_L - [e_L(r_L) + e_L(r_L)] \geq 0, \text{ (IR)}$$

and the incentive compatibility conditions:

$$\delta \bar{w}_H - [e_H(r_1) + e_H(r_2)] \geq \delta \bar{w}_L - [e_H(r_L) + e_H(r_L)],$$
$$\delta \bar{w}_L - [e_L(r_L) + e_L(r_L)] \geq \delta \bar{w}_H - [e_L(r_1) + e_L(r_2)]. \quad (2.1)$$

Consider a maximization problem and denote by (r_1^*, r_2^*) a solution to (2.2).

$$\max_{(r_1, r_2)} \delta \bar{w}_H - [e_H(r_1) + e_H(r_2)] \text{ subject to } (r_1, r_2) \in B, \quad (2.2)$$

where

$$B := \{(r_1, r_2) \in \mathbb{R}_+^2 \mid \delta \bar{w}_L - [e_L(r_L) + e_L(r_L)] \geq \delta \bar{w}_H - [e_L(r_1) + e_L(r_2)]\}. \quad (2.3)$$

Note that if (IR) is satisfied, no pooling equilibrium exists, and the set of equilibrium strategies is the same as the set of solutions to (2.2). We identify conditions under which with PGEO in a one-stage game, an equilibrium exists and (r_1^*, r_2^*) is greater than the high type's regulation rate without PGEO.[8]

Theorem 3 *With PGEO in a one-stage game:*

(i) *if* $\delta[-(a+\theta)+b] < \frac{1}{2}$, *(IR) is not satisfied, and*

(ii) *if* $\delta[-(a+\theta)+b] \geq \frac{1}{2}$, *there is a unique equilibrium* $(r_1^*, r_2^*) \gg (r_H, r_H)$.

We sketch a proof here. (IR) is $\delta \bar{w}_L - [e_L(r_L) + e_L(r_L)] = \delta [-(a+\theta)+b] - \frac{1}{2} \geq 0$. Proposition 1 in Majumdar and Yoo (2012) shows that there exists an equilibrium. Since, $\frac{e'_L(r)}{e'_H(r)} = \frac{-1+2r}{-1+r}$ is strictly monotone on $(r_H, +\infty)$, it follows from corollary 1(ii) in Majumdar and Yoo (2012) that $r_1^* = r_2^*$ and the equilibrium regulation profile is unique. Let $(r_1^*, r_2^*) = (r_H, r_H)$.

Then, $\delta \bar{w}_H - [e_L(r_1^*) + e_L(r_2^*)] = \delta \left[-\frac{1}{2}(a+\theta) + b \right] - \frac{1}{4}$, and $\delta \bar{w}_L - [e_L(r_L) + e_L(r_L)] - \{\delta \bar{w}_H - [e_L(r_1^*) + e_L(r_2^*)]\} = -\frac{1}{2}\delta(a+\theta) - \frac{1}{4} < 0$, which entails $(r_H, r_H) \notin B$. Hence, by corollary 1(i) in Majumdar and Yoo (2012), $(r_1^*, r_2^*) \gg (r_H, r_H)$.

Hence, the existence of PGEO in a one-stage game is beneficial to society since the qualified regulator voluntarily wishes to increase the regulation rates for both firms in order to deter the unqualified regulator from imitating the qualified regulator's strategy. In a one-stage game, with PGEO, the qualified regulators have no incentive other than to signal their qualifications through the regulation rates, which leads to greater regulation rates. On the other hand, the

---

[8] Since the incentive compatibility condition for the low type is a strictly convex function of r, we have to utilize SMP and necessary conditions of the maximization problem to characterize the solution to (2). Hence, this problem is not as trivial as it might look.

firms do not have a *strong* incentive not to comply with regulations and laws since they obtain zero profits either way. However, in an infinitely repeated game, a sequence of qualified regulators and a firm can collude in order to attain higher payoffs.

In an infinitely repeated game in which there is a sequence of regulators, and in each period, two regulators and two firms play the one-stage game described in the previous section. Hence, each regulator lives for two periods, and the firms live infinitely, so the regulators are 'short-run players', and the two firms are 'long-run players'. M-Y show that given a collusion-maximizing equilibrium in the infinitely repeated game (CME), the qualified bureaucrat *manipulates* regulation rates for two firms by regulating the colluding firm leniently for the maximized sum, but regulating the non-colluding firm stringently for the signalling in order to 'compensate' for the lenient regulation toward the colluding firm. For policy implications on the much-discussed and widely practiced restrictions on PGEOs, one can show that the negative (positive) *direct* effect is offset by the *indirect* effect from the collusion maximization, and M-Y suggest an alternative policy; as the magnitude of the marginal expected penalty strictly increases, the regulation rate for the colluding firm strictly increases.

* * *

Mathematical models are expected to capture some important themes in a particular context in a precise way. But precision and rigour also expose limited scope. A fundamental difficulty with the game-theoretic approach is the multiplicity of equilibria, and the issue of moving from a 'bad' to a 'good' equilibrium. In the model of investment, a natural question, in the Lange-Lerner tradition, is to introduce competition among tracks of bureaucrats, and to design a compensation mechanism that can periodically supervise and assess the success of a track in attracting investment, and penalize 'non-performance' (relative to the cost of maintaining the track). In the model of revolving doors, it is of interest to study how PGEOs and regulation rates affect the former bureaucrats' wages earned. These, and others, are directions for further exploration.

References

Adams, G. 1982. *Politics of Defense Contacting*. New Brunswick, NJ: Transactions Publishers.

Ades, A. and R. Di Tella. 1996. 'The Causes and Consequences of Corruption; A Review of Recent Empirical Contributions', *Institute of Development Studies Bulletin, University of Sussex*, 27: 6–11.

Aidt, T.S. 2003. 'Economic Analysis of Corruption: A Survey', *The Economic Journal*, 113: 632–52.

Andvig, J.C. 1991. 'The Economics of Corruption: A Survey', *Studi Economica*, 46: 55–94.

Bardhan, P. (1997), 'Corruption and Development: A Review of Issues', *Journal of Economic Literature*, 35: 1326–46.

Brezis, E., and A. Weiss 1997. 'Conscientious Regulation and Post-regulatory Employment Restrictions', *European Journal of Political Economy*, 13: 517–36.

Che, Y.K. 1995. 'Revolving Door and the Optimal Tolerance for Agency Collusion', *Rand Journal of Economics*, 26: 378–97.

Cho, I.K., and D.M. Kreps 1987. 'Signaling Games and Stable Equilibria', *Quarterly Journal of Economics*, 102: 179–222.

Eckert, R.D. 1981. 'The Life Cycle of Regulatory Commissioners', *Journal of Law and Economics*, 24: 113–20.

Elliott, K.A. 1997. *Corruption and The Global Economy*. Washington, DC: Institute for International Economics.

Gely, R., and A. Zardkoohi. 2001. 'Measuring the Effects of Post-government-employment Restrictions', *American Law and Economics Review*, 3: 288–301.

Klitgaard, R. 1988. *Controlling Corruption*. Berkeley: University of California Press.

Lafont, J.J., and J. Tirole. 1996. *A Theory of Incentives in Procurement and Regulation*. Cambridge, MA: MIT Press.

Lambert-Mogiliansky, A., M. Majumdar, and R. Radner. 2007. 'Strategic Analysis of Petty Corruption: Entrepreneurs and Bureaucrats', *Journal of Development Economics*, 83: 351–67.

———. 2008. 'Petty Corruption: A Game-theoretic Approach', *International Journal of Economic Theory*, 4: 273–97.

———. 2009. 'Strategic Analysis of Petty Corruption with an Intermediary', *Review of Economic Design*, 13: 45–57.

Lambsdorff, J.G. 1999. 'How corruption in government affects public welfare, a review of theories', Center for Globalization and Europeanization of the Economy. Discussion Paper, Vol. 9. University of Gottingen, Germany, OR 01.

Majumdar, M. and S.H. Yoo. 2012. Strategic analysis of influence peddling, to appear at *International Journal of Game Theory*.

Martimot, D. 1999. 'The Life Cycle of Regulatory Agencies: Dynamic Capture and Transaction Costs', *Review of Economic Studies*, 66: 929–47.

Mauro, P. 1995. 'Corruption and Growth', *Quarterly Journal of Economics*, 110: 681–712.

———. 1997. 'The Efects of Corruption on Growth, Investment and Government Expenditure: A Cross-country Analysis', in K. Elliot (ed.), *Corruption and Global Economy*. Institute for International Economics.

Mookherjee, D., and I.P.L. Png. 1992. 'Monitoring vis-à-vis Investigation in Enforcement of Law', *American Economic Review*, 82: 556–65.

———. 1995. 'Corruptible Law Enforcers: How Should They Be Compensated?', *The Economic Journal*, 105: 145–59.

Rangarajan, L.N. (ed.). 1992. *Kautilya: The Arthashastra*. New Delhi: Penguin Books.

Rose-Ackerman, S. 1999. *Corruption and Government*. Cambridge, UK: Cambridge University Press.

———. 2010. 'Law and Economics of Briber and Extortion', *Annual Review of Law and Social Science*, 6: 217–38.

Roy, J. 2003. 'Feeling good, but the Vision is Still Needed', The Financial Express (Co-ed page, 20 October). Available at: www.financialexpress.com/archive.html.

Scott, J.S. 1972. *Comparative Political Corruption*. Englewood Cliffs, New Jersey: Prentice-Hall.

Shleifer, A., and R.W. Vishny. 1993. 'Corruption', *Quarterly Journal of Economics*, 108: 599–612.

Yoo, S.H. 2008. 'Petty Corruption', *Economic Theory*, 37: 267–80.

SECTION II

GROWTH, POVERTY, AND MARKETS

3

Inefficiency and the Golden Rule
Phelps–Koopmans Revisited

Tapan Mitra and Debraj Ray

A planned path of consumptions is *efficient* if there is no other feasible planned path that generates just as much consumption at every date, with strictly more consumption at some date. This innocuous-looking definition contains one of the most interesting problems in classical growth theory: what criteria must one invoke to determine the efficiency of a planned path?

It isn't surprising that such a question was born in the early second half of the twentieth century. With the end of the Second World War, the newly-won independence of colonial nations, and the rising influence of socialist politics in Europe and elsewhere, planners and academics placed growing reliance on planned growth: on the deliberate allocation of resources, both across sectors and over time, to achieve economic development.

Of course, this relatively narrow definition of efficiency comes nowhere close to addressing the manifold complexities of such a development. But it is a *necessary* requirement, and it is a fundamental consideration. It is also a subtle criterion, as the work of Edmond Malinvaud, Edmund Phelps, Tjalling Koopmans, David Cass, and others was to reveal. When time (and the number of commodities) is finite, efficiency is no more involved than an old-fashioned maximization problem; indeed, in the aggregative growth model with a single malleable commodity, efficiency is identical to the simple absence of waste. However, when the time-horizon is open-ended, and therefore infinite, new considerations appear. It is entirely possible for a path to not involve any waste at any particular point in time, and yet be inefficient.

It is in this context that the so-called *Phelps–Koopmans theorem* provides a celebrated necessary condition for efficiency. As a historical note, Phelps (1962) actually conjectured the necessity of the condition, while Koopmans proved that conjecture; the resulting theorem appears in Phelps (1965). The work merited a Nobel citation. In awarding the 2006 Prize to Edmund Phelps, the Royal Swedish Academy of Sciences observed that:

> Phelps…showed that all generations may, under certain conditions, gain from changes in the savings rate.

Briefly, the Phelps–Koopmans theorem lays the blame for inefficiency at the doorstep of capital *over*-accumulation. The extreme cases are easy enough: if *all* capital is forever accumulated, then the outcome must perforce be inefficient, and if all capital is instantly consumed in the first period, the outcome must be efficient (after all, all other paths must yield lower consumption in the first period).[1] But the theorem throws light on the intermediate cases as well. Define a *golden rule* capital stock to be one at which output net of capital is maximized.[2] The Phelps–Koopmans theorem states that:

---

[1] The latter example underscores the fact that efficiency is a weak requirement: stronger optimality criteria such as the maximization of time-separable utility would generally rule out such paths. See Ray (2010) for a discussion of this case.

[2] With a standard production function $f(k)$ satisfying the usual curvature and end-point restrictions, such a stock is characterized by the condition $f'(k) = 1$.

If the capital stock of a path is above and bounded away from the golden rule stock, from a certain time onward, then the path is inefficient.

Later characterizations that seek a complete description of inefficiency (not just a sufficient condition), such as the work of Cass (1972), rely fundamentally on the Phelps–Koopmans insight. It is not our intention to survey the sizeable literature that works towards a complete characterization of efficiency. Rather we seek to investigate the original theorem in a more general context, one that allows for non-convexity of the production technology. The motivation behind such an investigation should be obvious. The vast bulk of literature assumes diminishing returns in production. This flies squarely in the face of empirical reality, in which minimum scales of operation (and the resulting non-convexities) are the rule rather than the exception. It is of some interest that this case has received little attention as far as the Phelps–Koopmans theorem is concerned. It is of even greater interest that without substantial qualification, the theorem actually fails to extend to this context.

To begin with, the setting is still the same: non-convexity is no impediment to the existence of a golden rule stock provided that suitable end-point conditions hold. Indeed, there may now be several such stocks; refer to the smallest of them as the *minimal* golden rule. Our recent paper (Mitra and Ray 2012) breaks up the Phelps–Koopmans assertion into three progressively stronger formats:

1. Every stationary path with capital stock in excess of the minimal golden rule is inefficient.
2. If a (possibly non-stationary) path converges to a limit capital stock in excess of the minimal golden rule, then it is inefficient.
3. If a (possibly non-stationary) path lies above, and bounded away from the minimal golden rule from a certain time onwards, then it is inefficient.

Obviously, version 3 nests version 2, which in turn nests version 1.

It is very easy to see that the weakest version, 1, of the Phelps–Koopmans theorem must be true. But version 2 of the theorem is false. In Mitra and Ray (2012), we present an example of an *efficient* path that converges to a limit stock that exceeds the minimal golden rule. The circumstances under which version 2 is true is completely characterized in that paper—in terms of the curvature of the production function at the golden rules.

In short, while a variant of the Phelps–Koopmans theorem does hold when technology is non-convex, the 'over-accumulation of capital', as defined by Phelps, need not always imply inefficiency.

A corollary of our characterization is that version 2 is indeed true provided that the golden rule stock is *unique*. It turns out; however, that version 3 of the theorem is not true even if the golden rule is unique. Proposition 3 in Mitra and Ray (2012) provides a stringent condition on the production function under which version 3 is guaranteed to fail (see condition F.4 in that paper). However, the stringency of the condition precludes its necessity. Our paper is silent on the possibility of *completely* characterizing an economic environment for which version 3 stands or falls. Indeed, we ended our introduction to our paper thus:

> An interesting research question is to describe conditions under which version III is valid. We suspect that such conditions will involve strong restrictions on the production technology. Whether those conditions usefully expand the subset of convex technologies remains an open question.

The goal of the present chapter is to address this question. Under some mild restrictions on the allowable family of production technologies, we provide a complete characterization of what one might call the *Phelps–Koopmans property*, one that allows for all non-stationary paths, as in version 3. The property may be stated as:

> A path is inefficient if its capital stock sequence lies above and bounded away from the minimal golden rule capital stock from a certain time onwards.

We prove that the Phelps–Koopmans theorem must fail whenever the net output of the aggregate production function $f(x)$, given by $f(x) - x$, is increasing in any region between the golden rule and the maximum sustainable capital stock. As a corollary of our result, suppose that the production function $f(x)$ is continuously differentiable, with a strictly positive derivative and admits a unique golden rule. Then if f is concave, the Phelps–Koopmans assertion holds, but if we perturb the function *ever so slightly* to the right of the golden rule (but below the maximum sustainable stock), so that it now admits a region over which $f'(x) > 1$, the Phelps–Koopmans property must fail. We return to this discussion after the statement of the main theorem.

Preliminaries

Consider an aggregative model of economic growth. At every date, capital x_t produces output $f(x_t)$, where $f : \mathbb{R}_+ \to \mathbb{R}_+$ is the production function. We assume throughout that:

[F] The production function $f : \mathbb{R}_+ \to \mathbb{R}_+$ is continuous and increasing on $\mathbb{R}_+$ with $f(0) = 0$, and there is $B \in (0, \infty)$ such that $f(x) > x$ for all $x \in (0, B)$ and $f(x) < x$ for all $x > B$. Further, the left hand derivative of f, denoted by f^-, exists and is positive for all $x > 0$.

We can think of B as the maximum sustainable stock.

Notice that [F] includes the standard convex technology, as well as technologies in which there are one or more regions of non-convexity. The somewhat awkward assumption that the left-hand derivative of f is always well-defined (but not necessarily the full derivative) allows us to accommodate cases in which f is the upper envelope of two or more neoclassical production functions, as described in Mitra and Ray (2012) and in the discussion later in this chapter.[3]

A *programme* from $\kappa \geq 0$ is a sequence of *capital stocks* $\boldsymbol{x} = \{x_t\}$ with:

$$x_0 = \kappa \text{ and } 0 \leq x_{t+1} \leq f(x_t)$$

for all $t \geq 0$. Let $c_{t+1} = f(x_t) - x_{t+1}$ be the associated consumption programme. With no real loss of generality, we presume that $\kappa \in [0, B]$.

A programme $\boldsymbol{x}'$ from κ *dominates* a programme $\boldsymbol{x}$ from κ if the associated consumption sequences satisfy:

$$c'_{t+1} = f(x'_t) - x'_{t+1} \geq f(x_t) - x_{t+1} = c_{t+1}$$

---

[3] We conjecture that the differentiability restriction on f can be dropped at no cost.

for every t, with strict inequality for some t. A programme x from κ is *inefficient* if there is a programme x' from κ which dominates it. It is *efficient* if it is not inefficient.

Define $s(x) \equiv f(x) - x$ for all $x \geq 0$. Under [F], s is continuous on $[0, B]$ with $s(0) = s(B) = 0 \geq s(x)$ for all $x \geq B$, so there is $x^* \in (0, B)$ such that:

$$s(x^*) \geq s(x) \text{ for all } x \geq 0.$$

Call x^* a *golden rule* stock, or simply a *golden rule*. Clearly, the set of golden rules lies in $(0, B)$ and is compact, so there is a smallest or *minimal* golden rule; denote it by k.

The Main Theorem

THEOREM 1 The Phelps–Koopmans property holds if and only if:

$$s(x) \text{ is non-increasing for all } x \in [k, B], \tag{3.1}$$

where k is the minimal golden rule.

Proof [If] Suppose $\{x_t\}$ is a programme from $\kappa \geq 0$, and there is $\alpha > 0$ and $T \in \mathbb{N}$ such that $x_t \geq k + \alpha$ for all $t \geq T$. Define $\{x'_t\}$ by $x'_t = x_t$ for $t = 0,\ldots, T - 1$, and $x'(t) = x(t) - \alpha$ for $t \geq T$. Then $x'_t = x_t \geq 0$ for all $t \in \{0,\ldots, T - 1\}$, and $x'_t \geq k$ for all $t \geq T$. Further, $c'_t = c_t$ for $t \in \{1,\ldots, T - 1\}$ if any, and $c'_T = c_T + \alpha > c_T$. For $t \geq T$, we have:

$$\begin{aligned} c'_{t+1} &= f(x'_t) - x'_{t+1} = f(x_t - \alpha) - f(x_t) + f(x_t) - x_{t+1} + \alpha \\ &= c_{t+1} + f(x_t - \alpha) - f(x_t) + \alpha \\ &= c_{t+1} + \left[f(x_t - \alpha) - (x_t - \alpha) \right] - \left[f(x_t) - x_t \right] \\ &\geq c_{t+1}, \end{aligned}$$

by virtue of the fact that (3.1) holds. Thus, $\{x_t\}$ is inefficient.[4]

---

[4] The 'if' part is standard, and is inspired by the original proof of the Phelps–Koopmans theorem, as suggested by Koopmans. We include it here for a self-contained treatment.

[Only If] Suppose that (3.1) is violated. Then, there exist numbers b and b' such that $b' > b > k$ and $s(b') > s(b)$.[5] Furthermore, there is $w \in (b, b')$ such that $\eta \equiv f^-(w)$ exceeds 1.[6] Since, η is the left-hand derivative of f at w, we can find $0 < e < w - b < w - k$ such that whenever $x \in (w - e, w)$, we have:

$$\left| \frac{f(w) - f(x)}{w - x} - \eta \right| < (\eta - 1)/2.$$

In particular, for all $x \in (w - e, w)$:

$$\frac{f(w) - f(x)}{w - x} \geq \eta - [(\eta - 1)/2] = [(\eta + 1)/2] \equiv h > 1,$$

so that:

$$f(w) - f(x) \geq h(w - x) \text{ for all } x \in (w - e, w]. \tag{3.2}$$

Next, pick $z \in (k, w - e)$, with z sufficiently close to k, so that if we define $y \equiv z - e$, then:

$$f(x) - x < f(z) - z \text{ for all } x \leq y. \tag{3.3}$$

To see that this can be done, suppose by way of contradiction that such a construction is impossible. Then there exists a sequence $z^n \downarrow k$ such that for every n, there is $x^n \leq z^n - e$ with $f(x^n) - x^n \geq f(z^n) - z^n$. By passing to the limit (and taking a subsequence of $\{x^n\}$ if necessary), we contradict the fact that k is the minimal golden rule.

To complete the preliminaries, define:

$$\delta \equiv [f(z) - z] - \max_{x \leq y}[f(x) - x],$$

---

[5] That $b > k$ is guaranteed by virtue of the fact that k is a golden rule.
[6] Suppose, on the contrary, that $f^-(x) \leq 1$ for all $x \in (b, b')$. Define $S(x) = -s(x)$ for all $x \in I \equiv [b, b']$. Then, S is continuous on I, and its left hand derivative is non-negative for all $x \in (b, b')$. By Proposition 2 of Royden (1988: 99), we must then have $S(b') \geq S(b)$, so that $s(b') \leq s(b)$, a contradiction.

and note that δ must be strictly positive. Choose a positive integer M such that:

$$M\delta > k. \tag{3.4}$$

Now define a cyclical programme x as follows. The programme starts at z and stays there for M periods, where M is defined by (3.4). The programme then steadily accumulates to reach w (to be concrete, think of this as pure accumulation with some adjustment in consumption in at most one period so as to hit w exactly). Say this takes N periods, thereby passing through $(N+1)$ distinct values of capital.

To describe the remainder of the programme, we need some more notation. Denote the distinct values of the stock by $(z_0, z_1,..., z_N)$, with $z_0 = z$, and $z_N = w$. The left-hand derivative of f exists and is positive at each of these points, and so $\mu \equiv \min\{f^-(z_0),...,f^-(z_N)\}$ is strictly positive. For each $j \in \{0, 1,..., N\}$, there is $0 < \theta_j < z$ such that for all $x \in (z_j - \theta_j, z_j)$:

$$\left| \frac{f(z_j) - f(x)}{z_j - x} - f^-(z_j) \right| < \mu/2.$$

so that for all $x \in (z_j - \theta_j, z_j)$:

$$\frac{f(z_j) - f(x)}{z_j - x} \geq f^-(z_j) - \mu/2 \geq \mu/2$$

and therefore:

$$f(z_j) - f(x) \geq (\mu/2)(z_j - x) \text{ for all } x \in (z_j - \theta_j, z_j).$$

Define $\theta \equiv \min\{\theta_0,..., \theta_N\}$. Then, for all $j \in \{0, 1,..., N\}$:

$$f(z_j) - f(x) \geq (\mu/2)(z_j - x) \text{ for all } x \in (z_j - \theta, z_j) \tag{3.5}$$

Consider the function $L(x) \equiv f(x) - f(x - \theta)$ for all $x \in [z, B]$. Then $L(x)$ is a positive continuous function on $[z, B]$, and has a minimum

Inefficiency and the Golden Rule 51

value, which we call $\bar{L}$. Define $\beta = \bar{L}/B$, and $\ell = \min\{\beta,(\mu/2)\}$. Note that $\ell > 0$. We now claim that for each $j \in \{0, 1,..., M\}$,

$$f(z_j) - f(x) \geq \ell(z_j - x) \text{ for all } x \in [0, z_j] \tag{3.6}$$

For $x = z_j$, this is trivially true. So, consider $x \in [0, z_j)$. Either (i) $x \in (z_j - \theta, z_j)$, or (ii) $0 \leq x \leq z_j - \theta$. In case (i), using (3.5) we have $[f(z_j) - f(x)] \geq (\mu/2)(z_j - x) \geq \ell (z_j - x)$. In case (ii), we have:

$$\begin{aligned} f(z_j) - f(x) &\geq f(z_j) - f(z_j - \theta) \\ &\geq \bar{L} = \beta B \geq \beta(z_j - x) \geq \ell(z_j - x) \end{aligned}$$

This establishes our claim (3.6).

Choose a positive integer Q so that:

$$h^Q \ell^{M+N} \equiv \lambda > 1. \tag{3.7}$$

Because $h > 1$ and $\ell > 0$, Q can always be chosen to satisfy (3.7).

We now complete the description of the programme. After accumulating to w, it stays there for Q periods, and then returns to z, whereupon the cycle is indefinitely repeated.

We claim that x is efficient.

If not, there is a dominating programme x'. Let $t(i)$ be the date at which a fresh round i starts. We claim that there is i such that $\varepsilon_i \equiv x_{t(i)} - x'_{t(i)} \geq e$.

To establish the claim, notice that at every date t:

$$f(x'_t) - x'_{t+1} \geq f(x_t) - x_{t+1,}$$

so that:

$$x_{t+1} - x'_{t+1} \geq f(x_t) - f(x'_t) \text{ for all } t \geq 0. \tag{3.8}$$

Since $x_0 = x'_0$, we have $x_t \geq x'_t$ for all $t \geq 0$ by using (3.8).

Now, during the first $M + N$ periods of any round, we know from (3.6) that:

$$f(x_t) - f(x'_t) \geq \ell[x_t - x'_t],$$

so that combining this information with (3.8), we see that during the first $M + N$ periods of any round:

$$x_{t+1} - x'_{t+1} \geq \ell[x_t - x'_t]. \tag{3.9}$$

Let us refer to the phase, in which the stock is kept stationary at w in the original programme, as the 'upper phase'. There are two possibilities to consider: (i) there is some date t in the upper phase, in some round, for which $x'_t \leq w - e$, and (ii) $x'_t > w - e$ at every date in the upper phase for every round. In case (i), using (3.8) again:

$$x_{t+1} - x'_{t+1} \geq f(x_t) - f(x'_t) \geq f(w) - f(w - e) \geq e,$$

because $f(x) - x$ is increasing over the range $[w - e, w]$. Thus, $x'_{t+1} \leq w - e$, and this step can be repeated for all subsequent dates of the upper phase of that round to obtain $x_\tau - x'_\tau \geq e$ where τ is the first period of the next round. This establishes our claim in case (i).

In case (ii), using (3.8) yet again, along with (3.2):

$$x_{t+1} - x'_{t+1} \geq h[x_t - x'_t] \tag{3.10}$$

for every date t of the upper phase of every round. Combining (3.9) and (3.10), we must conclude that:

$$\varepsilon_{i+1} \geq \ell^{M+N} h^Q \varepsilon_i = \lambda \varepsilon_i,$$

where $\lambda > 1$; see (3.7). So ε_i expands geometrically across rounds once it turns positive. But it must turn positive at some round, because x' is a dominating programme.

So in this case too, the claim is proved.

Consider any round i, then, at which $\varepsilon_i \geq e$. For the next M periods, we have $x'_t < y$ by induction, using (3.3), and moreover:

$$\begin{aligned} x'_{t+1} &\leq f(x'_t) - [f(z) - z] \\ &\leq [f(x'_t) - x'_t] - [f(z) - z] + x'_t \\ &\leq \max_{x \leq y}[f(x) - x] - [f(z) - z] + x'_t \\ &\leq x'_t - \delta \end{aligned}$$

But, this means that by the end of M more periods, we must have $x'_t < y - M\delta < k - M\delta < 0$, a contradiction. So no dominating programme can exist, and x must be efficient.

Discussion

We can illustrate the main theorem as follows. Call a production function F *neoclassical* if it satisfies condition [F] and in addition:

[C] F is strictly concave on $\mathbb{R}_+$ and twice continuously differentiable on $\mathbb{R}_{++}$, with $F''(x) < 0$ for all $x > 0$.

Consider a production function f that can be written as the pointwise maximum of two neoclassical functions; call them h and g:

$f(x) = \max \{h(x), g(x)\}$ for all $x \geq 0$.

Suppose that first h, then g, occupies the envelope, that is, there exists u such that:

$f(x) = h(x) > g(x)$ for $x < u$.
$f(x) = g(x) > h(x)$ for $x > u$.

Suppose, moreover, that:

$f(u) = h(u) = g(u) > u$.

Then f satisfies [F].

Denote the (unique) golden rule of h by k_h, and the golden rule of g by k_g. Assume that these two values lie on either side of u:

$k_h < u < k_g$.

Clearly, the technology set defined by f is non-convex (note that f is not, in general, differentiable). Observe that the minimal golden rule of f is k_h if:

$$h(k_h) - k_h \geq g(k_g) - k_g \tag{3.11}$$

with k_h the unique golden rule of f if and only if strict inequality holds in (3.11). Similarly, the minimal (and only) golden rule of f is k_g if (3.11) fails. In the latter case, since f is concave on $[k_g, B]$, the standard Phelps–Koopmans theory applies to paths which are above and bounded away from the golden rule stock k_g. So the Phelps–Koopmans property clearly holds in this case.

Our main theorem implies, however, that this is the *only* situation in which the Phelps–Koopmans theorem is valid. As soon as (3.11) holds, the Phelps–Koopmans theorem fails, no matter how briefly g occupies the outer envelope that comprises f. This is a remarkable fact that requires some explanation. Figure 3.1 illustrates a situation in which g occupies the frontier for a relatively short stretch. The proof of the theorem constructs a cycle that starts from a point z close to the minimal golden rule k_h, stays there for M periods, and then goes up into the zone where g occupies the envelope, but to the left of k_g; see the point w in Figure 3.1. The programme stays there for Q periods, and then drops back to z again, whereupon the cycle starts all over again.

A comparison programme that dominates this cycle must ultimately have lower stocks relative to the cycle at every date. If the cycle reaches its peak in a zone where h still occupies the envelope, this is not a problem; indeed, there is some surplus to be gained by lowering stocks by a tiny amount. However, if the peak is reached when g occupies the envelope, control over the comparison stocks is weaker: in the region in which w is being repeated for Q periods, the comparison programme must steadily drift further away from w, because the surplus $s(x)$ falls locally to the left of w. This drift magnifies over rounds until no matter how alike the comparison programme was to start with, the difference in the stocks is pronounced. At this point, the comparison programme drops below a point such as y to the *left* of the golden rule k_h, and generates *lower* surplus than z. Once here, though, it cannot recover. The M subsequent

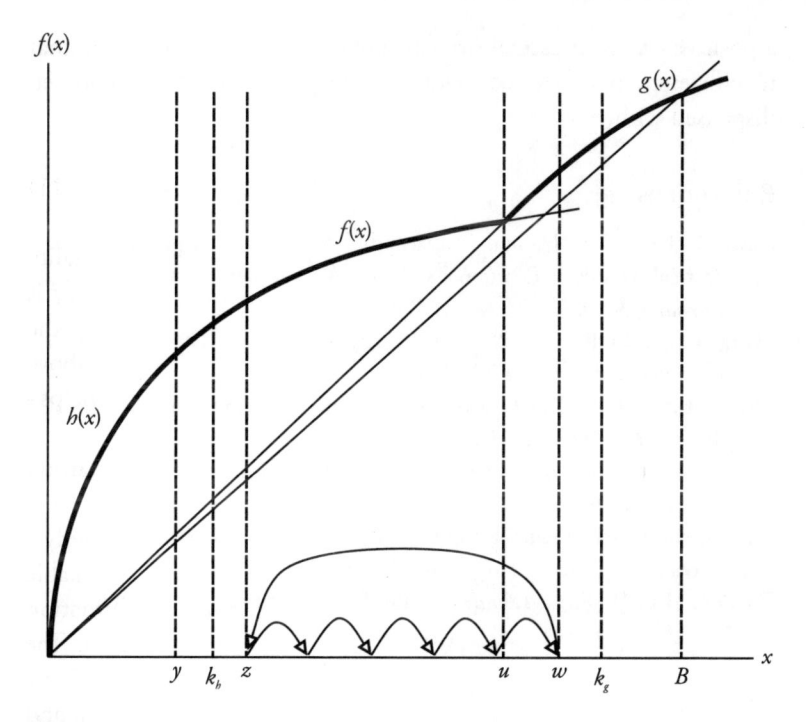

Figure 3.1 An Illustration of Theorem 1

repetitions of z force the comparison programme to fall ever lower in stocks, until feasibility is violated. So the cycle is efficient. It is in this way that a tiny 'intrusion' of the second neoclassical technique g destroys the Phelps–Koopmans property.

* * *

This paper studies the well-known Phelps–Koopmans theorem in an environment with a non-convex production technology. We argue that in such a setting, the Phelps–Koopmans result generally fails to hold, and that this failure is quite robust. Specifically, we prove that the theorem fails whenever the net output of the aggregate production function $f(x)$, given by $f(x) - x$, is increasing in *any* region between the golden rule and the maximum sustainable capital stock. That is, in such cases, it is always possible to find an *efficient* program in which capital stocks ultimately lie above (and stay bounded away from) the golden rule. Thus the 'overaccumulation of capital', as captured by a positive excess of capital over the golden rule, is no longer related to efficiency, once the convexity of the production technology is dispensed with.

References

Cass, D. 1972. 'On Capital Overaccumulation in the Aggregative Neoclassical Model of Economic Growth: A Complete Characterization', *Journal of Economic Theory*, 4: 200–23.

Mitra, T., and D. Ray. 2012. 'On the Phelps–Koopmans Theorem', *Journal of Economic Theory*, 147: 833–49.

Phelps, E.S. 1962. 'The End of the Golden Age in Solovia: Comment', *American Economic Review*, 52: 1097–9.

———. 1965. 'Second Essay on the Golden Rule of Accumulation', *American Economic Review*, 55: 793–814.

Ray, D. 2010. 'The Phelps–Koopmans Theorem and Potential Optimality', *International Journal of Economic Theory*, 6: 11–28.

Royden, H.L. 1988. *Real Analysis,* Third Edition. New York: Macmillan.

4

A Multidimensional Poverty Index[*]

Asis Kumar Banerjee

Dipankar Dasgupta and Amitava Bose have been among the leading economic theorists of India for a long time. I have had the privilege of knowing them for more than three decades and have witnessed, first hand, not only their devotion to deep theoretical analyses of important economic problems but also their human qualities. In this chapter, I take up one of the areas of my research interest (measurement of poverty in the multidimensional context) and try to bring to bear upon it the rigour of analysis for which Dasgupta and Bose are so well-known in the fields of their interests (which include but are not limited to this particular topic).

---

[*] An earlier version of the chapter was presented as a paper at the 2011 Annual Conference of the Indian Econometric Society at Indore, India. Closely related materials were also used for a presentation at the Economic Research Unit, Indian Statistical Institute, Kolkata, India in 2009. I am indebted to the comments and criticism from the participants in these discussions. However, the usual caveat applies.

It is by now widely recognized that the standard of living of a country is determined not only by the incomes of its citizens but also by a host of other attributes such as their education and health and that, therefore, the methods of measuring the standard of living and the extent of poverty prevailing in a country need to be extended from the unidimensional to the multidimensional framework.

In this chapter it is assumed that there is a given list of attributes. The purpose here is to construct a poverty index. Therefore, it is assumed that the list contains only those attributes which are considered to be basic necessities. In any society there is likely to be a broad social consensus regarding which attributes are to be included in the list. We shall not enter into the question about how this social consensus is (or should be) arrived at.

There have been several attempts at obtaining multidimensional poverty indices (MPIs). Some of these are generalizations of a widely used class of unidimensional indices of poverty or deprivation (the class proposed by Foster, Greer, and Thorbecke 1984 [FGT]). Some of the MPIs mentioned in Bourguignon and Chakravarty (2003) are of this type. For instances of other types of MPIs, see Chakravarty et al. (2008), Massoumi and Lugo (2008), and Tsui (2002).

The acceptability of an index depends on the conditions that it satisfies. This chapter suggests a new multidimensional poverty index (MPI) satisfying a number of conditions or axioms which seem to be reasonable. Two of the axioms considered in the chapter need mention. One of these is the axiom of Correlation Increasing Majorization (CIM) which states that a rearrangement of the entries in the poverty matrix which increases the correlation among the columns of the matrix increases the value of the poverty index. This axiom was introduced in economic literature by Tsui (1999) in the context of measuring inequality. Since a poverty index is usually desired to be sensitive to the inequality in the distribution of well-being among the poor, the axiom retains relevance in the present context (see Tsui 2002). The concept of Correlation Increasing Transfers (CITs) on which this axiom is based was discussed by Atkinson and Bourguignon (1982) and by Epstein and Tanny (1980).

An axiom called Prioritization of Attributes under Comonotonicity (PAC) is also introduced. In this context it is convenient to describe the poverty of the individuals with respect to the different attributes by means of a poverty matrix X in which the (p-th row, j-th column) term, x_p^j indicates the poverty of the p-th individual with regard to (w.r.t.) the j-th attribute. X is non-negative and each entry in X is normalized to ensure that it lies in the closed unit interval.

Suppose that the poverty matrix X is comonotonic (that is, if individual p is poorer than individual q w.r.t. to any given attribute, then p is poorer than q w.r.t. any other attribute). Thus, there is no scope for compensating for, say, a higher level of poverty of p w.r.t. one attribute by a lower level of poverty w.r.t. another. It then seems reasonable to require that if x^i, the i-th column of X, dominates its j-th column, x^j, that is, $x^i - x^j$ is non-negative and non-zero, then it is more beneficial (in terms of reduction in the value of the MPI) to reduce all the individuals' poverty levels w.r.t. attribute i to some target level than to reduce their poverty levels w.r.t. attribute j to the same level.

It is shown that CIM and PAC are independent conditions.

Taken individually, neither CIM nor PAC seem to be very restrictive conditions. Examples of MPIs satisfying CIM are easily found; and the same is true of those satisfying PAC.

Surprisingly, however, taken jointly, these two conditions severely restrict the admissible class of MPIs. In fact, existing literature does not seem to contain any MPI that satisfies CIM and PAC simultaneously. Therefore, the question arises as to whether such an MPI exists.

This chapter is an attempt at giving an affirmative answer to this question. It suggests an MPI that has not appeared so far in literature. The suggested class is a multidimensional generalization of the FGT class in the sense that it coincides with that class when there is only one attribute. However, it will be seen to be different from all the other MPIs in literature (whether related to the FGT class or not).

In the next section we introduce the notations, definitions, and axioms and also note the difficulties faced by the indices suggested in existing literature in satisfying the axioms. The section that follows introduces the index suggested in this chapter and shows that it satisfies both CIM and PAC. It also studies other properties of the suggested index. The last section provides a conclusion to the discussion.

Notations, Definitions, and Axioms

Consider the problem of constructing a poverty index for n individuals whose standard of living depends on their level of m attributes. Let the non-negative number s_p^j denote the level of attribute j for individual p ($p = 1, 2,\ldots, n$; $j = 1, 2,\ldots, m$). $N = \{1, 2,\ldots, n\}$ and $M = \{1, 2,\ldots, m\}$ will denote the set of individuals and the set of attributes respectively. The matrix S in which the (p-th row, j-th column) term is s_p^j is the *achievement matrix*. For all p in N and j in M, s_p and s^j will denote the p-th row and the j-th column of S respectively. The set of all achievement matrices will be denoted by S.

Let the positive number z_j be the threshold level (or poverty line) with respect to attribute j, that is, individual p is poor w.r.t. attribute j if $z_j \geq s_p^j$. Let z be the m-vector of threshold levels and z the set of all threshold vectors.

Let A be the set $\{s_p^j : S \; \varepsilon \; S, p \; \varepsilon \; N, j \; \varepsilon \; M\}$ and B be the set $\{z_j : z \; \varepsilon \; z, j \; \varepsilon \; M\}$. Let f be a mapping from $A \times B$ into $\Re+$, the set of non-negative real numbers, such that, for all a in A and all b in B: 1 f takes its minimal value at all a and b such that $a \geq b$; and 2 at all a and b such that $a < b$, f is decreasing in a and increasing in b. $f(s_p^j, z_j)$ is interpreted as the poverty of individual p w.r.t. attribute j. f will be called the Individual Deprivation Gaps Function (IDGF).

Example 1 The following are two specific examples of IDGFs: For all (S, z) in $S \times z$, for all p in N and for all j in M:

$$f^\beta(s_p^j, z_j) = (1 - s_p^j/z_j)^\beta \text{ for some } \beta > 0 \text{ if } s_p^j < z_j; \text{ and}$$

$$= 0, \text{ otherwise.}$$

f^1 will denote the IDGF f^β where $\beta = 1$.

(2) For all (S, z) in $S \times z$ such that $S > 0$, for all p in N and for all j in M:

$$h^\beta(s_p^j, z_j) = [z_j/min\,(s_p^j, z_j)]^\beta \text{ for some } \beta > 0.$$

h^1 will denote h^β when $\beta = 1$.

While the range of f^β is $[0, 1]$, that of h^β is $[1, \infty]$.

A Multidimensional Poverty Index

For all (S, z) in $\mathbf{S} \times \mathbf{z}$, the matrix in which the (p-th row, j-th column) term is $f(s_p^j, z_j)$ will be called the poverty matrix corresponding to (S, z) and will be denoted by $G(S, z)$. $G(S, z)$ will depend on f but this will be understood rather than made explicit in the notations. Poverty matrices are, by definition, non-negative. Moreover, for technical reasons we shall assume that, for all (S, z) in $\mathbf{S}, \mathbf{z}$ and for all IDGF f, $G(S, z)$ has at least one positive row, that is, there is at least one individual who has a positive level of deprivation w.r.t. all the attributes. $\mathbf{G(S, z)}$ (or $\mathbf{G}$) will denote the set of all poverty matrices with this characteristic.

Given an IDGF, f, not only is the poverty matrix (uniquely) given by a pair (S, z) in $\mathbf{S} \times \mathbf{z}$ but, for any matrix X in which all the entries are in the range of f, we can obtain a (not necessarily unique) pair (S, z) in $\mathbf{S} \times \mathbf{z}$ such that $X = G(S, z)$.

For any (S, z) in $\mathbf{S} \times \mathbf{z}$, let $D(S, z)$ denote the value of a (cardinal) poverty index D. For all (S, z) and (S', z') in $\mathbf{S} \times \mathbf{z}$, $D(S, z) \geq D(S', z')$ will be interpreted as implying that degree of overall poverty in the economy described by (S, z) is at least as great as that in the economy described by (S', z').

As in the unidimensional theory, a poverty index is desired to be sensitive to the distribution of poverty among the poor. In the multidimensional case, one aspect of such sensitivity is captured by the condition of Uniform Pigou-Dalton Majorization borrowed from literature on multidimensional *inequality* (see, for instance, Gajdos and Weymark (2005) and Weymark (2006)). It is a generalization of the notion of the unidimensional (Pigou-Dalton) principle of transfer *among the poor*.

Definition 1 For any (S, z) and (T, z') in $\mathbf{S} \times \mathbf{z}$, $X = G(S, z)$ is said to be obtained by a uniform Pigou-Dalton transfer from $Y = G(T, z')$ if $X \neq Y$ and if there exist p and q in N and k in $[0, 1]$ such that:

1. $x_p^j = k y_p^j + (1 - k) y_q^j$ for all j in M;

2. $x_q^j = (1 - k) y_p^j + k y_q^j$ for all j in M; and

3. $x_r = y_r$ for all r in $N - \{p, q\}$.

In this case it can be checked that $X = BY$ where $B = kI_n + (1-k)C_{p,q}$, I_n is the identity matrix of order n and $C_{p,q}$ is the permutation matrix which interchanges the p-th and q-th rows of Y. A matrix B of this form is called a 'T-transformation' matrix. Such matrices are special cases of bistochastic matrices, that is, matrices in which all rows and columns sum to 1. Not every bistochastic matrix, however, has the form of a T-transformation matrix.

Example 2 Let $n = m = 3$. Let (S, z) and (T, z') be such that:

$$Y = G(T, z') = \begin{pmatrix} a & b & c \\ d & e & f \\ g & h & k \end{pmatrix} \text{ and}$$

$$X = G(S, z) = \begin{pmatrix} (1/3)a + (2/3)d & (1/3)b + (2/3)e & (1/3)c + (2/3)f \\ (2/3)a + (1/3)d & (2/3)b + (1/3)e & (2/3)c + (1/3)f \\ g & h & f \end{pmatrix}.$$

This is a uniform Pigou-Dalton transfer between individuals 1 and 2 with $k = 1/3$. It is easily seen that $X = BY$ where:

$$B = K \begin{pmatrix} 1 & 0 & 0 \\ 0 & 1 & 0 \\ 0 & 0 & 1 \end{pmatrix} + (1-k) \begin{pmatrix} 0 & 1 & 0 \\ 1 & 0 & 0 \\ 0 & 0 & 1 \end{pmatrix} = \begin{pmatrix} k & 1-k & 0 \\ 1-k & k & 0 \\ 0 & 0 & 1 \end{pmatrix}.$$

Definition 2 For all X and Y in G, X is said to uniformly Pigou-Dalton majorize Y if X can be obtained from Y by a *finite sequence* of uniform Pigou-Dalton transfers.

The following axiom will be imposed on D:

Uniform Pigou-Dalton Majorization (UPDM): For all (S, z) and (T, z') in S, z, $D(S, z) \leq D(T, z')$ if $X = G(S, z)$ uniformly Pigou-Dalton majorizes $Y = G(T, z')$.

A stronger version of this requirement will replace the weak inequality in the earlier statement by a strict inequality and would require k in Definition 1 to lie in $(0, 1)$. In this chapter, however, we shall work with the weaker version proposed here.

Definition 3 An MPI is a mapping D: $(S \times z) \to \Re^+$ with the following properties:

1. It is a continuous mapping.
2. For all (S, z) in $S \times z$, for all p in N and j in M such that $s_p^j \leq z_j$, $D(S, z)$ increases if s_p^j decreases.
3. For all (S, z) in $S \times z$ and for all p in N and j in M such that $s_p^j > z_j$, $D(S, z)$ is invariant w.r.t. changes in s_p^j which do not violate this inequality.
4. For all (S, z) in $S \times z$ and for all $m \times m$ diagonal matrices Λ with positive scalars along the main diagonal, $D(S\Lambda, z\Lambda) = D(S, z)$.
5. For all (S, z) in $S \times z$, $D(S, z)$ is invariant w.r.t. permutations of the rows of S.
6. For all (S, z) in $S \times z$, if T is the k-fold population replication of S for some positive integer k, that is, for all p in N:

    $$s_p = t_p = t_{n+p} = \ldots = t_{n(k-1)+p},$$

    then $D(S, z) = D(T, z)$.
7. D satisfies UPDM.

As is easily checked, properties 2, 3, 4, 5, and 6 are respectively, multidimensional generalizations of the well-known properties of monotonicity, focus, ratio, scale invariance, anonymity, and population replication invariance of unidimensional theory and will be referred to by the same names in the present context.

Property 7 of Definition 3 ensures that D is distribution-sensitive. It may be noted that inequality literature contains several other transfer axioms which could have been adapted for the purpose. For instance, Uniform Majorization (Kolm 1977), Between Type Principle of Transfer (Ebert 2000; Ebert and Moyes 2003), etc. However, most of these other axioms are *stronger than* UPDM and are not proposed here as parts of the *definition* of a deprivation index. UPDM is one of the weakest and most straightforward generalizations of the unidimensional transfer principle.

Measures of inequality are, by definition, concerned with equity considerations. One aspect of such considerations is captured by extensions (such as UPDM) of the unidimensional transfer principle. In the multidimensional context, however, there are other aspects of the matter. One of these is sought to be captured by the axiom of CIM. To state this axiom we first state the concept of CITs.

Let X and Y be in G. For all p in N, let x_p and y_p be the p-th row of X and Y respectively. For all X in G and for all p, q in N, let $x_p \wedge x_q$ denote the vector $\{\min(x_p^1, x_q^1), \min(x_p^2, x_q^2),..., \min(x_p^m, x_q^m)\}$ and $x_p \vee x_q$ the vector $\{\max(x_p^1, x_q^1), \max(x_p^2, x_q^2),..., \max(x_p^m, x_q^m)\}$.

Definition 4 For all X and Y in G, X is said to be obtained from Y by a CIT if there exist p and q in N such that:

1. $x_p = y_p \wedge y_q$;
2. $x_q = y_p \vee y_q$; and
3. $x_r = y_r$ for all r in $N - \{p, q\}$.

The poverty index D is required to satisfy the following axiom:

Correlation Increasing Majorization (CIM) An MPI, D, is said to satisfy the axiom of CIM if, for all (S, z) and (T, z') in $\mathbf{S} \times \mathbf{z}$ such that $G(S, z)$ is obtained from $G(T, z')$ by a finite sequence of CIT's, $D(S, z) > D(T, z')$.

CIM was introduced in economic literature by Tsui (1999) in the context of inequality measurement. In statistical literature it was proposed by Boland and Proschan (1988). The concept of CIT on which it is based was studied in Atkinson and Bourguignon (1982) and in Epstein and Tanny (1980). In the context of measurement of poverty, a weaker version of the condition has been called the condition of Poverty Non-decreasing Rearrangement in Tsui (2002). An essentially similar condition has been called an Equity Principle in Pattanaik et al. (2008). Although the condition has been stated here in terms of *inequality among the poor*, the nomenclature of inequality literature has been retained.

The acceptability of an axiom depends on its intuitive plausibility. CIM seems to have a strong intuitive appeal. Consider, for instance, the following example. Let $n = 2 = m$. Let (S, z) and (T, z') be such that:

$$X = G(S, z) = \begin{pmatrix} 0.9 & 0.7 \\ 0.6 & 0.3 \end{pmatrix} \text{ and } Y = G(T, z') = \begin{pmatrix} 0.9 & 0.3 \\ 0.6 & 0.7 \end{pmatrix}.$$

X is obtained by a switch of the entries in the second column of Y. It is easily checked that this is a CIT. If it is now asked whether the level of overall poverty in the economy increases as we go from Y to X, there seems to be intuitive grounds for an affirmative answer. In Y individual 1 has a higher level of poverty than individual 2 w.r.t. attribute 1. But this is at least partially compensated for by the fact that w.r.t. attribute 2 individual 1 has a lower level of poverty. In X the effect of the higher poverty level of individual 1 w.r.t. attribute 1 is compounded by the fact that individual 1 also has a higher poverty level w.r.t. attribute 2, that is, there is greater *correlation* between the columns of the poverty matrix. It seems reasonable to require that overall poverty is higher in X than in Y. The social value judgement implicit here is that a higher poverty level of an individual w.r.t. an attribute can be compensated for by a lower level w.r.t. another. In other words, the different attributes are not independent: they are substitutes of one another.

To state the next axiom we need the concept of *comonotonic* matrices (see, for instance, Gajdos and Weymark (2005)).

For all poverty matrices X and for all j in M, x^j is *non-increasing monotonic* if $x_1^j \geq x_2^j \geq \ldots \geq x_n^j$. It is *non-decreasing monotonic* if $x_1^j \leq x_2^j \leq \ldots \leq x_n^j$. The individuals are called equally poor w.r.t. attribute j if x^j is both non-increasing monotonic and non-decreasing monotonic. For all poverty matrices X and for all i and j in M, x^i and x^j are *comonotonic* if either both x^i and x^j are non-increasing monotonic or both of them are non-decreasing monotonic; they are called *counter-monotonic* if one of them is non-increasing monotonic, the other is non-decreasing monotonic, and the individuals are not equally poor w.r.t. either i or j.

Definition 5 A poverty matrix X is comonotonic if either x^j is non-increasing monotonic for all j in M or it is non-decreasing monotonic for all j in M.

Now confine attention to comonotonic poverty matrices so that there is no scope for compensating for a greater poverty level of an individual than that of another w.r.t. one attribute by a lower poverty level w.r.t. some other attribute.

In the practical context it often becomes necessary to decide on the relative importance of the tasks of eliminating poverty w.r.t. the different attributes. This is especially true of non-income attributes such as education or health for which public action often takes the form of subsidizing the relatively worse-placed individuals rather than that of progressive transfers from the better-placed ones. (In fact, for such attributes it is not clear what such transfers would mean or how these would be implemented.) In such cases the resource constraints of the government or other social agencies make prioritization among the attributes a necessary part of policy formulation. (To an extent, this is also true of income. Indeed, poverty would not be a pervasive problem if the scope of income support to the poor by subsidization financed by transfers from the non-poor was not limited in practice by other considerations such as economic efficiency.)

In such circumstances it may be appropriate to assume that higher importance should be attached to the task of reducing those deprivations which are more acute.

At this point a potential misunderstanding regarding this assumption may be dealt with. In any society, deprivation w.r.t. luxury items (for instance, diamond jewellery or expensive cars) may be more acute than that w.r.t. necessities. A question may arise as to whether it is being suggested here that in such a society reducing deprivations w.r.t. luxuries should be considered to be more urgent. It may be noted that the answer is negative. As stated earlier, the list of attributes that we start with is assumed to include only the basic necessities of life.

We now formalize the assumption. For any (S, z) in $S \times z$, replacing the j-th column of the poverty matrix $X = G(S, z)$, x^j, by a column of ks where k is a constant such that $x^j \geq k.1_n$, $x^j \neq k.1_n$, can be interpreted to mean reducing all the individual poverty levels w.r.t. attribute j to the common level k. Obviously, this is feasible only if $k \geq u$ where u is the minimal value of the IDGF. For the IDGF f^β of Example 1 $u = 0$ while, for h^β, $u = 1$.

For all X in G and for all j in M, let $X^{-j,k}$ denote the matrix obtained by replacing the j-th column of X by $k.1_n$.

The following axiom is proposed:

Prioritization of Attributes under Comonotonocity (PAC) Let u be the minimal value of IDGF. Let (S, z) in $S \times z$ be such that $X = G(S, z)$ is comonotonic; and let i and j in M be such that $x^i \geq x^j \geq k1_n$, $x^i \neq x^j$ and $k \geq u$.

If (T, z') and (V, z'') in $\mathbf{S} \times \mathbf{z}$ are such that $X^{-i,k} = G(T, z')$ and $X^{-j,k} = G(V, z'')$, then $D(T, z') < D(V, z'')$.

PAC requires that if no individual is less poor w.r.t. attribute i than w.r.t. attribute j and at least one individual is poorer w.r.t. i, then it is considered more beneficial (in terms of reduction in the value of the index D of overall poverty) to reduce all the individual poverty levels w.r.t. attribute i to some given common feasible level than to reduce the individual poverty levels w.r.t. attribute j to the same level.

Example 3 Consider the IDGF f^1 mentioned in Example 1. Here $u = 0$.

Let $n = m = 2$. Let $S = \begin{pmatrix} 0 & 0 \\ 5 & 15 \end{pmatrix}$ and $z = (10, 20)$. Then $X = G(S, z)$

$= \begin{pmatrix} 1 & 1 \\ 1/2 & 1/4 \end{pmatrix}$ is comonotonic. Since $x^1 = \begin{pmatrix} 1 \\ 1/2 \end{pmatrix} \geq \begin{pmatrix} 1 \\ 1/4 \end{pmatrix} = x^2$

$> \begin{pmatrix} 1/10 \\ 1/10 \end{pmatrix} > \begin{pmatrix} 0 \\ 0 \end{pmatrix}$, and $x^1 \neq x^2$, PAC would require $D(T, z') < D(V, z'')$

if $T = \begin{pmatrix} 54/5 & 0 \\ 54/5 & 45/2 \end{pmatrix}$, $z' = (12, 30)$, $V = \begin{pmatrix} 0 & 45/2 \\ 15/2 & 45/2 \end{pmatrix}$ and $z'' =$

$(15, 25)$ since $G(T, z') = \begin{pmatrix} 1/10 & 1 \\ 1/10 & 1/4 \end{pmatrix} = X^{-1, 1/10}$ and $G(V, z'') =$

$\begin{pmatrix} 1 & 1/10 \\ 1/2 & 1/10 \end{pmatrix} = X^{-2, 1/10}$.

It is noted that the prioritization of the attributes implied by PAC depends on the poverty matrix. It does not refer to an *ex ante* prioritization.

PAC does not appear to be a very strong requirement. In fact, it is easily checked that one of the simplest MPIs, which is the arithmetic mean of the poverty indices of the different attributes (using any of the standard distribution-sensitive *unidimensional* formulas available in literature), will give us an MPI in the sense of Definition 3 and will satisfy PAC (such an MPI will, however, violate CIM).

The MPIs mentioned in the preceding paragraph show that PAC does not imply CIM. It is also true that CIM does not imply PAC. Consider the following MPI:

For all (S, z) in $S \times z$, $D(S, z) = [\sum_{p=1}^{n} (\sum_{j=1}^{m} w_j x_p^j)^2] / (n \times m)$ where $w_j \geq 0$ for all j in M, $\sum_{j=1}^{m} w_j = 1$ and $X = G(S, z)$ is obtained from the IDGF f^1 of Example 1.

Since CIM is stated in terms of a *finite* sequence of CITs, to show that D satisfies CIM it suffices to show that, for all (S, z) and (T, z') in $S \times z$ such that $X = G(S, z)$ is obtained from $Y = G(T, z')$ by a single CIT but $X \neq Y$ and X is not a permutation of the rows of Y, $D(S, z) > D(T, z')$.

In this case there exists a partition $\{U, V\}$ of the set of attributes M such that 1 for all j in U, $x^j = y^j$ and 2 there exist p and q in N such that, for all j in V, $x_p^j = y_q^j$, $x_q^j = y_p^j$ and $x_r^j = y_r^j$ for all r in $N - \{p, q\}$.

It can now be checked that the requirement that $D(S, z) > D(T, z')$ reduces to:

$$\sum_{i \in U} \sum_{j \in V} w_i w_j [(x_p^i \vee x_q^i) - (x_p^i \wedge x_q^i)] [(x_p^j \vee x_q^j) - (x_p^j \wedge x_q^j)] > 0.$$

Since each of the square-bracketed terms in the summation on the l.h.s. is non-negative by definition, the l.h.s. is non-negative. The facts that $X \neq Y$ and that X is not a permutation of the rows of Y imply that there is at least one positive term in the summation. The required strict inequality is, therefore, satisfied.

However, there exist cases in which the stated poverty index violates PAC. For instance, let $n = 2 = m$. Let $w_1 = 1/4$ and $w_2 = 3/4$. With the same IDGF, f^1, as before, so that $u = 0$, let (S, z) in $S \times z$ be such that:

$$X = G(S, z) = \begin{pmatrix} 1 & 1 \\ 1/2 & 1/4 \end{pmatrix}$$

Since X is comonotonic, $x^1 \geq x^2$ and $x^1 \neq x^2$, PAC requires that

$$D(T, z') < D(V, z'') \ldots (*)$$

where (T, z') and (V, z'') in $S \times z$ are such that $G(T, z') = \begin{pmatrix} a & 1 \\ 0 & 1/4 \end{pmatrix}$, $G(V, z'') = \begin{pmatrix} 1 & a \\ 1/4 & 0 \end{pmatrix}$

and $0 < a < 1$. However, it can be seen that, with the stated index and with the specified values of w_1 and w_2, (*) is contradicted since it would imply $a^2 > 133/128 > 1$.

Thus, CIM and PAC are independent axioms.

These two axioms taken together, however, seem to limit the applicability of many of the MPIs that have been proposed in theoretical literature or have been empirically applied. The general approach has been either to use a unidimensional poverty index (UPI) formula for each of the n columns of a poverty matrix and then to combine the m different UPIs into a single index by a weighting formula or to first arrive at a scalar indicator of each individual's poverty by combining the entries in the relevant row according to some formula and then to apply a UPI formula to the resulting n-vector of individual deprivations. As in Pattanaik et al. (2008) these two approaches may be called the 'columns first' and the 'rows first' approaches respectively. In that paper axioms are imposed on a ranking relation on the space of poverty matrices. However, the proof of one of the main results of that paper can be used to prove a proposition which, in terms of our notations and terminology, would read as follows: A MPI constructed by a 'columns first' approach violates CIM in the presence of other standard assumptions.

While UNDP's (2009) human poverty indices are built on the basis of a 'columns first' approach, academic literature contains examples of both the approaches. Most of these indices, however, face difficulties in satisfying CIM and PAC simultaneously. The nature of these difficulties is indicated now in the cases of a few of the indices that have been suggested in recent years.

Consider, for instance, the following index studied in Bourguignon and Chakravarty (2003). For all (S, z) in $S \times z$:

$$D(S, z) = (1/n) \sum_{j \in M} \sum_p \varepsilon_{S(j)} a_j (1 - s_p^j / z_j)^{b_j} \tag{4.1}$$

where $a_j \geq 0$ for all j in M, $\sum_{j=1}^{m} a_j = 1$; $b_j > 0$ for all j in M and, for all j in M, $S_j = \{p \varepsilon N : s_p^j < z_j\}$, that is, the set of individuals who are poor w.r.t. attribute j.

IDGF implicit in the index is the same as the one used in the examples discussed before, that is, f^1.

It is easily checked that if the number of attributes m is 1, the class of indices in (4.1) coincides with the FGT class of unidimensional poverty indices, that is, it is a generalization of the FGT class.

However, the class of indices described by (4.1) does not satisfy CIM and PAC simultaneously. In fact, the violation takes a strong form: not only is it the case that there *exists* a member of the class which fails to satisfy these axioms simultaneously; in fact, for *any* specified values of the parameters there will exist some S and z such that the poverty index (4.1) violates either CIM or PAC. The proof of this proposition is indicated here for the case where $n = m = 2$. The argument extends to the general case in a straightforward way.

Consider first the case in which $a_1 < a_2$. In this case $a_2 \neq 0$.

Let $z = (10, 20)$ and $S = \begin{pmatrix} 0 & 0 \\ 0 & 20(1-k) \end{pmatrix}$ for k such that $0 < k < 1$.

Then $G(S, z) = \begin{pmatrix} 1 & 1 \\ 1 & k \end{pmatrix}$.

PAC requires $D(T, z') < D(V, z'')$ where (T, z) and (V, z'') are such that $G(T, z') = \begin{pmatrix} c & 1 \\ c & k \end{pmatrix}$

and $G(V, z'') = \begin{pmatrix} 1 & c \\ 1 & c \end{pmatrix}$ if $0 \leq c < k$.

It can be checked that the index formula (4.1) would then imply the requirement:

$[(1 + k^{b_2} - 2c^{b_2}) / (1 - c^{b_2})] < 2(a_1/a_2)$.

It is possible to choose c and k such that this inequality is violated. For instance, if c is put at 0, the requirement becomes: $k < [2(a_1/a_2) - 1]^{1/b_2} = \alpha$ (say) < 1 (since $a_1 < a_2$). Since a_1, a_2, b_2 and, therefore,

A Multidimensional Poverty Index 71

α are pre-specified, it is possible to choose a value of k such that $\alpha < k < 1$ so that PAC is violated (it is possible to get similar violations with positive values of c if these are sufficiently small).

On the other hand, consider the case where $a_1 > a_2$. Now $a_1 \neq 0$.

Keeping the labelling of the attributes unchanged, we can change the specification of S and z so that we now have:

$$X = \begin{pmatrix} 1 & 1 \\ k & 1 \end{pmatrix} \text{ where, as before, } 0 < k < 1.$$

Proceeding in the same way as earlier, we now get the following implication of PAC if $c = 0$: $k < [2(a_2/a_1) - 1]^{1/b_1} = \phi$ (say). Noting that in the present case $\phi < 1$, we can, again, obtain a violation of PAC by a suitable choice of k.

The problem is avoided *only* if $a_1 = a_2$ (= a, say). However, in that case, choosing (S, z) and (T, z') in **S** × **z** so that:

$$X = G(S, z) = \begin{pmatrix} 1 & 1 \\ 1/2 & 1/2 \end{pmatrix} \text{ and } Y = G(T, z') = \begin{pmatrix} 1 & 1/2 \\ 1/2 & 1 \end{pmatrix},$$

and applying the index formula (4.1), it is seen that $D(S, z) = D(T, z')$ although X is obtained from Y by a CIT. Thus, CIM is violated.

Consider now the following MPI which is one of the indices proposed by Tsui (2002) (also see Massoumi and Lugo [2008]):

For all (S, z) in **S** × **z**:

$$D(S, z) = (1/n) \sum_{p=1}^{n} \sum_{j=1}^{m} a_j \log [z_j / min (s_p^j, z_j)] \tag{4.2}$$

where a_j's are as in (4.1) and it is assumed that the matrix S is positive.

Here the underlying IDGF is h^1 of Example 1.

However, it can be seen, by an argument similar to that in the case of (4.1), that for any specified values of the parameters a_j, if these are not the same for all j in M, then, for some (S, z), (T, z') and (V, z'')

in $S \times z$, (4.2) will violate PAC while if these are the same, then it will violate CIM.

The special case of equal a_j's in (4.2) corresponds to the Multidimensional Watts Index mentioned in Chakravarty et al. (2008). It is defined as:

For all (S, z) in $S \times z$,

$$D(S, z) = (1/n) \sum_{p=1}^{n} \sum_{j=1}^{m} \log [z_j/\min(s_p^j, z_j)] \qquad (4.3)$$

This is a multidimensional version of one of the earliest distribution-sensitive measures of poverty suggested by Watts (1968). However, from the discussion earlier it is clear that (4.3) would violate CIM.

From the viewpoint of the present discussion the case of another MPI studied in Bourguignon and Chakravarty (2003) is only slightly different. This index is defined as:

For all (S, z) in $S \times z$,

$$D(S, z) = (1/n) \sum_{p=1}^{n} [\{\sum_{j=1}^{m} a_j (x_p^j)^\beta\}^{1/\beta}]^\alpha \qquad (4.4)$$

where $\alpha > 0$, $\beta > 0$ and, for all p in N and j in M,

$x_p^j = (z_j - s_p^j)/z_j$ if $z_j > s_p^j$

$= 0$, otherwise.

For any specified values of the parameters a_j such that these are not the same for all j in M, it is, again, possible to construct examples of (S, z), (T, z'), and (V, z'') in $S \times z$ for which (4.4) would violate PAC. However, if these are the same for all j in M, then, under *some additional restrictions* on the relative magnitudes of the parameters α and β, it will satisfy both CIM and PAC.

Tsui (2002) also discussed another deprivation index which can be stated as:

For all (S, z) in $S \times z$ such that S is positive:

$$D(S, z) = (1/n) \sum_{p=1}^{n} [\prod_{j=1}^{m} \{z_j/\min(s_p^j, z_j)\}^{a_j} - 1] \qquad (4.5)$$

where $a_j > 0$ for all j in M.

So far as its compatibility with the axioms is concerned, the case of this index is essentially similar to that of (4.4): it satisfies both CIM and PAC only if a_j is the same for all j in M.

An assumption of equal weights for all attributes under all circumstances (that is, whatever the number and the nature of the specific attributes may be) does not seem to be justifiable. As has been remarked, this assumption is 'obviously convenient but also universally considered to be wrong' (see Chowdhury and Squire (2006: 762). Also, see the discussion in Decancq and Lugo (2010: 15–16)).

It should be noted that the discussion here does not constitute a general critique of the MPIs that have been mentioned. Indeed, as is shown in the cited references, each of these indices has its own supporting set of axioms. However, these remarks seem to indicate that in existing literature it is hard to find examples of MPIs that satisfy both CIM and PAC without precluding unequal weights on the attributes. Therefore, the question arises as to whether such an index (or a class of such indices) exists. The next section suggests an affirmative answer.

A Multidimensional Poverty Index

Consider the IDGF, f^β, of Example 1. Let P_β be the following mapping on (S, z):

Definition 6 $P_\beta : (S \times z) \to \Re^+$ is such that, for all (S, z) in $S \times z$:

$$P_\beta(S, z) = \lambda^* (X'X)/(nm)$$

where $X = G(S, z)$ and $\lambda^* (X'X)$ is the maximal eigenvalue (that is, the Perron-Frobenius characteristic root) of the $m \times m$ non-negative non-zero matrix $X'X$.

We shall prove the following:

Proposition 1 The mapping P_β in Definition 6 is a MPI satisfying CIM and PAC.

In proving Proposition 1 we shall use the Perron-Frobenius theorem for positive (or non-negative indecomposable) square matrices. We shall also use the following three Lemmas:

Lemma 1 For any square positive matrix B let $\lambda^*(B)$ be its maximal eigenvalue. Then:

1. λ^* is continuous and increasing in all the entries in B; and
2. $\lambda^*(kB) = k\lambda^*(B)$ for all positive scalars k.

Lemma 2 Let S_m be the set of all real square *symmetric* matrices of order m. For any A in S_m let $\lambda_i(A)$, $i = 1, 2,..., m$, be the eigenvalues of A arranged in non-increasing order: $\lambda_1(A) \geq \lambda_2(A) \geq ... \geq \lambda_m(A)$. Let A, B, and C in S_m be such that $A = B + C$. If $\lambda_m(C) \geq 0$, then $\lambda_i(A) \geq \lambda_i(B)$ for all $i = 1, 2,..., m$.

Lemma 3 Let S_m be as in Lemma 2. Let C in S_m be such that:

1. The main diagonal entries in C are non-negative; and
2. The minor of each entry in C is zero.

Then the eigenvalues of C are: 0 with multiplicity $(n-1)$, and the sum of the main diagonal terms of C.

Part 1 of Lemma 1 is a well-known result in the Perron-Frobenius theory of non-negative square matrices. For proof and discussion see, for instance, Debreu and Herstein (1953) and Horn and Johnson (1985). Part 2 is easily checked. Lemma 2, quoted in, for instance, Boroojeni (2008), is a special case of Weyl's Inequalities. For proof and discussion see Horn and Johnson (1991: Chapter 3). Lemma 3 is established by solving the characteristic equation. It is noted that C in Lemma 3 is not necessarily non-negative. If $m = 3$, the following would be an example of a matrix satisfying the conditions stated in Lemma 3:

$$C = \begin{pmatrix} aa & ab & ac \\ ba & bb & bc \\ ca & cb & cc \end{pmatrix}$$

where a, b, and c are real numbers, not necessarily of the same sign. As is easily seen, the eigenvalues of C are: 0, 0 and $a^2 + b^2 + c^2$.

Proof of Proposition 1 For any (S, z) in $S \times z$, since $X = G(S, z)$ has a positive row, $X'X$ is a positive square matrix of order m. By the Perron-Frobenius theorem, therefore, $\lambda^*(X'X)$ is real, positive and unique. Hence, the mapping P_β in Definition 6 is well-defined.

Under IDGF, f^β, $X = G(S, z)$ is continuous in any entry of S or z. By Part 1 of Lemma 1, therefore, P_β satisfies Continuity (part i of Definition 3). Since, for any (S, z) in $\mathbf{S} \times \mathbf{z}$, an increase in an entry in $X = G(S, z)$ implies an increase in some entries in $X'X$, 1 of Lemma 1 also implies Monotonicity of P_β (part ii of Definition 3). It is easily checked that P_β satisfies the conditions of Focus and Ratio Scale Invariance (parts iii and iv of Definition 2.3). Anonymity (part 5 of 3) follows the fact that, for any (S, z) in $\mathbf{S} \times \mathbf{z}$, a permutation of the rows of S induces the same permutation in the rows of $X = G(S, z)$ and leaves $X'X$ and, hence, λ^* unchanged. To check Population Replication Invariance (part vi of Definition 3), note that for any (S, z) and (T, z) in $\mathbf{S} \times \mathbf{z}$, such that T is a k-fold population replication of S for some positive scalar k, if $X = G(S, z)$ and $Y = G(T, z)$, then $Y'Y = kX'X$. By Part 2 of Lemma 1, therefore, $\lambda^*(Y'Y) = k\lambda^*(X'X)$. Hence, $P_\beta(T, z) = k\lambda^*(X'X)/knm = \lambda^*(X'X) / nm = P_\beta(S, z)$.

To see that P_β satisfies UPDM (part vii of Definition 3), note that uniform Pigou-Dalton majorization involves a finite sequence of uniform Pigou-Dalton transfers.

Hence, it suffices to show that, for any (S, z) and (T, z') in $\mathbf{S}, \mathbf{z}$ such that $X = G(S, z)$ is obtained from $Y = G(T, z')$ by a single transfer of this type, $P_\beta(S, z) \leq P_\beta(T, z')$. For X and Y as stated, it follows that $X = BY$ where B is a 'T-transformation matrix' (see Definition 1 and the remarks following it). Calculations which are notionally straightforward but space-consuming (and, therefore, omitted here) now establish the following equality: For some k in $[0, 1]$:

$$Y'Y = X'X + 2k(1-k)C$$

where C is a square symmetric matrix of order m in which the main diagonal entries are non-negative and the minors of all the entries are zero. With the notations as in Lemmas 2 and 3, therefore, it follows from Lemma 3 that $\lambda_m(C) = 0$. Since $Y'Y$ and $X'X$ are square symmetric matrices of order m, we get from Lemma 2: $\lambda_1(Y'Y) \geq \lambda_1(X'X)$. Also, since these matrices are positive, $\lambda^*(Y'Y) = \lambda_1(Y'Y)$ and a similar equality holds for $X'X$. Therefore, $P_\beta(T, z') \geq P_\beta(S, z)$. This completes the proof of the fact that P_β is a MPI.

It is easily seen that if (S, z) and (T, z') are such that $X = G(S, z)$ is obtained from $Y = G(T, z')$ by a CIT, then $X'X \geq Y'Y$ and $X'X \neq Y'Y$. Hence, $P_\beta (S, z) > P_\beta (T, z')$ by Part 1 of Lemma 1. Since CIM involves a finite sequence of CITs, it follows that P_β satisfies CIM.

To show that P_β satisfies PAC, let (S, z), (T, z') and (V, z'') in $S \times z$ be such that (4.1) $X = G(S, z)$ is such that, for some i and j in M, $x^i \geq x^j \geq k1_n$, $x^i \neq x^j \neq k1_n$ for some positive scalar k, (2) $Y = X^{-i, k} = G(T, z')$ and (3) $Z = X^{-j, k} = G(V, z'')$. As is easily seen, for any (S, z), $P_\beta (S, z)$ is invariant w.r.t. permutations of columns of $X = G(S, z)$. Using this fact, it can be shown that $Y'Y \leq X'X$ and $Y'Y \neq X'X$. Therefore, Part 1 of Lemma 1 implies that $P_\beta (T, z') < P_\beta (V, z'')$, as required.

Q.E.D.

We end this section with some remarks on the nature of the MPI suggested in Proposition 1.

(1) For all (S, z) in $S \times z$, $P_\beta (S, z) > 0$. If (S, z) is such that all the entries in $X = G(S, z)$ are 1, $X'X$ is a square matrix of order m in which all the entries are n. In this case $\lambda^*(X'X) = nm$. Hence, $P_\beta (S, z) = 1$. Thus, the MPI, P_β, has the range $(0, 1)$.

(2) In the special case where there is only one attribute ($m = 1$), P_β coincides with the well-known class of indices suggested by FGT. S in this case is an achievement *vector* and z, a scalar, rather than a matrix and a vector respectively. In the notations of this chapter, the FGT index can be stated as follows: For all (S, z) in $S \times z$:

$$F_\alpha (S, z) = (1/n) \sum_{p=1}^{n} x_p^\alpha \text{ for some } \alpha > 0$$

where x_p is the p-th entry in the vector $X = G(S, z)$, obtained from the IDGF, f^1.

It can be seen from Definition 6 that if $m = 1$, then P_β is essentially the same class of indices as F_α in the sense that there is a one-to-one correspondence between the members of the two classes: for any $\alpha > 0$ there exists a unique $\beta > 0$ (which is, $\beta = \alpha/2$) such that $P_\beta (S, z) = F_\alpha (S, z)$ for all (S, z) in $S \times z$; and vice versa. In this sense P_β is a multidimensional version of the FGT class of poverty indices.

(3) It is obvious from Definition 6 that P_β does not constitute either a 'columns first' or a 'rows first' approach to the problem of obtaining an index of aggregate poverty. For any poverty matrix X,

A Multidimensional Poverty Index 77

the maximal eigenvalue of $X'X$, obtained as the maximal root of the relevant characteristic equation, will depend simultaneously on all the entries of $X'X$ and, therefore, on those of X.

(4) However, P_β can be given an interpretation which would make the underlying approach comparable to that of the other MPIs in literature. For this purpose we make use of a particular member of the FGT class which has been widely applied empirically, which is, the one for which $\alpha = 2$.

As is well-known, the maximal eigenvalue of a positive (or non-negative indecomposable) square matrix has the special feature that it is the only eigenvalue of the matrix such that the associated eigenvector is positive (this eigenvector is often called the 'first eigenvector' of the matrix). The index P_β is related to the idea of using, for every (S, z), the components of the first eigenvector of $X'X$, where $X = G(S, z)$, as the weights on the attributes and then using the formula, F_2. The notion is illustrated here with the case where $n = m = 2$.

Let (S, z) in $\mathbf{S} \times \mathbf{z}$ be such that $X = G(S, z)$, obtained from IDGF f^β, is $\begin{pmatrix} a & b \\ c & d \end{pmatrix}$. Let the first eigenvector of $X'X$ be $w = (w_1, w_2) > 0$. Components of eigenvectors, however, are determined only up to ratios. The vectors are made unique by choosing a normalization rule. In mathematical literature, a frequently used normalization is to put the squared sum of the components equal to 1: $w_1^2 + w_2^2 = 1$. If we follow this rule, the index P_β can be given the following interpretation. If we use w as the vector of weights on the attributes and consider the weighted sum of the entries in a row of X to be the scalar indicator of the poverty level of the relevant individual, we get $(aw_1 + bw_2)$ and $(cw_1 + dw_2)$ as the two individuals' poverty levels. If we now use the unidimensional F_2 formula, we get the following value for overall deprivation for this extended version of F_2, F_2^E (say):

$$[(aw_1 + bw_2)^2 + (cw_1 + dw_2)^2]/2 = [(a^2 + c^2)w_1^2 + (b^2 + d^2)w_2^2 + 2(ab + cd)w_1 w_2]/2 \quad (**)$$

On the other hand, by definition of eigenvalues, $(X'X)w' = \lambda^* w'$. With the specified X this implies: $(a^2 + c^2)w_1 + (ab + cd)w_2 = \lambda^* w_1$; and $(ab + cd)w_1 + (b^2 + d^2)w_2 = \lambda^* w_2$. Multiplying the last two equations by w_1 and w_2 respectively, adding the resultant equations, and using the normalization specified earlier, it is seen that $\lambda^*(X'X)$ equals the expression within square brackets in the numerator of (**). Hence, $P_\beta(S, z) = \lambda^*(X'X) / 4 = F_2^E(S, z)/2$. Thus, P_β is a constant multiple of F_2^E. A similar result will be valid for the general nm case.

(If other normalization rules are used, for instance, if the components of the first eigenvector are required to sum to 1, the precise result of the preceding paragraph will be disturbed. But P_β will continue to be closely related to F_2^E.)

Thus, it is as if P_β takes a 'rows approach' to the problem of constructing an MPI by using the first eigenvector of $X'X$ as the vector of weights on the attributes.

However, it is noted that this interpretation of P_β also highlights its important distinguishing characteristic. Unlike the exogenously given weights used in MPIs mentioned in the section, 'Notations, Definitions, and Axioms', the weights on the attributes which are implicit in the index suggested in this chapter depend on the poverty matrix.

* * *

This chapter suggested an MPI, satisfying a number of axioms. If the poverty matrix is X, the value of the index is the maximal eigenvalue of $X'X$ scaled by $(1/nm)$ where n and m are the number of individuals and the number of attributes respectively. This particular index does not seem to appear in existing literature. One of its main features is that the weights on the attributes, which are implicit in the index, are given by the first eigenvector of $X'X$. Hence, these implicit weights are functions of the poverty matrix unlike the exogenously given weights in most of the other multidimensional indices in literature.

The index suggested here is to be contrasted from an approach first suggested in the 1980s literature on measuring well-being in a multidimensional framework. In that approach a scalar indicator for each row of a well-being matrix will be obtained by constructing the 'first principal component' of the corresponding row, that is, that linear combination of the entries in the row in which the first eigenvector of the empirical *covariance* (or *correlation*) matrix is used as the weight vector (see Ram (1982)).

A central difference in the approach taken in this chapter from the framework of principal component analysis is that, even for non-negative data, the covariance matrix is not necessarily non-negative. For instance, as is easily seen, it will fail to be non-negative whenever a pair of columns in the poverty matrix are counter-monotonic. Hence, the Perron-Frobenius theorem does not apply to that framework. Therefore, the non-negativity of the weight vector is not guaranteed in the principal components approach.

In contrast, in the approach taken in this chapter the Perron-Frobenius theorem lies at the heart of the matter. In economic terms, a strong point of the index suggested here is that while complying with the axioms, it pays attention to the need for ensuring that the implicit weight on any attribute does not turn out to be negative.

References

Atkinson, A.B., and F. Bourguignon. 1982. 'The Comparison of Multidimensional Distributions of Economic Status', *Review of Economic Studies*, 49: 183–201.

Boland, D.J., and F. Proschan. 1988. 'Mulidimensional Arrangement Increasing Functions with applications in Probability and Statistics', *Journal of Multivariate Analysis*, 25: 286–98.

Bourguignon, F., and S.R. Chakravarty. 2003. 'The Measurement of Multidimensional Poverty', *Journal of Economic Inequality*, 1: 25–49.

Boroojeni, J.E. 2008. 'Sum of the Largest Eigenvalues of Symmetric Matrices and Graphs', MSc thesis, Department of Mathematics, Simon Fraser University.

Chakravarty, S.R., J. Deutsch, and J. Silber. 2008. 'On the Watts Multidimensional Poverty Index and its Decomposition', *World Development*, 36: 1067–77.

Chowdhury, S., and L. Squire. 2006. 'Setting Weights for Aggregative Indices: An Application to the Commitment to Development Index and Human Development Index', *Journal of Development Studies*, 42: 761–71.

Decancq, K., and M.A. Lugo. 2010. 'Weights in Multidimensional Indices of well-being: An overview', Working Paper, Centre for Economic Studies, Catholic University of Leuven, pp. 1–31.

Debreu, H., and I.N. Herstein. 1953. 'Non-negative Square Matrices', *Econometrica*, 21: 597–607.

Ebert, U. 2000. 'Sequential Generalized Lorenz Dominance and Transfer Principles', *Bulletin of Economic Research*, 52: 113–23.
Ebert, U., and P. Moyes. 2003. 'Equivalence Scales Reconsidered', *Econometrica*, 71: 319–43.
Epstein, L.G., and S.M. Tanny. 1980. 'Increasing Generalized Correlation: A Definition and Some Economic Concepts', *Canadian Journal of Economics*, 13: 16–34.
Gajdos, T., and J.A. Weymark. 2005. 'Multidimensional Generalized Gini Indices', *Economic Theory*, 26: 471–95.
Foster, J.E., J. Greer, and E. Thorbecke. 1984 'A Class of Decomposable Poverty Measures', *Econometrica*, 52: 761–6.
Horn, R.A., and C.R. Johnson. 1985. *Matrix Analysis*. Cambridge: Cambridge University Press.
———. 1991. *Topics in Matrix Analysis*. Cambridge: Cambridge University Press.
Kolm, S.C. 1977. 'Multidimensional Egalitarianisms', *Quarterly Journal of Economics*, 91: 1–13.
Massoumi, E., and M.A. Lugo. 2008. 'The Information Basis of Multivariate Poverty Assessments', in N. Kakwani and J. Silber (eds), *Quantitative Approaches to Multidimensional Poverty Measurement*. London: Palgrave Macmillan, pp. 1–29.
Pattanaik, P.K., S.G. Reddy, and Y. Xu. 2008. 'On Procedures for Measuring Deprivation and Living Standards of Societies in a Multi-attribute Framework', Working Paper 08–02, Andrew Young School of Policy Studies, Georgia State University.
Ram, R. 1982. 'Composite Indices of Physical Quality of Life, Basic Needs Fulfilment and Income', *Journal of Development Economics*, 11: 227–47.
Tsui, K.Y. 1999. 'Multidimensional Inequality and Multidimensional Generalized Entropy Measures: An Axiomatic Derivation', *Social Choice and Welfare*, 16: 145–77.
———. 2002. 'Multidimensional Poverty Indices', *Social Choice and Welfare*, 19: 69–93.
United Nations Development Program. 2009. *Human Development Report 2009*. New York: Oxford University Press.
Watts, H.W. 1968. 'An Economic Definition of Poverty', in D.P. Moynihan (ed.), *On Understanding Poverty*. New York: Basic Books, pp. 316–29.
Weymark, J.A. 2006. 'The Normative Approach to the Measurement of Multidimensional Inequality', in F. Farina and E. Savaglio (eds), *Inequality and Economic Integration*. London: Routledge, pp. 303–28.

5

Transaction Costs and Optimal Market Structure

Meenakshi Rajeev[*]

A competitive economy is characterized by the matching of aggregate demand for and aggregate supply of each commodity. For example, while agent 'a' has an excess demand for good 'c', there is a trading partner who has excess supply of that good. However, even in such an economy, lack of a double coincidence of wants at the individual level can create serious problems in attaining one's desired bundle of goods (Ostroy and Starr 1990). The earliest recognition of the problem emerged in Menger (1892); later Hicks (1967) posed it in

[*] I am immensely grateful to Dipankar Dasgupta and Amitava Bose for rousing my interest in this area. Their intellectual support and encouragement have always been critical for my academic career. I worked in this research area jointly with Dipankar Dasgupta, who was my PhD supervisor, and I benefited greatly from his guidance. I also thank Randall Wright and Ross Starr for useful discussions on the topic of money and markets. Usual disclaimer applies.

the context of Walrasian economy (Walras 1956). In recent times a considerable body of literature has emerged (see Ostroy and Starr (1974, 1990) and Kiyotaki and Wright [1989]) that examines the problems associated with decentralized process of exchange and consequently highlights how money as a medium of exchange helps to facilitate exchange process and reduces transactions costs like time or storage cost.[1] In the literature, agents are usually assumed to be randomly searching for trading partners in order to attain the goods they finally wish to consume by exchanging either directly or indirectly the goods they produce or are endowed with. We would call such a trading process 'market-less trade' or synonymously 'pure random search'. In the process of indirect exchange, an agent may accept a good not because s/he wishes to consume it but because it can be exchanged for a good s/he finally demands. Such a commodity then takes the role of a medium of exchange.

A medium of exchange undoubtedly aids the process of exchange, but equally important is a market institution which facilitates the transaction process by acting as a meeting point for the buyers and sellers. Some authors have theoretically examined the coexistence of money and markets as facilitators of exchange (see Starr (2002), Howitt (2002), Rajeev (1997, 1999), Rajeev and Dasgupta (2007)) and highlighted the role of markets in the process of exchange. The market setup considered in the literature consists of trading posts for different possible pairs of commodities and is visited by both demanders and suppliers of the goods concerned. Such an institution is intended to minimize/avoid direct meetings between the agents. This chapter examines the steady-state utility levels derived by the agents trading in a market setup vis-à-vis the process of pure random search, and establishes the superiority of a market setup.

However, notwithstanding the obvious advantages of a market setup where buyers and sellers of a particular good can meet with respect to the goods they want to trade (as against a pure random

---

[1] There are several recent models that theoretically formulate monetary exchange, for example, see Schindler et al. (2001); Corbae et al. (2003); Starr (1976, 2003); Dasgupta and Rajeev (1997); Jones (1976); Kiyotaki and Wright (1993); Ostroy (1973); Wright and Trejos (1993); and Starr and Stinchcombe (1999).

search for a matching trading partner amongst all agents in the economy) market-less trade is not uncommon in developing economies. For example, hawkers trying to sell a variety of goods—ranging from perishable goods like fish or vegetables to non-food items like clothing or utensils—call out in residential areas essentially in search for a possible trading opportunity. In the larger cities, at any traffic signal stop, one's vehicle is surrounded by vendors peddling their fares. This type of trading process is close to the pure random search process illustrated in the literature. In other words, though a market setup can reduce the search cost to a great extent, random search still persists even for the commodities having established markets. Can one theoretically show meaningful equilibrium where random search coexists with markets? This issue is discussed briefly in the current paper. A more elaborate discussion on the topic can be found in Rajeev and Dasgupta (2007) and Rajeev (2012).

In this chapter we consider trading possibilities in a pair-wise trading post arrangement vis-à-vis a combined market where all goods are traded against each other (à la supermarket). Given these two types of trading arrangements, which one will prevail and under what conditions? In this chapter, conditions for arriving at sustainable equilibria are drawn up, and the steady-state utility levels (synonymously termed as welfare levels) are compared.

The basic framework considered in the chapter is by Kiyotaki and Wright (1989) where there are three different types of goods in terms of storage cost and three types of agents who specialize in production and consumption of goods. We however, modify this framework to introduce different types of markets or, alternatively, trading posts. In section 2.1, possible equilibria in a trading post setup are considered, and the welfare levels are compared amongst themselves and with the market-less setup.

Subsequently, we take into account the fact that in addition to time or storage costs, there may be additional resources necessary for one to engage in trade through a market setup. These may include taxes payable, rentals or power charges, and so on. Keeping this in mind, we have introduced the concept of 'cost' of participating in a market setup, which is measured like other costs by instantaneous disutility. Like Kiyotaki and Wright (1989), we consider an economy with different types of agents characterized by their excess demand

and supply, and all agents belonging to a particular type are assumed to be identical. Finally, to make the multi-commodity market setup meaningful, it is also necessary to diversify the consumption bundle of the agents. More precisely, we assumed later that though the agents remain specialized in production they nevertheless have diversified consumption needs. The concept of equilibrium considered here is a steady-state Nash equilibrium, involving the optimal trading strategies of agents engaged in a process of exchange, given the strategies of the other agents of the economy.

Given this background, the next section describes the basic framework under consideration. The subsequent two sections examine the possible equilibrium strategies under different trading arrangements. Following them is a concluding section, with an appendix providing the technical details, thereafter.

Framework

As the basic framework used here is similar to that of Kiyotaki and Wright (1989) (though tailored appropriately to introduce different types of market setups), it is essential to re-state the important features of the original Kiyotaki and Wright (1989) framework (see also Rajeev 2012).

The economy is considered as one having three types of agents (referred to as types 1, 2, and 3), and three distinct commodities; each of these types (comprising equal number of agents, N) produces and consumes specialized goods and in one unit only. In notation: Type k agents derive utility from the consumption of good k only and produce k^*. It is assumed that $1^* = 2, 2^* = 3, 3^* = 1$ (that is, a type 1 agent produces good 2, etc.). As and when a type k agent obtains good k, s/he consumes it instantaneously and, in turn, produces one unit of her/his specified production good, k^*. During the search process for appropriate trading partner, the good needs to be stored and in this regard it is assumed that each good can be stored but at a cost, and not more than one unit can be stored at a time. It is assumed that b_{kc} represents the cost (measured in terms of instantaneous disutility) to the type k agents of storing good c and, without loss of generality (WLOG), the following relation holds good $0 < b_{k1} < b_{k2} < b_{k3}$, for all k.

Suppose $\overline{U}_k$ signifies the immediate utility from consumption of good k, L_{k^*} immediate disutility of creating k^* for a type k trader and $\beta \in (0, 1)$ is the discount factor (common to all types). Thus, expected lifetime utility, discounted over time for a type k trader as represented by Kiyotaki and Wright (1989) (see also Rajeev 2012) is:

$$E\left[\sum_{t=0}^{\infty}\beta^t \{I_k^{\overline{U}}(t)\overline{U}_k - I_{k^*}^L(t)L_{k^*} - I_{kc}^b(t)b_{kc}\}\right]$$

where $I_k^{\overline{U}}(t)$ is a random indicator function with:

$I_k^{\overline{U}}(t)$ = 1, if a type k agent consumes good k in period t
     = 0, otherwise.

Similarly,

$I_{k^*}^L(t)$ = 1, if a type k agent produces good k^* in period t
     = 0, otherwise

Also,

$I_{kc}^b(t)$ = 1, if a type k agent stores any good c in period t
     = 0, otherwise.

The trading process in the model is conceived as follows. In each time period, the agents look for possible trading opportunities in a random manner with a suitable trading partner. Naturally trade occurs when both traders find it optimal to do so. For a meaningful model it is necessary to presume that the net utility of consumption plus production $u_k = U_k - L_{k^*}$ is large enough so that agents do not have stimulus to drop out of the economy. As mentioned in Kiyotaki and Wright (1989), the following condition is sufficient to ascertain this phenomenon (see also Rajeev 2012):

$u_k > (b_{kk^*} - b_{kc})/(1-\beta)$, for all type k agents and commodities c

Two types of pure-strategy Nash equilibria are derived under the basic framework of Kiyotaki and Wright (1989). As per the definition, a steady-state Nash equilibrium consists of a set of trading strategies $\{S_k\}$, one for each type k, along with a steady state distribution of inventories $\bar{p}$ (which represents the proportion of type k agents with good *c and consequently ascertains the probability of meeting a type k agent with good c*) that satisfies the following conditions:

(i) each individual k chooses S_k to maximize her/his expected discounted lifetime utility, given the optimal trading strategies of other agents and the distribution $\bar{p}$; and
(ii) given S_k, $\bar{p}$ is the resultant steady-state distribution.

The two types of equilibria that are established can be summarized as below.

1. *Fundamental equilibrium*: where good 1 (*the good with the lowest storage cost*) evolves itself as the unique medium.
2. *Speculative equilibrium*: where both goods, that is, good 1 (the lowest storage cost good) and good 3 (the highest storage cost good) begin to assume the role of media of exchange through the agents' optimizing trading behaviour.

To establish the equilibria, one needs to first calculate and then compare the steady-state levels of expected discounted lifetime utility for each type of agents for going through direct barter vis-à-vis indirect trade (given the assumed strategies of the others). Further, weighing the individual welfare levels (measured by the steady-state utility level related to each equilibrium for each type of agents), one can establish that these two equilibria are Pareto non-comparable. In an interesting paper, by using experimental methods, Duffy and Ochs (1999, 2002) express that their subjects were able to coordinate easily on efficient monetary exchange equilibria in Kiyotaki–Wright model characterized by *fundamental*, cost-minimizing strategies, but the subjects had much greater difficulty coordinating on equilibria that required them to adopt *speculative* strategies. In this backdrop, we would first consider pair-wise commodity markets without any additional market-related costs and consider all possibilities, i.e., fundamental and other equlibria and show that fundamental equilibrium dominates the other equilibria in a trading post setup. Hence this exercise in a sense supports the results from experimental exercise conducted by Duffy and Ochs (1999, 2002).

Thus, we first extend the basic framework discussed so far to incorporate markets or trading posts and call this economy '$\mathcal{E}$'. For comparison purposes, we first consider two types of trading arrangements, viz., the market-less arrangement, as considered by Kiyotaki and Wright (1989), and the trading post setup. As mentioned earlier, in a market-less arrangement (Kiyotaki and Wright 1989; Aiyagari and Wallace 1991), the agents try to explore trading possibilities through random meetings and the exchange of goods takes place when it is mutually beneficial. In a trading post setup however, there exist separate markets and, in this case, three markets to deal with good 1 against good 2, good 1 against good 3 and good 2 against good 3. In the (c, c') trading post (or market) good c is exchanged against good c' where the agents desiring to trade good c against c' visit the trading post. We assume that the buyers and sellers (of c against c') *can readily discover each other* and meet and trade. Thus, many unnecessary meetings between the agents may be avoided in a trading post setup which is not possible in a market-less trading arrangement. We have first considered different possible equilibria in a trading post setup and compared the welfare levels associated with each equilibrium. *Finally we seek to show that the fundamental equilibrium is Pareto superior to all other equilibria and it also dominates the equilibria that can be derived for a market-less setup. As mentioned earlier, this result supports the experiment based conclusions derived by Duffy and Ochs (2002), and also proves that in general a market setup cannot be dominated by market-less trade.*

Like the Kiyotaki and Wright (1989) model, for a trading post setup as well, it is essential to assume that the utility u_k is large enough in comparison to the costs (measured through instantaneous disutility) such that no agent drops out of the market economy. This may be ascertained on the basis of the following sufficient condition (see also Rajeev 2012).

$$u_k - \frac{b_{kk^*}}{1-\beta} \geq -\frac{b_{kc}}{1-\beta}, \forall good\ c \neq k^* \qquad (*)$$

It is essential to note that the above-mentioned framework is modified in the next stage by assuming that though by trading through a trading post setup, one can save time cost, certain additional costs (in addition to the storage costs) need to be incurred for the setting up and maintenance of a market system. In notation, let $\gamma_{cc'}$ be the per period cost to be incurred to run the market (it includes tax payable, electricity charges, etc.)[2] by an agent trading in (c, c') trading post. We then explore possible trading equilibria under different types of markets viz., single pair of goods vs. multiple goods market.

Comparing Trading Post Setup and Random Search: Fundamental versus Other Equilibria

We consider an economy, as described earlier, where trade is taking place through a pair-wise trading post setup and the agents are trying to attain their desired good, starting with their production good through a decentralized process of trade. In such a setup, each good acting as a medium of exchange can be sustained as a steady-state Nash equilibrium. However, we show that the equilibrium with fundamental strategies Pareto dominates the other two equilibria. More precisely, it means that the type of agents for whom the storage cost of the good they produce is the highest, would opt for indirect trade by using a good with lesser transactions cost (a good which they neither produce nor use for final consumption) as the medium of exchange. Naturally, the trading post that would have been relevant for their direct barter will not function. To show this we first prove that good 2 acting as a unique medium of exchange forms a steady-state Nash equilibrium. Existence of the other two equilibria, where good 1 and good 3 can act as unique medium of exchange, can be established in a similar manner.

Proposition 1 In a trading post setup, good 2 acting as a unique medium of exchange forms a steady-state Nash equilibrium.

Proof Suppose good 2 is uniquely chosen as a medium of exchange. Given the production and consumption profile of the agents, this is possible if, in equilibrium, the type 3 agents opt for indirect trade

---

[2] Here we have made these costs market specific. Similar exercise can be carried out if one makes these costs agent specific or, alternatively, dependent on the good which one wants to sell in that market.

by selling good 1 against good 2 and then using good 2 to buy good 3; and the type 1 and 2 agents go for direct barter. Our purpose is to examine whether these trading strategies form steady-state Nash equilibrium strategies.

(i) We begin with a type 1 agent's expected utility in opting for direct barter. As soon as a type 1 agent produces good 2 she pays the storage cost b_{12}. Next period (discounted by β) she can meet a type 3 agent (visiting the (1,2) trading post to sell good 1) and acquire the medium of exchange, that is, good 2 in this case. Let p'_{31} be the proportion of type 3 agents in the (1,2) trading post. Let $\bar{U}_k^B$ and $\bar{U}_k^I$ be the expected discounted lifetime utility (synonymously 'value functions') of a type k agent who goes through direct barter and indirect trade respectively. Thus, with probability p'_{31}, a type 1 agent can meet a type 3 agent in trading post (1,2) and acquire her consumption good, that is, good 1. She consumes it and derives utility u_1 and instantaneously produces good 2 again and remains with the utility level $\bar{U}_1^B$ or $\bar{U}_1^I$, whichever is maximum. On the other hand, with probability $(1-p'_{31})$ she is not able to meet a type 3 agent and remains with the same utility level. Using Bellman's equation in dynamic programming (see Bertsekas 1976) the steady state expected utilities can be written as:

$$\bar{U}_1^B = -b_{12} + \beta[p'_{31}(u_1 + \max(\bar{U}_1^B, \bar{U}_1^I)) + (1-p'_{31}) \max(\bar{U}_1^B, \bar{U}_1^I)]$$

Let us now concentrate on $\bar{U}_1^I$. To go through indirect trade a type 1 agent needs to sell her production good, i.e., good 2 against good 3 in (2,3) market and then attain good 1 against good 3 in the (1,3) trading post. It can be easily checked that:

$$\bar{U}_1^I = -b_{12} + \beta[p'_{12}\bar{U}_{13}^I + (1-p'_{12}) \max(\bar{U}_1^I, \bar{U}_1^B)] \tag{5.1}$$

where, p'_{12} is the probability of meeting a complementary trading partner in the (2,3) trading post and $\bar{U}_{13}^I$ is the indirect utility of acquiring good 3 by a type 1 agent. However, given the strategies of the other two types, no trader will be present in the (1,3) market. Hence a type 1 agent visiting (1,3) market needs to wait indefinitely for a complementary trading partner and pay lifetime storage cost. This can be written as:

$$\therefore \bar{U}'_{13} = -b_{13} + \beta\left[\frac{-b_{13}}{1-\beta}\right]$$

To compare $\bar{U}_1^I$ and $\bar{U}_1^B$:

$$\bar{U}_1^I = -b_{12} + \beta\left[p'_{12}(-b_{13})\left\{1+\frac{\beta}{1-\beta}\right\} + (1-p'_{12})\max\left(\bar{U}_1^I, \bar{U}_1^B\right)\right]$$

$$< -b_{12} + (1-p'_{13})\max\left(\bar{U}_1^I, \bar{U}_1^B\right) \Rightarrow \bar{U}_1^I < \bar{U}_1^B \quad (5.1)$$

Otherwise we would get a contradiction.

(ii) We now consider a type 2 agent. Let p'_{32} be the proportion of type 3 agent in trading post (2,3). Then, as before,

$$\bar{U}_2^B = -b_{23} + \beta\left[p'_{32}\{u_2 + \max\left(\bar{U}_2^B, \bar{U}_2^I\right)\}\right.$$

$$\left. + (1-p'_{32})\max\left(\bar{U}_2^B, \bar{U}_2^I\right)\right]$$

$$\Rightarrow (1-\beta)\bar{U}_2^B \geq -b_{23} + \beta p'_{32} u_2 \quad (5.2)$$

and

$$\bar{U}_2^I = -\frac{b_{23}}{1-\beta} \Rightarrow (1-\beta)\bar{U}_2^I = -b_{23}$$

Using equation 5.2 we get:

$$\bar{U}_2^B > \bar{U}_2^I$$

(iii) Finally, we consider a type 3 agent. Clearly,

$$\bar{U}_3^B = \frac{-b_{31}}{1-\beta}$$

If a type 3 agent opts for indirect trade, he has to first visit (1,2) trading post and then the (2,3) trading post. Given the strategies of type 1 and type 2 agents, he would meet a complementary trading partner in both these trading posts with probability 1.

$$\therefore \bar{U}_3^I = -b_{31} + \beta\left[-b_{32} + \beta(u_3 + \max\{\bar{U}_3^B, \bar{U}_3^I\})\right]$$

$$\Rightarrow (1-\beta^2)\bar{U}_3^I \geq -b_{31} - \beta b_{32} + \beta^2 u_3$$

$$\Rightarrow \bar{U}_3^I \geq -\frac{b_{31}}{1-\beta^2} + \frac{\beta}{1-\beta^2}[-b_{32} + \beta u_3]$$

$$= -\frac{b_{31}}{1-\beta} + \frac{\beta}{1-\beta^2}b_{31} + \frac{\beta}{1-\beta^2}[-b_{32} + \beta u_3]$$

$$= -\frac{b_{31}}{1-\beta} + \frac{\beta}{1-\beta^2}[(b_{31} - b_{32}) + \beta u_3]$$

$$\therefore \bar{U}_3^B < \bar{U}_3^I \text{ if}$$

$(b_{31} - b_{32})\beta u_3 > 0$, where $b_{31} - b_{32} < 0$

Condition (*) implies that

$$u_k > \frac{b_{kk^*} - b_{kc^*}}{1-\beta}, \forall k \in K, \forall c^* \in C$$

$\therefore$, or a type 3 agent (taking $c^* = 2$) we have,

$$u_3 > \frac{b_{31} - b_{32}}{1-\beta},$$

$$\Rightarrow (1-\beta)u_3 > b_{31} - b_{32}$$

$\therefore$ if $\beta > 1 - \beta$ we have

$$\beta u_3 > b_{31} - b_{32}$$

$$\Rightarrow \bar{U}_3^B < \bar{U}_3^I$$

Thus, $\beta > 1 - \beta$ or $\beta > 1/2$ gives a sufficient condition under which there will be a steady-state Nash equilibrium with good 2 acting as a unique medium of exchange. It can be easily checked that in the steady-state equilibrium $p'_{31} = p'_{32} = 1/2$.

Welfare Comparisons

Let us now define the welfare derived by a type k agent as:

$$WF_k = (1-\beta)\sum_c p_{kc} \bar{U}_{kc}$$

where, p_{kc} is the proportion of type k agents with good c in the steady state and $\bar{U}_{kc}$ is the utility derived by a type k agent by acquiring good c.

Let us now consider the welfare derived by a type k agent for a steady-state Nash equilibrium with good 2 acting as a unique medium of exchange.

Using the steady-state utility levels corresponding to the equilibrium strategies derived above one can arrive at the welfare levels as follows:

$$\overline{WF}_1 = -b_{12} + \frac{u_1\beta}{2}$$

$$\overline{WF}_2 = -b_{23} + \frac{u_2\beta}{2}$$

$$\overline{WF}_3 = \frac{-(b_{31}+b_{32})}{2} + \frac{u_3\beta}{2}$$

Corresponding to the equilibrium, where good 1 is acting as a unique medium of exchange, one can compute the welfare levels as follows:

$$\overline{WF}_1 = -b_{12} + \frac{u_1\beta}{2}$$

$$\overline{WF}_2 = -\frac{b_{23}+b_{21}}{2} + \frac{u_2\beta}{2}$$

$$\overline{WF}_3 = -b_{31} + \frac{u_3\beta}{2}$$

We can then compare the welfare levels of these two equlibria.

$$\overline{\overline{WF_1}} = -b_{12} + \frac{u_1\beta}{2} = \overline{WF_1}$$

$$\overline{\overline{WF_2}} = -b_{23} + \frac{u_2\beta}{2} < -\frac{b_{23} + b_{21}}{2} + \frac{u_2\beta}{2} = \overline{WF_2}$$

$$\overline{\overline{WF_3}} = \frac{-(b_{31} + b_{32})}{2} + \frac{u_3\beta}{2} < -b_{31} + \frac{u_3\beta}{2} = \overline{WF_3}$$

Thus, we see that welfare levels are lower for type 2 and type 3 agents and it is the same for type 1, when good 2 is the medium of exchange. Thus, the fundamental equilibrium (that is, good 1 acting as the medium of exchange) Pareto dominates the equilibrium where good 2 is the medium of exchange.

Proceeding in an exactly parallel fashion, it can be shown that good 3, acting as a unique medium of exchange, can be established as a steady-state Nash equilibrium (for $\beta > 1/2$). However, the equilibrium, where good 1 is acting as a medium of exchange, remains Pareto superior welfare-wise. Thus, we have:

Proposition 2 For the economy ε (described above), there exists, a steady-state Nash equilibrium with good 1 acting as the unique medium of exchange under all parameter values. On the other hand, under the condition $\beta > 1 - \beta$, there can exist steady-state Nash equilibria with good 2 or good 3 acting as the unique medium of exchange. However, the equilibrium with good 1 acting as a unique medium of exchange Pareto dominates the other two equilibria.

Welfare Comparisons: Trading Post versus Market-less Trading Arrangements

In the context of a market-less trading arrangement we consider the welfare associated with the non-equilibrium strategy (see Kiyotaki and Wright (1989: 948) of 'always trading regardless of the match', as it Pareto dominates the equilibrium strategies (both fundamental and speculative, in a market-less setup). Welfare levels are derived in Kiyotaki and Wright (1989) as follows:

Type 1 agent's welfare level:

$$WF_1^* = \frac{\beta u_1}{3} - \frac{1}{3}(b_{13} - b_{12}) - b_{12}$$

For the type 2 agent,

$$WF_2^* = \frac{\beta u_2}{3} - \frac{b_{23} + b_{21}}{2} - \frac{1}{6}(b_{23} - b_{21})$$

For the type 3 agent

$$WF_3^* = \frac{\beta u_3}{3} - \frac{1}{3}(b_{32} - b_{31}) - b_{31}$$

Comparing these values with $\overline{WF}_1, \overline{WF}_2$, and $\overline{WF}_3$ of the trading post setup, we can easily check that:

$$WF_1^* < \overline{WF}_1, WF_2^* < \overline{WF}_2, WF_3^* < \overline{WF}_3$$

Thus we have the following.

Proposition 3 For the economy ε (described above), the fundamental strategies in a trading post setup, that is, where type 1 and 3 agents go for direct barter and type 2 agents go for indirect trade, Pareto dominates all possible equilibria in a market-less trading arrangement.

Remark 1 Thus, trade through markets cannot be dominated by trade without markets.

Remark 2 As mentioned above, we next examine the case where one needs to incur additional costs (above the storage costs) for the setting up and maintenance of a market system. More precisely, let $\gamma_{cc'}$ be the per period cost to be incurred to run the market (it includes, for example, tax payable and electricity charges)[3] by an agent trading in (c, c') trading post.

---

[3] Here we have made these costs market specific. Similar exercise can be carried out if one makes these costs agent specific or alternatively dependent on the good one wants to sell in that market.

In that case it can be shown that the fundamental strategies can be sustained as steady-state Nash equilibria under the following condition:

$$\gamma_{13} - \gamma_{12} < \frac{\beta}{2} u_3$$

And the welfare of every agent is higher under the fundamental strategies in a trading post setup as compared to that of the market-less trading arrangement, if the following conditions hold (for details of proof, see Rajeev 2012):

$$\frac{\beta u_1}{3} > \gamma_{12}, \frac{\beta u_3}{3} > \gamma_{13}, \frac{\beta u_2}{3} > \frac{1}{2}(\gamma_{12} + \gamma_{13})$$

Thus, as expected, with additional costs in a market setup, certain upper bound on the market-related costs become necessary to show the superiority of the trading post set up.

Remark 3 It can also be shown (see Rajeev 2012) that if the costs of running some markets are high then a subset of agents may optimally choose to trade through a market-less arrangement even in the presence of markets. Thus random search can coexist with a market setup in equilibrium. This is a phenomenon often seen in the developing countries where hawkers somewhat randomly search for buyers at traffic signals or in residential areas by calling out loudly.

Pair-wise Trading Post versus Combined Market

Specialized Production as well as Consumption

We first consider our basic setup of the section, 'Comparing Trading Post Setup and Random Search: Fundamental versus other equilibria', where we discussed pair-wise markets (c, c'). We next introduce one combined market where goods 1, 2, and 3 can be exchanged against each other. As this is a market setup, buyers and sellers can identify each other (unlike in a pure random search case). As mentioned above, looking at reality we assume that one needs to incur additional costs (above the storage costs) for the setting up and maintenance of a pair-wise market system (measured in terms of instantaneous disutility) which is denoted by $\gamma_{cc'}$ as per period cost to be incurred to participate in the (c,c') market by an agent.

Depending on the relation that prevails amongst the costs different equilibria may be derived. We would consider a specific relation amongst the costs to be incurred in a trading post setup.

Relation I: $b_{k2} + \gamma_{12} < b_{k1} + \gamma_{31} < b_{k3} + \gamma_{23}$, $\gamma_{12} \leq \gamma_{31} \leq \gamma_{23}$

All other possible relationships can be considered and dealt with by following similar methods.

Similarly, let us assume that the *one-time cost* of participating in the combined market is γ (independent of the number of goods one transacts). But the agents need to pay a transport cost τ to travel to this market (measured again in terms of instantaneous disutility and assumed to account for fuel cost, etc.). Further, WLOG we assume that there is an additional time cost of 1 unit needed to travel to this market. Thus we perceive a combined market to be something like a supermarket at a central location and the pair-wise trading posts are perceived as smaller specialized local shops, visits to which do not cost any transport cost. Suppose a type k agent can decide to trade either in a pair-wise trading post or in a combined market setup. Considering welfare criterion, we confine ourselves to the fundamental equilibrium. Hence we compute value functions under the strategy profile: Type 1 and type 3 agents go for direct barter and type 2 agents go for indirect trade.

Under pair-wise trading post setup the value functions can be derived following exactly similar method as that of the section, 'Comparing Trading Post Setup and Random Search: Fundamental versus other equilibria' (see proof of proposition 1). Here, as before, the superscripts B and I stand for (direct) barter and indirect trade respectively. We have also used *'pair-wise'* and *'comb'* to denote pair-wise trading post and combined market setup.

$$\bar{U}_1^{Bpair\text{-}wise} = -(b_{12} + \gamma_{12}) + \beta \left[p_{21}\left(u_1 + \max(\bar{U}_1^{Bpair\text{-}wise}, \bar{U}_1^{Ipair\text{-}wise})\right) \right] +$$
$$\left[(1 - p_{21}) \max\left(\bar{U}_1^{Bpair\text{-}wise}, \bar{U}_1^{Ipair\text{-}wise} \right) \right]$$

Under combined market setup, value function for a type 1 agent can be written as follows:

$$\bar{U}_1^{Bcomb} = -(b_{12}+\tau) - \beta(b_{12}+\gamma) + \beta^2\left[p_{21}\left(u_1 + \max(\bar{U}_1^{Bcomb}, U_1^{Icomb})\right)\right] + \left[(1-p_{21})\max\left(\bar{U}_1^{Bcomb}, \bar{U}_1^{Icomb}\right)\right]$$

Similarly value functions for other types can be written. We then have the following results.

Proposition 4 Under Relation I, the fundamental strategies in a trading post setup, that is, where type 1 and type 3 agents go for direct barter and type 2 agents go for indirect trade in a pair-wise trading post setup, form a set of equilibrium strategies under a feasible set of parametric values.

Similarly, where type 1 and type 3 agents go for direct barter and type 2 agents go for indirect trade in a combined market setup, the fundamental strategies form a set of equilibrium strategies under a feasible set of parametric values.

Proof It is straightforward and follows from the fact that if type i and type j go for trade in a particular market setup say, combined market setup, by trading in a pair-wise trading post the third type, which is type k, will incur lifetime storage and market costs as s/he meets no complementary trading partner.

Proposition 5 Pair-wise trading post setup gives higher steady-state utility levels compared to combined market setup under the following sufficient condition:

$$\gamma - \gamma_{cc'} > -\frac{\beta}{2(1+\beta)}u_k \qquad (5.3)$$

Proof See Appendix A5.

Remark 4 Thus condition (5.3) implies that for the pair-wise trading post setup to be utilized by the agents, cost differentials between combined market and pair-wise trading posts should not be sufficiently high vis-à-vis (discounted) utility derived from consumption.

We next modify our setup to introduce the notion of economies of scale in trading.

Specialized Production and Diversified Consumption

We extend our basic structure to consider the fact that while the agents are specialized in their production, they have diversified consumption needs. More precisely, the type 1 agents produce two units of good 2 and consume one unit of good 1 and one unit of good 3. The type 2 agents produce two units of good 3 and consume one unit of good 2 and one unit of good 1, and the type 3 agents produce two units of good 1 and consume one unit of good 2 and one unit of good 3. After the consumption of the two goods, the agents can again produce two units of their respective production goods. Given this production and consumption structure, let us first consider a pair-wise trading post arrangement. Following proposition 1 one can easily derive Propositions 6 and 7.

Proposition 6 Type 1 agents going for direct barter in (1,2) and (2,3) trading posts, type 2 agents going for direct barter in (1,3) and (2,3) trading posts and type 3 agents trading in (1,3) and (1,2) trading posts will form a steady-state Nash equilibrium. In each trading post 1/2 of each type of agents will be present in the steady state and there will be perfect mutual coincidence of wants.

We next consider the same consumption and production structure and trade in a combined market. We get:

Proposition 7 Each type of agents, opting for direct barter in a combined market, forms a steady-state Nash equilibrium.

Comparing the steady-state utility levels for each type of agents under strategy profiles described in Proposition 6 and 7 we get the following result.

Proposition 8 If discount factor β is sufficiently small (< 0.6) and transport cost is not too low then pair-wise trading post setup is superior to the combined market.

Proof See Appendix.

Remark 5 It is interesting to observe that when there is an urgent need for consumption (given by small β) pair-wise local trading posts are better.

We have not considered any transportation cost for visiting any of the pair-wise trading posts. Thus it is indirectly assumed that all pair-wise trading posts exist in the neighbourhood. If, on the other hand, there is any transport cost for travelling between one trading post and another, then the utility of pair-wise trading post further diminishes and it becomes easier to dominate a pair-wise market set up by a combined market.

Thus, from this exercise, one gets the indication that in a sense, specialized local shops (dealing with limited commodities) can survive better if they exist together in a marketplace and can complement each other and sell commodities, consumption of which is of urgent nature (for example, consumer durables may not satisfy this requirement).

* * *

This chapter looks into the possibility of trade through a trading post setup together with a market-less trading arrangement in a dynamic framework. While the literature so far considers the role of markets and medium of exchange in facilitating trade, this chapter also discusses briefly the co-existence of market-less random search and market setup in order to examine whether a mix of both can provide a stable equilibrium. This corroborates what one observes in a developing economy. It also provides theoretical justification to this unique feature of *random search in the presence of markets* in the less developed nations. Finally, in the background of recent debate concerning opening up of retail business segment in India and the resulting possibility of extinction of small local shops, the model considers the case of specialized markets vs. multi-commodity markets (supermarkets), and examines under what conditions one can dominate the other. The model utilized in the chapter no doubt can be extended further to introduce several complexities such as a flexible price regime. One interesting extension of the work can be the introduction of fiat money to examine the characteristics of resultant equilibria.

Appendix A5

Proof of Proposition 5

We first compare the value functions of a type 1 agent when she trades through direct barter in a pair-wise trading post setup (to be denoted by $\bar{U}_1^{Dpair\text{-}wise}$) as against in a combined market (to be denoted by $\bar{U}_1^{Dcomb}$).

Following methods of Proposition 1 we get:

$$\bar{U}_1^{Dpair\text{-}wise} = -(b_{12} + \gamma_{12}) + \frac{\beta}{2}(u_1 + \bar{U}_1^{Dpair\text{-}wise}) + \frac{\beta}{2}\bar{U}_1^{Dpair\text{-}wise}$$

We note that with probability of ½ she will meet a complementary trading partner (a type 2 agent) in the (1,2) market.

If she wishes to trade through direct barter in a combined market setup she needs to pay the transportation cost τ, one-time market participation cost γ and one period additional travel-time cost. Thus

$$\bar{U}_1^{Dcomb} = -(b_{12} + \tau) - \beta(\gamma + b_{12}) + \beta^2 \frac{1}{2}(u_1 + \bar{U}_1^{Dcomb}) + \frac{1}{2}\beta^2 \bar{U}_1^{Dcomb}$$

$$\therefore (1-\beta)\bar{U}_1^{Dpair\text{-}wise} = -(b_{12} + \gamma_{12}) + \frac{\beta}{2}u_1$$

$$\& \ (1-\beta^2)\bar{U}_1^{Dcomb} = -(b_{12} + \tau) - \beta(\gamma + b_{12}) + \frac{\beta^2}{2}u_1$$

$$\Rightarrow (1-\beta)\bar{U}_1^{Dcomb} = -\frac{(b_{12} + \tau)}{1+\beta} - \frac{\beta}{1+\beta}(\gamma + b_{12}) + \frac{\beta^2}{2(1+\beta)}u_1$$

Thus, $\bar{U}_1^{Dpair\text{-}wise} > \bar{U}_1^{Dcomb}$

$$\Rightarrow -(b_{12} + \gamma_{12}) + \frac{b_{12} + \tau}{1+\beta} + \frac{\beta}{1+\beta}(\gamma + b_{12}) \quad \quad (A5.1)$$

$$> -\frac{\beta}{2}u_1 + \frac{\beta^2}{2(1+\beta)}u_1$$

R.H.S. of inequality (A5.1)

$$= \frac{\beta}{2}u_1\left[\frac{\beta}{1+\beta} - 1\right] = -\frac{\beta}{2}u_1\left(\frac{1}{1+\beta}\right)$$

$$= -\frac{\beta}{2(1+\beta)}u_1 < 0$$

L.H.S. of inequality (A5.1)

$$-(b_{12}+\gamma_{12})+\frac{b_{12}+\tau}{1+\beta}+\frac{\beta}{1+\beta}(\gamma+b_{12})$$
$$=-b_{12}+b_{12}-\gamma_{12}+\frac{\beta\gamma+\tau}{1+\beta}$$

WLOG, let min $(\gamma, \tau) = \gamma$.
Then we get the sufficient condition as follows:

$$\gamma-\gamma_{12} > -\frac{\beta}{2(1+\beta)}u_1 \qquad (A5.2)$$

Thus sufficient condition derived in (A5.2) indicates that utility derived from consumption needs to be sufficiently large compared to the costs differentials of participating in these two different market setups.

Proof of Proposition 8

Let us consider the case of a type 1 agent; other types can be dealt with in an exactly similar fashion. Before moving further, it is important to note that in this setup of specialized production and diversified consumption, there is perfect mutual coincidence of wants and hence only direct barter will take place. Hence, we have not used the superscript 'D' in this case. In case a type 1 agent trades through a pair-wise trading arrangement, she would go for *direct* barter in (1,2) and (2,3) trading post. On the other hand, if she trades through a combined market arrangement, she would go to one market, thereby incurring a transport cost τ, a one-time market participation cost γ, and a time cost of one period for travelling. We assume that there is economies of scale with respect to time taken for trade in a combined market as all goods are available under one roof. In the present setup, we assume that it takes one period of time to acquire two goods that an agent wishes to consume. We note that same trade takes two periods in a pair-wise trading post setup as the agent visits two separate markets.

Let $\bar{U}_1^{\text{Pair-wise}}$ and $\bar{U}_1^{\text{comb}}$ be the value function corresponding to pair-wise trading post and combined market setup, respectively. A type 1 agent now has two units of good 1 and hence pays a storage cost of $2b_{12}$ to begin with. After she visits the (1,2) trading post, she acquires one unit of good 1 and gets utility of u_1. Next period she visits the (2,3) market, paying storage and market participation cost of $b_{12} + \gamma_{23}$ and then acquires good 3 for consumption, and so on. In the steady state, each type of agent will be equally distributed between two of their respective markets and, therefore, the number of buyers and sellers would match in each trading post. Each agent will, therefore, take one period in each trading post. Thus, following the similar method as before we can write:

$$\bar{U}_1^{\text{Pair-wise}} = -(2b_{12} + \gamma_{12}) + \beta[u_1 - b_{12}] - \beta^2[b_{12} + \gamma_{23}] + \beta^3 u_1 + \beta^3 \bar{U}_1^{\text{Pair-wise}}$$

where u_1 is the utility attained by a type 1 agent by consuming one unit of good 1 or good 3. For notational simplicity, we assume both these utility levels to be equal. On the other hand, in the combined market, the agent needs to pay storage and transport cost first. Next period she needs to also incur storage and market participation cost as there is one period of travel time. Thus we have:

$$\bar{U}_1^{\text{comb}} = -(2b_{12} + \tau) - \beta(2b_{12} + \gamma) + \beta^2(2u_1) + \beta^2 \bar{U}_1^{\text{comb}}$$

$$\therefore \bar{U}_1^{\text{Pair-wise}} > \bar{U}_1^{\text{comb}}$$

$$\Rightarrow \frac{-[(2b_{12} + \gamma_{12}) + \beta b_{12} + \beta^2(b_{12} + \gamma_{23})]}{1 - \beta^3} + \frac{\beta u_1 + \beta^3 u_1}{1 - \beta^3}$$

$$> \frac{-[(2b_{12} + \tau) + \beta(2b_{12} + \gamma)]}{1 - \beta^2} + \frac{\beta^2 2u_1}{1 - \beta^2} \quad (\text{A5.3})$$

The sufficient conditions for equation A5.3 to hold are that:

$$\frac{+[2b_{12} + \gamma_{12} + \beta b_{12} + \beta^2(b_{12} + \gamma_{23})]}{1 - \beta^3} < + \frac{2b_{12} + \tau + \beta(2b_{12} + \gamma)}{1 - \beta^2}$$

$$(\text{A.5.4})$$

And $\dfrac{\beta u_1 + \beta^3 u_1}{1-\beta^3} > \dfrac{\beta^2 2 u_1}{1-\beta^2}$ (A.5.5)

Now, $1-\beta^3 > 1-\beta^2 \Rightarrow \dfrac{1}{1-\beta^3} < \dfrac{1}{1-\beta^2}$

Thus, for equation A5.4 to hold, it is sufficient that:

$2b_{12} + \gamma_{12} + \beta b_{12} + \beta^2 (b_{12} + \gamma_{23}) < 2b_{12} + \tau + \beta(2b_{12} + \gamma)$, which can be reduced to a sufficient condition:

$\gamma_{12} + \gamma_{23} - \gamma < \tau$ (A.5.6)

Thus, if the additional cost of trading in pair-wise trading posts vis-à-vis a combined market is less than the travel cost to the combined market then agents would prefer to trade in the pair-wise trading posts. Loosely speaking, if the travel cost to a supermarket is large enough vis-à-vis additional market participation cost to be incurred to trade in a local market, then the latter would be preferred.

To find the condition under which:

$\dfrac{\beta u_1 + \beta^3 u_1}{1-\beta^3} > \dfrac{\beta^2 2 u_1}{1-\beta^2}$

$\Rightarrow \dfrac{\beta + \beta^3}{1-\beta^3} > \dfrac{2\beta^2}{1-\beta^2}$

$\Rightarrow (\beta + \beta^3)(1-\beta^2) > 2\beta^2(1-\beta^3)$

$\Rightarrow 1 > 2\beta - \beta^4$ (A.5.7)

$\Rightarrow 2\beta - \beta^4 < 1$ is another sufficient condition (along with equation A5.6) for a pair-wise trading post setup to be welfare-wise superior. Let us consider, $f(\beta) = 2\beta - \beta^4$. Differentiating with respect to β gives $f'(\beta) = 2 - 4\beta^3$. Thus $f(\beta)$ will increase in β if:

$\Rightarrow \beta < \dfrac{1}{\sqrt[3]{2}} = 0.79$ (approx.)

Further, $f''(\beta) = -12\beta^2 < 0$.

Therefore considering this function we get:

β	0	.6	½	$\dfrac{1}{\sqrt{2}}$	$\dfrac{1}{\sqrt[3]{2}}$	1
$f(\beta)$	0	1.01	.93	1.16	1.99	1

The above table shows that if β is sufficiently small, say, if $\beta < 0.6$, then trading post setup dominates the equilibrium arrived under combined market setup.

References

Aiyagari, S.R., and N. Wallace. 1991. 'Existence of Steady States with Positive Consumption in Kiyotaki-Wright Model', *Review of Economic Studies*, 58: 901–16.

Bertsekas, D.P. 1976. *Dynamic Programming and Stochastic Control*. New York: Academic Press.

Corbae, D, T. Temzilides, and Rendall Wright. 2003. 'Directed Matching and Monetary Exchange', *Econometrica*, 71: 731–56.

Dasgupta, D., and M. Rajeev. 1997. 'Feasibility Criteria in Monetary Trade', *The Japanese Economic Review*, 48: 453–61.

Duffy, J., and J. Ochs. 1999. 'Emergence of Money as a Medium of Exchange: An Experimental Study', *American Economic Review*, 89(4): 847–77.

———. 2002. 'Intrinsically Worthless Objects as Media of Exchange: Experimental Evidence', *International Economic Review*, 43: 637–73.

Hicks, J. 1967. *Critical Essays in Monetary Theory*. Oxford: Clarendon Press.

Howitt, Peter. 2002. 'Beyond Search: Fiat Money in Organized Exchange', Working Paper, Department of Economics, University of Brown.

Jones, R.A. 1976. 'The Origin and Development of Media of Exchange', *Journal of Political Economy*, 84: 757–75.

Kiyotaki, N., and R. Wright. 1989. 'On money as a medium of exchange', *Journal of Political Economy*, 97: 927–54.

———. 1993. 'A Search Theoretic Approach to Monetary Economics', *American Economic Review*, 83: 63–77.

Menger, K. 1892. 'On the Origin of Money'. *Economic Journal*, 2: 239–5.

Ostroy, J.M. 1973. 'The Informational Efficiency of Monetary Exchange', *American Economic Review*, 63: 597–610.

Ostroy, J.M., and R.M. Starr. 1974. 'Money and the decentralization of exchange', *Econometrica*, 42: 1093–113.

———. 1990. 'The Transactions Role of Money', in B. Friedman and F.H. Hann (eds) *Handbook of Monetary Economics*, pp. 4–59. Amsterdam: North Holland.

Rajeev, Meenakshi. 1997. 'Large Monetary Trade, Market Specialization and Strategic Behaviour', in T. Parthasarathy, Bhaskar Dutta, J. Potters, et al. (eds) *Game Theoretic Applications to Economics and Operations Research*, pp. 291–300. Netherlands: Kluwer Academic Publishers.

———. 1999. 'Market-less Setup vs. Trading Posts: A Comparative Analysis', *Annales D'Economie Et De Statistique*, 53, 197–211.

———. 2012. 'Search Cost, Trading Strategies and Optimal Market Structure', *Economic Modelling*, 29: 1757–65.

Rajeev, Meenakshi and Dipankar Dasgupta. 2007. 'Random Search in the Presence of markets', Working Paper No. 204, Department of Economics and Finance, City University of Hong Kong, October.

Schindler, M., P. Rupert, and Rendall Wright. 2001. 'Generalised Bargaining Models of Monetary Exchange', *Journal of Monetary Economics*, 48: 605–22.

Starr, R.M. 1976. 'Decentralized Non-monetary Trade', *Econometrica*, 44: 1087–9.

———. 2002. 'Monetary General Equilibrium with Transactions Costs', UCSD Economics Department Discussion Paper No. 2002-01R, University of California, San Diego.

———. 2003. 'Why is there money? Endogenous Derivation of Money as the Most Liquid Asset: A Class of Examples', *Journal of Economic Theory*, 21(2–3): 455–75.

Starr, R.M., and M.B. Stinchcombe. 1999. 'Exchange in a Net-work of Trading Posts, Markets', in G. Chichilnisky (ed.), *Information and Uncertainty, Essays in honour of Kenneth Arrow*, pp. 216–34. Cambridge: Cambridge University Press.

Walras, L. (translated and edited by W. Jaffe). 1900. 'Elements of Pure Economics', Homewood, Illinois, Irwin.

Wright, Rendall, and Alberto Trejos. 1993. 'Search, Bargaining, Money and Prices: Recent Results and Policy Implications', *Journal of Money Credit and Banking*, 25: 558–76.

6

The Determination of Profits

Romar Correa

The problem of accounting for the emergence of profits in a capitalist economy is suddenly being attacked by scholars (see, for instance, Binswanger (2009)). Some impetus is provided by the recent financial crisis. The era of the so-called 'great moderation' was a period when profits, in contrast to wages, increased steadily. With the breakdown of financial circulation, real activity-generating profits came to an abrupt halt. The pioneering interventions of the Federal Reserve to support long-term productive activity must have the flowering of prospective positive profits as the underlying objective. The founding fathers wrestled with the concept analytically. In the case of an economy which is a circular flow that rejuvenates itself, the value of factor inputs must equal the value of output at nominal prices. Consequently, entrepreneurial profits as well as interest accruing must be nil. Besides, if owners of the factors of production command total revenues, no monetary resources should be left over for new investment. In turn, Marx, Keynes, and Schumpeter, for instance, allegedly threw up their hands in despair. Marx, for example, did not offer a rigorous account of how M, through the circulation of commodities, could transform to M'. The material for an accounting resolution was available in Keynes' *Treatise*. That work is rich in monetary and financial detail supported by the development of accounting relations. However, in the movement towards the 'General Theory', attention was deflected towards determining output as a whole. Schumpeter's model consists of an evenly-rotating engine moving goods and services that suddenly transforms itself into a non-linear system with risk-loving banks and profit-seeking entrepreneurs. The details of the transformation were never worked out.

The modern contribution is to not treat the real and monetary aspects of the issue separately. Thus, interest in Marx's manuscripts on banking, published posthumously, is not less than that in the volumes of *Capital*. For instance, little attention is paid to the 'transformation problem' of theorizing the trip from values into prices, the sine qua non of Marxian economics of yesteryears. The limits of algebra were stretched in providing examples and counter-examples of 'negative surplus value' and 'positive profits'. An emerging synthetic approach confronts the modern economy as a set of interrelated monetary and financial and real circuits. Support of the founding fathers has been secured towards that end (Tomasson and Bezemer 2010). Jeremy Bentham was a progenitor of the notion, subsequently associated with Keynes and the post-Keynesians, that banks could create credit out of 'thin air'. He distinguished between productive and unproductive credit. The former supported productive enterprises and melded with the circular flow. The latter, on the other hand, did not finance current production nor fresh investment and, therefore, did not cycle back to factor owners. For example, in consumption credit and mortgage loans lay the foundations of money profits and interest. Also, the contribution of Jean-Baptiste Say might not be the law for which he is famous. Inherent in supply is the 'wherewithal' for its own-consumption. 'Wherewithal' is understood to mean monetary means or purchasing power. Money is the intermediary in the logical relationship. No sooner has a product been produced that it affords a market for other products to the full extent of its value. The actual sale calls forth the funds that back the demand for goods. Finally, in the appraisal of one scholar, macro-economics did not begin with Keynes (Colander 2010). The classical mercantilist divide of the

1600s was imaginary. Scholars such as Thornton, Cantillon, and Law, for instance, were alive to the connection between finance and macro-economic activity, being intimately involved with the banking business themselves. Coming to the present, in the circuit approach in monetary macro-economics, bank money is emitted with the wage bargain. Correspondingly, businesses draw down their overdraft facilities with financial institutions and production gets underway. The expenditure of workers is the income of firms and the circuit ends when firms square their debts with the banks. Clearly, there is no room for a positive interest rate or bank profits when accounts are closed. The circuitistes have been critiqued for not accounting for the following inequalities: the initial loan, a stock, might generate flows that exceed the value of the stock. For instance, the wage bill could exceed the value of the initial finance (Keen 2010).

The Godley and Lavoie (2007) Model

For the reasons cited, we prefer the so-called consistent stock-flow modelling strategy associated with Godley and Lavoie (hereafter G&L) 2007. The canvas is national income accounts and the discipline is that of double-entry book keeping. Surplus and deficit items must be of opposite sign and identical magnitude. Thus, in a typical G&L matrix, the bottom row and the extreme right-hand column are vectors of zeroes. Our dilemma is underscored. How do we make room for positive profits in a model with no growth? A hint is provided by Bruun and Heyn-Johnsen (2009), who protest that G&L do not investigate the dynamics of changes in the prices of equity. The latter reflect the best guess of future cash flows and are not bound by the laws of conservation. Equity held is valued at current prices whereas equity issued is fixed at the issue price. Hence, the calculations of profits depend on financial markets. The net worth of an economy depends on the revaluations of the capital stock. We work with this insight. Only, private equity washes away when added up for the economy as a whole. Government bonds take the place of equity. Overall, G&L have left the agenda of working through the steady state properties of their models open (Taylor 2010).

Our first equation is given by the definition of 'entrepreneurial profits', F, by G&L (2007: 255). We resort to explicit time subscripts when necessary and substitute the value of consumption, C, for the value of sales, S. Thus:

$$F = C - WB + IN_t - IN_{t-1} - r_{lt-1} IN_{t-1} \qquad (6.1)$$

During the period, firms have to meet a wage bill, WB. The change in the value of inventories ΔIN are financed through bank loans, ΔL. In addition, as a legacy of the past, they must pay interest on their outstanding stock of loans/inventories.

Private Banking

The equations that follow are intended to mimic the banks of yesteryear which 'originated and held' loans made for productive purposes. At the other end, they received the savings flows of small and local borrowers. The following is taken from chapter 7 of G&L, the subscripts s and d denoting supply and demand respectively. Instantaneous quantity adjustments are assumed. That is to say:

$$\begin{aligned} C_s &= C_d \\ N_s &= N_d \\ \Delta L_s &= \Delta L_d \end{aligned} \qquad (6.2)$$

The first equation states that producers supply the goods demanded. Involuntary unemployment prevails. Workers will offer themselves for employment at the prevailing wage rate (the second equation). According to the final equation, banks satisfy all their loan applicants. With no government and, therefore, no taxes, the disposable income of households is the sum of wages and interest incomes from their bank accounts.

$$YD = WB + r_{ht-1} M_{t-1} \qquad (6.3)$$

The household budget constraint follows. In our one-asset world, income not spent on consumption goods must be deposited in banks. Thus:

$$\Delta M = YD - C \qquad (6.4)$$

Combining (6.3) and (6.4) we get:

$$M_t = (1 + r_{ht-1}) M_{t-1} + WB - C \qquad (6.5)$$

Rewriting Equation 1 (6.1) and recalling the bank financing of inventory accumulation:

$$L_t = (1 + r_{lt-1}) L_{t-1} + WB - C + F \qquad (6.6)$$

We take the stationary solution of these two equations and introduce the definition of bank profits $F_b = r_{lt-1} L_{t-1} - r_{ht-1} M_{t-1}$. Then subtracting (6.5) from (6.6) gives:

$$F_b + F = 0 \qquad (6.7)$$

G&L discipline is enforced. Profits must be extinguished in equilibrium. We underline that banks' profits earned from financing plant and machinery and so on and supporting the precautionary motives of households have a counterpart in profits in manufacturing activity. If profits in the ordinary business of banking dwindle so too do the profits of industry. Both are, consequently, propelled off balance sheet. Banks will approach wholesale funding sources and support esoteric financial instruments increasingly unrelated to real activity. In the mirror, entrepreneurial activity will be driven towards financial innovation and churning. Thereby runs the tale of the US of A (Kregel 2010). By separating commercial banks and investment banks, the Glass-Steagall Act guaranteed the profits of the former. Competition from non-banks forces banks to lower r_l. At the same time, reliefs in providing low-cost transaction balances on account of productivity increases have not taken place. That is to say, there has not been a downward pressure on r_h. Financial entities could challenge bank spreads through asset securitization.

Government Money

The money of Bentham and Say need not be private money. It could as well be paper issued by the state. The defining function of a central bank in a monetary laissez-faire economy is its establishing a unit of account. Outside the textbook, relative price discovery takes place through encountering nominal prices denominated in fiat money. Inter-temporal trades are possible if and only if people trust in the agency backing the paper (Aglietta and Mojon 2010).

We introduce long-term government bonds or consols BL (G&L 2007: chapter 5). Each perpetuity is a piece of paper that pays one unit of currency per unit of time. The total flow of interest payments on these assets in the current period is BL_{t-1}. The value of the bond in the current period is quantity times price or $p_{bLt} BL_t$. Households are characterised by an accumulation of wealth, V, equation, which goes as follows (G&L 2007: 140):

$$V_t - V_{t-1} = (YD - C) + \Delta P_{bL} BL_{t-1} \tag{6.8}$$

In what has been called the Haig-Simons definition of income, capital gains, the last term in the earlier equation, is included. For later reference, we will refer to the expression as the surplus of wage-earners and rentiers.

The government budget constraint is:

$$B_t - B_{t-1} = (G + r_{t-1} B_{t-1} + BL_{t-1}) - (T + r_{t-1} B_{cbt-1}) - p_{blt} \Delta BL \tag{6.9}$$

The government deficit is financed by freshly-issued bills, B. The first term in the parentheses is the total outlays of the government which consist of expenditures and interest payments on the outstanding debt. The second term is government revenues which comprises its income-tax receipts and central bank profits. We know that government deficit is private sector surplus. Then subtracting Equation 7.8 from Equation 7.9 should give aggregate profits. Recall that the central bank is the residual purchaser of government bills after household demands, B_{hh}, and bank portfolios, B_{bd}, are satisfied. That is, $B_s = B_{cb} + B_{hh} + B_{bd}$. Thus:

$$\Delta B - \Delta V = (C + G) - (YD + T - r_{t-1} B_{hht-1}) + r_{t-1} B_{bdt-1} + BL_{t-1} - p_{bLt} BL_t + p_{bLt-1} BL_{t-1}$$

Now, $Y = C + G = YD + T - r_{t-1} B_{hht-1}$ (G&L 2007: 103). The return on government bonds is a part of disposable income now.

Also denoting profits, the left-hand side of the equation, by the more familiar π:

$$p_{bLt} BL_t = (1 + P_{bLt-1}) BL_{t-1} - \pi + r_{t-1} B_{bdt-1} \qquad (6.10)$$

The stationary solution is given by:

$$\pi = BL_{t-1} + r_{t-1} B_{bdt-1} \qquad (6.11)$$

The superstructure for profits is the banking system, both private banks that hold government securities as well as the central bank that issues long-term bonds. As an illustration, the stability of post-War output of the US economy was on account of a large government deficit. Households and firms could access a risk-free asset, the government treasury bill, that was leveraged to deliver steady growth.

The strategy of going long was invented by the Federal Reserve (Fed) post the crisis (Gagnon et al. 2010; Nelson 2011). In the face of the zero-bound interest rate problem, the Fed purchased huge quantities of assets with medium and long-term maturities. These large-scale asset purchases (LSAPs) have ignited interest in the Fed balance sheet. They reduce the supply of riskier long-term assets. The risk premiums fall as do yields. The LSAPs caused a reduction in long-term interest rates not just on securities that had been purchased but on others as well. These drops in interest rates reflect a fall in risk premiums, not expectations of lower future short-term rates. With lower yields on government securities, investors will bid up the prices of corporate bonds and equities and, thereby, stimulate investment. Private borrowers should find their long-term borrowing costs lower. The value of long-term assets held by households and firms should be higher. Most of the lending on the long side is done by institutions such as pension funds and insurance companies which are more-or-less committed to purchasing long-term fixed income securities. The scope for central bank purchases to affect long-term interest rates for a given path of short-term rates is not slight. With a near-zero short-term rate, the relative immobility of short-term funds makes direct purchases in the long-term bond market necessary to effect a portfolio balance shift. The instrument might resuscitate moribund banks. At a null short-rate bound, central bank purchases of short-term riskless paper leaves commercial banks with an unchanged total of non-interest bearing assets, base money, and short-term treasuries. A central bank purchase of long-term debt, on the other hand, raises this total. If the bond purchase is from a commercial bank, its earning assets are reduced. Along with its enhanced liquidity, it is likely to respond by restoring and hiking its total earning assets. The aggregate level of deposits of the banking system will rise. If the bond purchase is from a non-bank seller, financed by the creation of reserves, the earning assets of commercial banks do not fall but their non-interest-bearing assets rise. Once again, there is a liquidity effect leading to an inducement to lend. The long-term government bond, in addition, might back Keynes' recommendation to separate the budget into a current (government consumption) and capital (government investment) budget (Pérez and Vernengo 2010). The capital budget is a summary of capital expenditures required for equality with savings. A policy of public works, if accounted for in the capital budget would, *ceteris paribus*, create surpluses in the current budget. Thereby, the deadweight debt would be replaced by productive debt. Deficit financing of capital spending is defensible in contrast to deficit financing of state expenditure. Productive state investment would be immune to the charge of crowding out which might be made of deficit-financed current spending.

* * *

Aggregate profits, it turns out, are a part of the solution of a difference equation in central bank funding of economic activity. They can grow or shrink, cause or be effected by capital gains on long-term government bonds. The context of the exercise is a set of ideas thrown up during the recent financial-real crises emanating in the US. The dilemma is to distinguish profits generated in the financial circulation from profits earned on the production of goods and services. The consensus is that there is need to recapture the distinction between banks supporting production and inventory accumulation and long-term investments backed by financial institutions through money market funds. The latter are uninsured and some scholars, endorsing the intervention of the Federal Reserve to back real investments, have opined that long-term government bonds might be the monetary instrument of the future.

References

Aglietta, M., and B. Mojon. 2010. 'Central Banking', in A. Berger, P. Molyneux, and J.O.S. Wilson (eds), *The Oxford Handbook of Banking*. Oxford: Oxford University Press, pp. 233–57.

Binswanger, M. 2009. 'Is There a Growth Imperative in Capitalist Economies? A Circular Flow Perspective', *Journal of Post Keynesian Economics*, 37(4): 707–27.

Bruun, C., and C. Heyn-Johnsen. 2009. 'The Paradox of Monetary Profits: An Obstacle to Understanding Financial and Economic Crisis', Economics Discussion Papers, 2009–52, Kiel Institute for the World Economy.

Colander, D. 2010. 'Review of "the Genesis of Macro: New Ideas from Sir William Petty to Henry Thornton"', Discussion Paper No. 10–04, Middlebury College Economics.

Gagnon, J., M. Raskin, J. Remache, and B. Sack. 2010. 'Large-Scale Asset Purchases by the Federal Reserve: Did they Work?', Federal Reserve Bank of New York Staff, Report No. 441.

Godley, W., and M. Lavoie. 2007. *Monetary Economics*. Hampshire: Palgrave Macmillan.

Keen, S. 2010. 'Solving the Paradox of Monetary Profits', *Economics*, the Open-Access, Open-Assessment E-journal, 4, 2010–31, 28 October 2010.

Kregel, J. 2010. 'Is This the Minsky Moment for Reform of Financial Regulation?' Working Paper No. 586, Levy Institute.

Nelson, E. 2011. 'Friedman's Monetary Economics in Practice', Finance and Economics Discussion Series, Divisions of Research & Statistics & Monetary Affairs. Washington, DC: Federal Reserve Board.

Pérez, E., and M. Vernengo. 2010. 'All is Quiet on the Fiscal Front: Fiscal Policy for the Global Economic Crisis', Working Paper No. 2010–02, Department of Economics, University of Utah.

Taylor, L. 2010. 'Keynesian Prospects for the US Economy', *Seoul Journal of Economics*, 23(1): 1–34.

Tomasson, G., and D.J. Bezemer. 2010. 'What is the Source of Profit and Interest? A Classical Conundrum Reconsidered', MPRA Paper 20320, University Library of Munich, Germany.

SECTION III

INFORMAL CREDIT AND MICRO-FINANCE

7

Vertical Linkage between Formal and Informal Credit Markets

Corruption and Credit Subsidy Policy

Sarbajit Chaudhuri and Krishnendu Ghosh Dastidar[*]

Forging a vertical linkage between formal and informal credit markets is considered to be one of many different ways of pursuing a liberalized policy in financial markets in emerging economies. Under this policy, formal credit is supplied to lenders in the informal sector with a view to enhancing competition between them so that the ultimate borrowers receive credit at a reasonable interest rate. Here the informal sector lenders act as financial intermediaries between the formal credit agency and the final borrowers of credit. This policy has been experimented with some success in the Philippines (see Umali 1990).

[*] Professor Amitava Bose and Professor Dipankar Dasgupta are among the finest minds in our country. The authors are deeply honoured to be able to contribute to this volume dedicated to them.

There is a small body of theoretical literature that analyses the economic effects of building such a vertical linkage. Some papers in this literature discuss as to why the policy may not ultimately succeed. Hoff and Stiglitz (1997) have argued that this policy may be counterproductive and actually raise the informal sector interest rate since extending formal credit to informal lenders paves the way for the entry of new lenders in the informal credit market which in turn makes loan recoveries from borrowers more difficult and this leads to an increase in the cost of loan administration for every lender. Bose (1998) has shown that the policy of vertical linkage may in fact produce adverse effects on the borrowing terms faced by small and marginal borrowers He considered a situation where informal sector lenders have asymmetric information regarding the borrowers' ability to repay loans and competition between them determines the interest rate in the informal credit market. In such a context, a credit subsidy policy will enable the better-informed informal sector lender to attract better borrowers (who have lower probability of default). Consequently, the remaining borrowers (with higher probability of default) will be forced to go to the other lender. As a result, the second lender may not find it profitable to continue the lending operations and may finally leave the credit market. In such a situation, the borrowing terms in the informal credit market will deteriorate. Furthermore, Floro and Ray (1997) have shown that credit flow to lenders in the informal credit market may strengthen the ability and incentive of informal lenders to collude among themselves, which will result in worse terms faced by borrowers in the informal credit market. Finally, Chaudhuri and Dastidar (hereafter referred to in the chapter as 'CD') (2011) have shown that presence of corruption in the distribution of formal credit might be another factor behind the failure of the policy of vertical linkages.

This chapter is an extension of CD (2011). We develop a model of a vertical linkage between the formal and informal credit markets that highlights the presence of corruption in the distribution of formal credit. The existing moneylender, bank officials, and new moneylenders move sequentially and the existing moneylender acts as a Stackelberg leader and unilaterally decides on the informal interest rate. The analysis distinguishes between two different ways of designing a credit subsidy policy. If a credit subsidy policy is undertaken through an increase in the supply of institutional credit, it is likely to increase the competitiveness in the informal credit market and lower the informal sector interest rate under reasonable parametric restrictions. This result is different from that of CD (2011). The present chapter goes on to show that any change in the formal sector interest rate has no effect on informal interest. However, an anti-corruption measure (increase in penalty) unambiguously lowers the interest rate in the informal credit market. Finally, the effects of alternative policies on the incomes of different economic agents are also examined. These effects have not been examined in CD (2011).

The Model

We closely follow CD (2011). There is a rural credit market with a single formal credit agency (a bank). The bank official is given the task of distributing a given amount, $\overline{C}$, of bank credit to people who re-lend the money to farmers in the village. Let N denote the *very large* number of homogeneous new moneylenders applying for bank credit. But how many of them, n, would ultimately get formal credit is decided by the bank official. The bank officer is corrupt and demands a bribe, z, per unit of bank credit given to the fringe moneylenders.[1] This amount is withheld as 'cut money' from the bank credit at the time of disbursal.

There are three stages of the game. In the first stage, the dominant moneylender determines the informal interest, i, as he knows the behavioural patterns of the bank official and the fringe moneylenders. In the second stage of the game the bank official decides on the bribing rate, z, and the number of new moneylenders, n, who actually get the credit. In the final stage of the game, each fringe moneylender determines the amount of formal credit that he would apply for. The amount of formal credit that each new moneylender receives, C^F, is also determined in the process.

We now analyse the behaviour and payoff functions of the different economic agents in this model.

---

[1] See Chaudhuri and Gupta (1996) and Gupta and Chaudhuri (1997) in this context.

Fringe moneylenders: We start with fringe moneylenders who move in the third stage. Each fringe moneylender decides the amount of formal credit that he will apply for. If fringe moneylender is formally approved of C^F amount of credit, the amount that he actually gets in hand is $C^F(1-z)$ as zC^F is to be paid as bribe to the bank official. He can now use this amount $(1-z)C^F$ to disburse as loan and earn an interest rate of i on it. Let r be the formal interest rate and $f(x)$ be the cost of loan enforcement. It is given that $f(0) = 0$. Also $f'(x) > 0$ and $f''(x) > 0$ for all $x > 0$. Since this person has been formally approved of C^F amount of credit, he has to pay back $(1+r)C^F$ to the bank.

The income of each fringe moneylender is therefore:

$$Y^F = \left[(1+i)(1-z)-(1+r)\right]C^F - f\left[C^F(1-z)\right].$$

We assume that the reservation income of each moneylender is zero. We now proceed to the bank official.

The bank official: The bank official moves in at the second stage and chooses the bribing rate, z, and the number of new moneylenders, n, who actually get the credit. Let C^F be the formal credit received by each of the n fringe moneylenders in the third stage. Let $P(z)$ be the probability of the bank official getting caught if he takes a bribe. $P(.)$ satisfies the following properties:

1. $P(0) = 0$
2. $P'(z) > 0 \ \forall z > 0$
3. $P''(z) > 0 \ \forall z > 0$.

K is the fixed money value of penalty in case bribery is detected. The bank official is assumed to be risk neutral and his expected income is:

$$Y^O = nzC^F - P(z)K.$$

It may be noted that the bank official while choosing z and n must see to it that $Y^F \geq 0$ (the reservation income constraint of each fringe moneylender) and $\bar{C} \geq nC^F$ (the credit constraint that he himself faces).

The dominant moneylender: The dominant moneylender moves in the first stage and chooses the informal interest, i. Let g be the opportunity interest rate of the dominant moneylender. $F(i)$, the aggregate demand function for credit by the ultimate borrowers (farmers). We assume $F'(.) < 0$ and $F''(.) \leq 0$. Note that $n(1-z)C^F$ is the aggregate supply of actual formal credit (after bribe has been paid) going to the fringe moneylenders. Since this amount is supplied to the farmers as loans, the net demand function of credit faced by the dominant moneylender is: $F(i) - n(1-z)C^F$. Hence, the income of the dominant moneylender is:

$$Y^M = (i - g)[F(i) - n(1-z)C^F].$$

We also assume that the dominant moneylender has no cost of enforcing loan repayment. This can be justified by the hierarchical structure of a rural society where the dominant moneylender enjoys enormous clout.

Solving for the Three-stage Game

Third Stage

The fringe moneylender moves and chooses $C^F \geq 0$ to maximize:

$$Y^F = [(1+i)(i-z) - (1+r)]C^F - f[C^F(1-z)].$$

The first and second order conditions for maximization are:

$$Y^F_C = \frac{\partial Y^F}{\partial C} = (1+i)(1-z) - (1+r) - f'[C^F(1-z)](1-z) = 0 \tag{7.1}$$

$$\text{and } Y^F_{CC} = \frac{\partial^2 Y^F}{\partial C^2} = -f''[C^F(1-z)](1-z)^2 < 0 \tag{7.1a}$$

Note that the second order condition $\left(Y^F_{CC} < 0\right)$ is always satisfied since $f''(.) > 0$. Solving (7.1) and (7.1a) we get C^F. Note that if

$(1 + i)(1 - z) - (1 + r) < 0$ then $C^F = 0$. Also, $C^F > 0$ Þ $(1 + i)(1 - z) - (1 + r) > 0$. Therefore:

$$Y^F = [(1+i)(1-z)-(1+r)]C^F - f[C^F(1-z)] > 0 \Rightarrow (1+i)(1-z)-(1+r) > 0 \qquad (7.2)$$

From (7.1) we get that if $C^F > 0$ then:

$$(1 + i)(i - z) - (1 + r) = f'[C^F(1 - z)](1 - z)$$

That is, if $C^F > 0$ we get that (from [7.1]):

$$C^F = \frac{1}{1-z} f'^{-1}\left(1+i-\frac{1+r}{1-z}\right) \qquad (7.3)$$

Note that $C_r^F = \dfrac{\partial C^F}{\partial r} < 0$ [since $f''(.) > 0$] $\qquad$ (7.3a)

and the sign of $C_z^F = \dfrac{\partial C^F}{\partial z}$ is ambiguous. $\qquad$ (7.3b)

Second Stage

We now fold the game backwards and solve the second stage. In this stage the bank official moves and chooses z and $n \leq N$ to maximize Y^O subject to $Y^F \geq 0$ and $\overline{C} \geq nC^F$. Using (7.2) it may be noted that the official maximizes:

$$Y^O = nzC^F - P(z)K$$
$$s.t.\, g^1(z,n) = -Y^F \leq 0$$
$$g^2(z,n) = nC^F - \overline{C} \leq 0$$
and $g^3(z,n) = n - N \leq 0$

The relevant Lagrangian is:

$$L = nzC^F - P(z)K + \lambda_1 Y^F + \lambda_2(\overline{C} - nC^F) + \lambda_3(N - n)$$

In an interior equilibrium, the IOCs and the complementary slackness conditions are:

$$L_z = \frac{\partial L}{\partial z} = nC^F + nzC_z^F - P'(z)K + \lambda_1 Y_z^F - n\lambda_2 C_z^F = 0 \quad (7.4a)$$

$$L_n = \frac{\partial L}{\partial n} = zC^F - \lambda_2 C^F - \lambda_3 = 0 \quad (7.4b)$$

$$L_{\lambda_1} = \frac{\partial L}{\partial \lambda_1} = Y^F \geq 0 \quad (7.4c)$$

$$\lambda_1 \left(\frac{\partial L}{\partial \lambda_1} \right) = \lambda_1 Y^F = 0 \quad (7.4d)$$

$$L_{\lambda_2} = \frac{\partial L}{\partial \lambda_2} = \overline{C} - nC^F \geq 0 \quad (7.4e)$$

$$\lambda_2 \left(\frac{\partial L}{\partial \lambda_2} \right) = \lambda_2 (\overline{C} - nC^F) = 0 \quad (7.4f)$$

$$L_{\lambda_3} = \frac{\partial L}{\partial \lambda_3} = N - n \geq 0 \quad (7.4g)$$

$$\lambda_3 \frac{\partial L}{\partial \lambda_3} = \lambda_3 (N - n) = 0 \quad (7.4h)$$

Note that in any non-trivial equilibrium $Y^F > 0$ and this implies (from 7.4d) that $\lambda_1 = 0$. Since we have assumed that N is very large, in equilibrium $n < N$. This means $\lambda_3 = 0$ (from 7.4h).

In equilibrium $\overline{C} - nC^F = 0$. This is because of the following reason. If $\overline{C} - nC^F > 0$ then the official can increase his payoff simply by increasing n. Therefore, $\overline{C} - nC^F > 0$ cannot arise in equilibrium. Hence, the *binding constraint* is the second constraint [which is $g^2(.)$]. Note that:

$$g_z^2 = \frac{\partial g^2(.)}{\partial z} = nC_z^F \text{ and}$$

$$g_n^2 = \frac{\partial g^2(.)}{\partial n} = C^F.$$

124 Emerging Issues in Economic Development

Therefore the second order condition for the maximization is:

$$\det \begin{vmatrix} L_{zz} & L_{zn} & -g_z^2 \\ L_{nz} & L_{nn} & -g_n^2 \\ -g_z^2 & -g_n^2 & 0 \end{vmatrix} > 0$$

Remark 1 It may be noted that the second order condition will be valid only if $P''(.) > 0$ (which we have assumed to be the case).

Then using the fact that $\lambda_1 = 0 = \lambda_3$ and that $g^2(.) = 0$ in equilibrium, we get the following from (7.4a) to (7.4h):

$$nC^F + n(z - \lambda_2)C_z^F - P'(z)K = 0 \qquad (7.5a)$$

$$(z - \lambda_2)C^F = 0 \qquad (7.5b)$$

$$\overline{C} = nC^F \qquad (7.5c)$$

From (7.5a) to (7.5c) we can solve for z, λ_2 and n. That is, we will get z and n as functions of i (which has been chosen by the existing moneylender in the first stage), $\overline{C}$, and r. Note that $\overline{C}$ and r are given exogenously.

From (7.5b) we get that $z - \lambda_2 = 0$, since $C^F > 0$ (in any non-trivial equilibrium). This implies (from 7.5a and 7.5c):

$$\overline{C} - p'(z)K = 0 \qquad (7.6)$$

Since $P'(.)$ is a strictly monotonic function, we have in equilibrium:

$$z = P'^{-1}\left(\frac{\overline{C}}{K}\right) \qquad (7.7)$$

Hence we have:

$$z_i = \frac{\partial z}{\partial i} = 0 \qquad (7.8a)$$

$$z_r = \frac{\partial z}{\partial r} = 0 \qquad (7.8b)$$

$$z_{\bar{C}} = \frac{\partial z}{\partial \bar{C}} = \frac{1}{KP''\left[P'^{-1}\left(\dfrac{\bar{C}}{K}\right)\right]} = \frac{1}{KP''(z)} \qquad (7.8c)$$

$$\text{and } z_K = \frac{\partial z}{\partial K} = -\frac{\bar{C}}{K^2 P''(z)} \qquad (7.8d)$$

First Stage

We now solve the first stage. In this stage, the dominant moneylender chooses i to maximize:

$$Y^M = (i-g)\,[F(i) - n(1-z)C^F].$$

Note that from the second-stage equilibrium condition we know that $z = z(i, \bar{C}, r)$ and $nC^F = \bar{C}$.

The dominant moneylender will take this into account (like a Stackelberg leader) to maximize:

$$Y^M = (i-g)\bigl[F(i) - (1-z)\bar{C}\bigr].$$

The conditions for maximization are as follows. We use (7.8a), (7.8b), and (7.8c) to derive them:

$$Y_i^M = \frac{\partial Y^M}{\partial i} = (i-g)F'(i) + F(i) - \bar{C}(1-z) = 0 \qquad (7.9a)$$

$$\text{and } Y_{ii}^M = \frac{\partial^2 Y^M}{\partial i^2} = (i-g)F''(i) + 2F'(i) < 0 \qquad (7.9b)$$

Note that (7.9b) is always satisfied since we have assumed that $F'(.) < 0$ and $F''(.) \le 0$.

Subgame perfect equilibrium Note that in our model the parameters are $\bar{C}$, K, r, and g. From (7.5c), (7.7), and (7.9a) we can compute the subgame perfect equilibrium values of i, z, and n (i^{eqm}, z^{eqm}, and n^{eqm}, respectively). Plugging in the values of i^{eqm} and z^{eqm} in (7.3) we will get the equilibrium value of C^F.

By using (7.8a), (7.8b) and (7.8c) and (7.9a) we get:

$$Y_{ir}^M = \overline{C}\left[(i-g)z_{ir} + zr\right] = 0 \tag{7.10a}$$

$$Y_{i\overline{C}}^M = -(1-z) + \overline{C}z_{\overline{C}} = -(1-z) + \frac{\overline{C}}{KP''(z)} \tag{7.10b}$$

$$\text{and } Y_{iK}^M = \overline{C}_{zK} = \frac{\overline{C}^2}{K^2 P''(z)_g} \tag{7.10c}$$

Also note that:

$$\frac{di^{eqm}}{dr} = -\frac{Y_{ir}^M}{Y_{ii}^M} \tag{7.11a}$$

$$\frac{di^{eqm}}{d\overline{C}} = -\frac{Y_{i\overline{C}}^M}{Y_{ii}^M} \tag{7.11b}$$

$$\text{and } \frac{di^{eqm}}{dK} = -\frac{Y_{iK}^M}{Y_{ii}^M} \tag{7.11c}$$

In any non-trivial equilibrium where $C^F > 0$ and $z \in (0,1)$ we get the following result:

Proposition 1

(i) $\dfrac{\partial i^{eqm}}{\partial \overline{C}} < 0$

(ii) $\dfrac{\partial i^{eqm}}{\partial \overline{C}} < 0$ provided <u>either</u> K is large enough compared to $\overline{C}$ <u>or</u> $P''(z)$ is large enough (that is, $P(z)$ is sufficiently convex)

(iii) $\dfrac{\partial i^{eqm}}{\partial K} < 0$

Proof (i) Note $Y_{ii}^M < 0$ (7.9b) and $Y_{ir}^M = 0$ (7.10a). Hence, from (7.11a) we get that $\dfrac{\partial i^{eqm}}{\partial r} = 0$. (ii) Since $P''(.) > 0$ then $\dfrac{\overline{C}}{KP''(z)} > 0$.

However, if K is large enough compared to $\overline{C}$ then $\dfrac{\overline{C}}{K}$ is sufficiently small. Since $z < 1$, $-(1-z) < 0$, and so we get that $Y\dfrac{M}{iC} = -(1-z) + \dfrac{\bar{C}}{KP''(z)} < 0$ for a sufficiently large K. For such a K we have $\dfrac{\partial i^{eqm}}{\partial \bar{C}} < 0$. Similarly, if $P''(z)$ is large enough then $Y\dfrac{M}{iC} = -(1-z) + \dfrac{\bar{C}}{KP''(z)} < 0$. This in turn implies that $\dfrac{\partial i^{eqm}}{\partial r} = 0$.

(iii) Since $Y_{ii}^M < 0$ the above result follows straight from (7.10c) and (7.11c).

Comment We now try to provide some intuition behind Proposition 1. If r decreases z does not change as (7.7) does not contain r. This means that the effective amount of formal credit injected into the system, $\bar{C}(1-z)$ remains unaffected which in turn implies that the informal interest rate, i, in the new equilibrium will remain unchanged.

An increase in $\bar{C}$, on the contrary, changes z. But the direction of change must depend on the curvature of the $P(.)$ function. As $P''(.) > 0$ in a stable equilibrium, z rises. However, either if K is sufficiently large relative to $\bar{C}$ or if $P(.)$ is sufficiently convex, the increase in z is small (relative to the increase in $\bar{C}$) so that $\bar{C}(1-z)$ rises. In this situation also i falls as the existing moneylender's demand for informal credit falls.

If the government resorts to anti-corruption measures in the form of an increase in K, $P'(z)$ has to fall (see (7.6)). Consequently, z must decrease in a stable equilibrium. It decreases as $P''(.) > 0$, which in turn, implies a rise in $\bar{C}(1-z)$. As a consequence, the demand for informal credit of the dominant moneylender falls which compels him to lower the informal interest rate, i.

We now proceed to provide a few remarks on n^{eqm} (the number of fringe moneylenders who actually get the credit in equilibrium). From (7.5c) we get that $n^{eqm} = \dfrac{\bar{C}}{C^F}$.

Therefore $\dfrac{\partial n^{eqm}}{\partial r} = -\dfrac{\dfrac{\partial C^F}{\partial r}}{\left(C^F\right)^2}$ (7.12a) and $\dfrac{dn^{eqm}}{d\bar{C}} = \dfrac{1}{(C^F)^2}\left[C^F - \bar{C}\dfrac{dC^F}{d\bar{C}}\right]$ (7.12b)

Since $z_r = 0$ (from 7.8b) and $C^F = \dfrac{1}{1-z}f'^{-1}\left(1+i-\dfrac{1+r}{1-z}\right)$ (from (7.3)) and $f''(.) > 0$ we get that $\dfrac{dC^F}{dr} < 0$.

Therefore $\dfrac{dn^{eqm}}{dr} = -\dfrac{\dfrac{dc^F}{dr}}{(C^F)^2} > 0$ (7.13)

Note that $\dfrac{dz^{eqm}}{d\bar{C}} = z_{\bar{C}}$. From (7.3) we have:

$$\dfrac{dC^F}{d\bar{C}} = \dfrac{1}{(1-z)^2}\left[\begin{array}{c}(1-z)\dfrac{1}{f''\left(1+i-\dfrac{1+r}{1-z}\right)}\left(\dfrac{di^{eqm}}{d\bar{C}} - z_{\bar{C}}\dfrac{1+r}{(1-z^{eqm})^2}\right)\\ +f'^{-1}\left(1+i-\dfrac{1+r}{1-z}\right)z_{\bar{C}}\end{array}\right]$$

(7.14)

Therefore from (7.12b) and (7.14) it is clear that the sign of $\dfrac{dn^{eqm}}{d\bar{C}}$ is ambiguous. We summarize this result in terms of the following proposition.

Proposition 2 n^{eqm} always rises with r. However, the effect of an increase in $\bar{C}$ on n^{eqm} is ambiguous.

Comment It may be noted that while the effect of increasing $\bar{C}$ on i^{eqm} is ambiguous, with reasonable restrictions on the parameters it is possible to have a scenario where n^{eqm} increases with $\bar{C}$. This will be shown in an example later.

We now provide some comparative static results. It may be noted that r, $\bar{C}$, and K are the parameters of our model. The results are as follows. From earlier discussions and using (7.8a–7.8d) we obtain:

$$\frac{dY^F}{dr} = -C^F - C^F[(1+i) - f'(.)]\frac{dz}{dr} = -C^F < 0. \left(\text{note that } \frac{dz}{dr} = 0\right)$$

$$\frac{dY^F}{d\overline{C}} = -C^F(1+r)\frac{dz}{d\overline{C}} < 0. \left(\text{note that } \frac{dz}{d\overline{C}} > 0 \text{ as } P''(.) > 0\right)$$

$$\frac{dY^F}{dK} = -C^F(1+r)\frac{dz}{dK} > 0. \left(\text{as } \frac{dz}{dK} < 0\right)$$

Proposition 3
(i) Y^F always increases with a fall in r.
(ii) Y^F increases following an increase in K.
(iii) Y^F falls following an increase in $\overline{C}$.

A decrease in the formal interest rate, r, lowers the opportunity cost of credit of every fringe moneylender which in turn raises his net income. Besides, an increase in the gross volume of formal credit, $\overline{C}$, raises the bribing rate, z, charged by the bank official, for each unit of formal credit disbursed to the new moneylenders as $P''(.) > 0$ in the stable SPE. This affects their profitability adversely and lowers their income. Finally, an anti-corruption measure on the bank official lowers z and hence improves earnings of the fringe moneylenders.

Differentiating the expression for Y^M and using (7.8a–7.8d) we get:

$$\frac{dY^M}{dr} = (i-g)\overline{C}\frac{dz}{dr} = 0$$

$$\frac{dY^M}{d\overline{C}} = -(i-g)\left(\frac{d(1-z)\overline{C}}{d\overline{C}}\right) < 0.$$

$$\left(\text{note that } \frac{d(1-z)\overline{C}}{d\overline{C}} > 0 \text{ if } K \text{ is sufficiently large} \atop \text{relative to } \overline{C} \text{ or if } P(.) \text{ is sufficiently convex.}\right)$$

$$\frac{dY^M}{dK} = (i-g)\overline{C}\frac{dz}{dK} < 0.$$

Proposition 4
(i) A change in r cannot affect Y^M.
(ii) An increase in $\bar{C}$ lowers Y^M in a stable equilibrium.
(iii) A rise in K lowers Y^M.

A credit subsidy policy in terms of a reduction in the formal interest rate cannot affect the income of the dominant moneylender as it does not change the bribing rate. On the other hand, although an increase in $\bar{C}$ raises the bribing rate, it may also lead to an increase in the net volume of formal credit, $\bar{C}(1-z)$, injected into the system, provided K is sufficiently large relative to $\bar{C}$ and/or $P(.)$ is sufficiently convex. If this happens, the aggregate demand for informal credit of the moneylender falls and this affects his profitably adversely. Furthermore, an increase in K lowers the official's bribing rate which in turn raises the net volume of formal credit injected into the system. The dominant moneylender in such a situation has no alternative but to charge a lower informal interest rate that also affects his profitability unfavourably.

From the bank officer's maximization exercise, the following may also be noted:

$$\frac{dY^O}{dr} = 0, \frac{dY^O}{d\bar{C}} = z > 0 \text{ and } \frac{dY^O}{dK} = -P(.) < 0 \qquad (7.15)$$

Consequently, we have the following result:

Proposition 5
(i) $dY^O/dr = 0$.
(ii) $dY^O/d\bar{C} > 0$.
(iii) $dY^O/dK < 0$.

A credit subsidy policy, if undertaken through a reduction in the formal interest rate, cannot affect the income of the official as the bribing rate that he charges remains unaffected. Besides, the official has to lower the bribing rate following an anti-corruption measure which in turn affects his income negatively. Finally, an increase in $\bar{C}$

enables the official to earn a higher bribe income when he behaves optimally and chooses the bribing rate.

An Example

Let us have the following:

$f(x) = \frac{1}{2}x^2, P(z) = z^\alpha$ where $\alpha > 0$ and $\alpha \neq 1$,
$F(i) = 100 - i$ and $g = 0$.

Note that $P'(z) = \alpha z^{\alpha-1} > 0$ for all $z > 0$. $P''(z) = \alpha(\alpha - 1) z^{\alpha-2}$. If $\alpha \in (1, \infty)$ then $P''(z) > 0$. This means all the assumptions of our model are satisfied in the example.

Using (7.3) we get:

$$C^F(i, z, r) = \frac{(i+i)(1-z)-(1+r)}{(1-z)^2} \qquad (7.16)$$

Routine computation shows that in our example:

$$z^{eqm} = \left(\frac{\bar{C}}{\alpha K}\right)^{\frac{1}{\alpha-1}} \qquad (7.17a)$$

$$i^{eqm} = \frac{1}{2}\left[100 - \bar{C}\left(1 - \left(\frac{\bar{C}}{\alpha K}\right)^{\frac{1}{\alpha-1}}\right)\right] \qquad (7.17b)$$

$$\text{and } n^{eqm} = \frac{\bar{C}\left[1 - \left(\frac{\bar{C}}{\alpha K}\right)^{\frac{1}{\alpha-1}}\right]^2}{\left[1 + \frac{1}{2}\left\{100 - \bar{C}\left(1 - \left(\frac{\bar{C}}{\alpha K}\right)^{\frac{1}{\alpha-1}}\right)\right\}\right]\left[1 - \left(\frac{\bar{C}}{\alpha K}\right)^{\frac{1}{\alpha-1}}\right] - (1+r)}$$

$$(7.17c)$$

132 Emerging Issues in Economic Development

Note that:

$$\frac{di^{eqm}}{d\bar{C}} = \frac{1}{2}\left[-1+\left(\frac{\bar{C}}{\alpha K}\right)^{\frac{1}{\alpha-1}}\left(\frac{\alpha}{\alpha-1}\right)\right] \qquad (7.18)$$

To illustrate the case of $\alpha > 1$ (that is, $P''(.) > 0$) we take $\alpha = 2$. For this particular value of α, we have:

$$\frac{di^{eqm}}{d\bar{C}} = \frac{1}{2}\left[-1+\frac{\bar{C}}{K}\right] < 0 \text{ if } K > \bar{C}.$$

$$n^{eqm} = \frac{\bar{C}\left(1-\dfrac{\bar{C}}{2K}\right)^2}{\left[1+\dfrac{1}{2}\left\{100-\bar{C}\left(1-\dfrac{\bar{C}}{2R}\right)\right\}\right]\left[1-\dfrac{\bar{C}}{2R}\right] - (1+r)} \qquad (7.19)$$

Here we have:

$$\frac{\partial n^{eqm}}{\partial \bar{C}} = 16(2K-\bar{C})K\frac{\begin{pmatrix}100K^2 - 150\bar{C}K - 2K^2 r + \\ 51\bar{C}^2 + 3K\bar{C}r\end{pmatrix}}{\begin{pmatrix}-400K^2 + 204\bar{C}K + 4K^2\bar{C} - \\ 4\bar{C}^2 K + \bar{C}^3 + 8K^2 r\end{pmatrix}^2}$$

$$= 16K^2(2K-\bar{C})\frac{(2K-3\bar{C})(50-r)+51\bar{C}^2}{\begin{pmatrix}-400K^2+204\bar{C}K+4K^2\bar{C}-4\bar{C}^2\\ K+\bar{C}^3+8K^2 r\end{pmatrix}^2}$$

(7.19a)

Note that since r is the formal sector rate of interest it is reasonable to suppose that $r < 50$ (that is, formal sector rate of interest is less than 5,000 per cent).

From (7.19a) we get that if $K > \dfrac{3}{2}\bar{C}$ then $\dfrac{\partial n^{eqm}}{\partial \bar{C}} > 0$.

Our example illustrates some of the main results derived in this chapter.

* * *

Development economists have concerns regarding the efficacy of the policy of forging a vertical linkage between the formal and informal credit markets in achieving its primary objective of enhancing competition and improving the borrowing terms faced by small and marginal farmers. It has been shown in literature that such a policy may be counterproductive under asymmetric information among informal sector lenders. In this context, we analysed some issues that have not been adequately examined in earlier works. In this chapter we showed that even without any asymmetric information problems, this policy may fail in the presence of corruption in the distribution of formal credit. We also showed that any change in the formal sector interest rate has no effect on the informal interest rate while an anti-corruption measure (increase in penalty) unambiguously lowers the interest rate in the informal credit market. Finally, we also examined the effects of alternative policies on the incomes of different economic agents.

References

Bose, P. 1998. 'Formal-informal Sector Interaction in Rural Credit Markets', *Journal of Development Economics*, 56: 265–80.

Chaudhuri, S., and K.G. Dastidar. 2011. 'Corruption in a Model of Vertical Linkage between Formal and Informal Credit Sources and Credit Subsidy Policy', *Economic Modelling*, 28: 2596–9.

Chaudhuri, S., and M.R. Gupta. 1996. 'Delayed Formal Credit, Bribing and the Informal Credit Market in Agriculture: A Theoretical Analysis', *Journal of Development Economics*, 51: 433–49.

Floro, M.S., and D. Ray. 1997. 'Vertical Links between Formal and Informal Financial Institutions', *Review of Development Economics*, 1: 34–56.

Gupta, M.R., and S. Chaudhuri. 1997. 'Formal Credit, Corruption, and the Informal Credit Market in Agriculture: A Theoretical Analysis', *Economica*, 64: 331–43.

Hoff, K., and J. Stiglitz. 1997. 'Moneylenders and Bankers: Price-increasing Subsidies in a Monopolistically Competitive Market', *Journal of Development Economics*, 52: 429–62.

Reserve Bank of India. 1981. *All India Rural Debt and Investment Survey, 1981*. Mumbai: RBI.

Umali, D. 1990. 'The Structure and Price Performance of the Philippine Rice Marketing System'. PhD dissertation, Stanford University.

8

Sequential Lending

Dynamic Institutions and Micro-finance

Prabal Roy Chowdhury

Lack of information and inadequate collateral regarding poor borrowers imply that formal sector lending to the poor is quite problematic, often characterized, for example, by inadequate coverage, very low rates of repayment, and imprecise targeting.[1] The recent success of the Grameen Bank in Bangladesh, at least as far as repayment rates are concerned,[2,3] however, raised hopes that group lending schemes might be used as a conduit for channelling formal sector credit to

---

[1] These problems are of serious concern given the linkage between finance and growth (see, for example, Goldsmith (1969); Gurley and Shaw (1955); and Levine (1997)).

[2] Hossein (1988) argues that the Grameen Bank has a repayment rate in excess of 95 per cent. Similar figures were obtained by Morduch (1999) and Christen et al. (1994).

[3] In this survey we are not concerned with the debate on whether microfinance has had a positive 'impact' on the borrowers. We refer the readers to Aghion and Morduch (2005) for a discussion of some of the issues.

the poor.[4] This led to a huge expansion of micro-finance schemes all across the world, including countries in Latin America, Africa, Asia, and even the United States of America.

Apart from its success, another interesting aspect of micro-finance has been the use of various innovative loan products. It may be useful to illustrate this point using the Grameen I programme which has been used by Grameen Bank for quite a long time. Under Grameen I, loans are given to a group of five borrowers. Initially loans are given to two of the borrowers. A few weeks after this, these borrowers are supposed to start their repayments. These repayments involve small but regular repayments, usually weekly. Once these two initial borrowers make the first few repayments, another two borrowers receive loans. These, in turn, start their repayments after a few weeks, and so on. Further, in case any one of the borrowers defaults, the other borrowers are supposed to repay for her.

As this discussion shows, there are lots of things going on here. First, the loans involve group lending. Further, there is what we call joint liability; that is, all borrowers are jointly responsible for repaying the loans. Moreover, loans are sequential, with some members receiving the loans earlier than the others, with the other borrowers receiving their loans only if the earlier borrowers are successful in their repayments. These are the two aspects that we focus on in this chapter.[5]

There have been several important contributions that seek to explain the success of such schemes.[6] Given that micro-finance schemes have these two unusual features, namely, the very high rates of repayment, and several innovative loan schemes, it seems natural to conjecture that their success may be connected to these loan products. This is the viewpoint that, along with much of the literature, we

---

[4] Group lending schemes, however, are not a recent phenomenon. See Ghatak and Guinnane (1999) for a discussion of an earlier group-lending scheme in Germany.

[5] Of course there are other interesting dynamic issues involved here. For example, micro-finance often involves gradual repayment, the practice of asking for repayment in small, but regular repayments. However, we touch on this aspect only briefly in the introduction.

[6] We refer the readers to Ghatak and Guinnane (1999); Morduch (1999); and Roy Chowdhury (2010) for recent surveys of the literature.

take in this survey. In this chapter we provide an analytical summary of some of the key ideas in the literature. We begin with an informal discussion of some of the ideas, before providing a more formal discussion in the main body of the chapter. Further, we focus on those papers whose ideas can be easily framed in the simple framework that we have in mind.

The initial surge of interest was focussed around the issue of joint liability lending. As we discuss later, the main idea was that such joint liability lending would trigger either monitoring by the borrowers themselves, or that it would lead to good borrowers bonding together, with attendant benefits for the lenders. While the monitoring literature was pioneered by, among others, Stiglitz (1990), Varian (1990), and Banerjee et al. (1994), the literature on assortative matching was pioneered by, among others, Ghatak (1999, 2000) and Tassel (1999).

The more recent literature has, however, started moving away from the static joint liability aspects of such schemes, and focuses on dynamic elements like sequential lending and gradual repayment. While Roy Chowdhury (2005, 2007) and Kumar (2007) discuss some aspects of sequential lending, Jain and Mansuri (2003), Chowdhury et al. (2010), and Fisher and Ghatak (2011) examine some aspects of gradual repayment.

In this chapter, we begin by discussing some of the salient features of literature, especially those dealing with joint liability lending and sequential financing. Many of these papers, however, use different frameworks, making it hard for an interested reader to quickly scan through some of the main ideas. In the rest of the chapter we therefore attempt to illustrate some of the key ideas using the same unified framework. Apart from the gain in accessibility, the exercise demonstrates that many of the key ideas are robust enough to survive a transplantation to a different framework. The downside of such an approach is, of course, that some of the ideas may suffer because of being forced into this framework. We offer an apology to all authors who suffer as a result of our approach.

We begin by discussing the papers on peer monitoring. The essential idea here is that the borrowers have much more information about one another compared to outsiders. The role of the innovative schemes (mentioned earlier) used in micro-finance is to allow the lenders to tap into this information.

We begin with the role of joint liability lending. Stiglitz (1990), Varian (1990), and Banerjee et al. (1994) provide explanations based on peer monitoring. They argue that since group members have better information compared to the lenders, peer monitoring will be relatively cheaper compared to bank monitoring, leading to greater monitoring and greater rates of repayments. Banerjee et al. (1994), in fact, argue that compared to other explanations, arguments based on the idea of peer monitoring are relatively more successful in explaining the success of group lending schemes.

Besley and Coate (1995) analyse a strategic repayment game with joint liability and demonstrate that successful group members may have an incentive to repay the loans of the less successful ones. They also highlight the effect of social collateral in ensuring repayments. Ghatak and Guinnane (1999), on the other hand, analyse moral hazard problems in group lending. In a model with moral hazard and monitoring they find that if the social sanctions are effective enough, or monitoring costs are low enough, joint liability lending will improve repayment rates through peer monitoring even when monitoring is costly.

Roy Chowdhury (2005) argues that this literature ignores the fact that in the presence of interlinked markets and informal mutual insurance schemes, the borrowers may have a strong incentive to collude. The critical idea is that in such a situation, monitoring by the borrowers in a group becomes strategic complements, so that peer monitoring may not be forthcoming at all. Sequential lending, however, incentivizes peer monitoring as it makes such collusion quite costly as the downstream borrowers may not receive a loan at all.

We then turn to literature on endogenous group formation. Some of the recent contributions focus on two aspects of such schemes, *endogenous group formation* and the presence of *social capital*. Ghatak (1999, 2000) and Tassel (1999) analyse the problem of endogenous group formation in the presence of *joint liability*, so that in case of default by some member, the other members have to make up the deficit. They demonstrate that there will be *positive assortative matching* in the sense that borrowers of the same type will club together. Ghatak (2000) and Tassel (1999) then go on to show that the lender can use an appropriate set of loan contracts to screen out the 'bad' borrowers.[7] Ghatak (1999), on the other hand, argues that positive assortative matching improves the mix of borrowers by attracting safe borrowers.

Roy Chowdhury (2007) focuses on the dynamic aspects of group lending, in particular sequential financing and contingent renewal, where contingent renewal refers to the fact that a group may receive further loans if and only if all embers of this group repay the current loans. This chapter examines the efficacy of these two schemes in harnessing social capital, finding that, for the appropriate parameter configurations, there is homogenous group formation so that the lender can ascertain the identity of a group without lending to all its members, thus screening out bad borrowers partially.

The rest of this chapter is concerned with formalizing some of these ideas. While the next section examines how joint liability and sequential lending fare in harnessing the force of peer monitoring, the section that follows examines the role of these institutions in generating positive assortative matching. The last section concludes with a brief summary of some other papers in literature.

Peer Monitoring

We begin by exploring the idea that various institutional innovations generate peer monitoring by the borrowers, thus solving some of the informational issues associated with informal lending.

The story begins with two borrowers, call them borrower 1 and borrower 2, B_1 and B_2 for short, and a single micro-finance institution (henceforth MFI). Both borrowers have access to project(s) that require a setup cost of Re 1. The borrowers, however, are poor and have neither money, nor assets. Thus, they must approach the MFI for this amount.

For simplicity, we take the gross interest rate charged by the MFI from its clients, r, to be exogenously given. This of course is realistic in many countries where the government decides the gross interest based on socio-political considerations. One unit of capital yields a

---

[7] Bad borrowers are more risky as per Ghatak (2000), and less able as per Tassel (1999).

return of one in its alternative use, and MFIs can themselves access capital at a gross interest of 1.

B_1 has access to a project, call it project 1, that yields a verifiable income of H, where $H > 1$, so that investing in this project is efficient. Thus, if borrower 1 obtains a loan, then there is a verifiable income of H, out of which she returns the interest factor r, where $r \geq 1$. Borrower 2, however, has access to two different kinds of projects. The first project is identical to project 1 of borrower 1, that is, it yields a verifiable income of H. The other project, however, yields a non-verifiable income of b. Further, project 2 is inefficient, in the sense that $b < 1$. Time and other resource constraints however ensure that borrower 2 can invest in at most one project, even if she has adequate financing. MFI does not know which borrower is which, and, moreover, it is prohibitively costly for it to obtain this information.

The central issue is one of moral hazard, in that the MFI cannot prevent borrower 2 from investing in project 2, in case she wants to do so. Would B_2 want to do so? If the borrower chooses the first project, her net utility is $H - r$. However, in case she invests in the second project, given that the return from this project is non-verifiable, the borrower will not pay the interest, so that her net utility is b itself. Moreover, we have:

$$b > H - r \qquad (8.1)$$

Thus, B_2 will choose the second project in case she obtains the loan, so that the moral hazard problem is potentially a serious one.

MFI maximizes borrowers' welfare and is therefore interested in offering a loan provided it can ensure that it can break even.

We first examine if individual lending is feasible, given that the MFI cannot identify which borrower is which. Note that in case the MFI lends to both borrowers, its expected payoff is $r - 2$. This is because in case of lending to both the borrowers, only borrower 1 will repay. Consequently, the MFI will not lend whenever $r - 2 < 0$. In order to focus on the case of interest, we assume that this indeed is the case:

$$r < 2. \qquad (8.2)$$

Joint Liability Lending with Simultaneous Loans

We then introduce group lending with joint liability. Thus, in case borrower i defaults, borrower j, $i \neq j$, is supposed to repay for both. How does this help? At this point we introduce one of the central themes in literature, the idea that the borrowers have much more information about one another, compared to outsiders. The question is whether joint liability lending can help MFIs to tap into this information.

We formalize the joint liability aspect by assuming that borrower 1, by spending an amount m on monitoring, can ensure that borrower 2 invests in the right project, which is project 1. For the MFI, however, doing so is much too expensive. We then examine if B_1 in fact has an incentive to monitor the other borrower. Note that borrower 1's payoff in case she does not monitor is $H - 2r$. This is because in that case she will have to repay for the other borrower who, in the absence of monitoring, will default. Whereas if she does monitor, then her payoff is $H - r - m$, as in this case she can force B_2 to invest in project 1 also, though at the cost of incurring m. Consequently, it is optimal for borrower 1 to monitor provided $m < r$.

Turning to the efficiency properties of this equilibrium, note that this is efficient vis-à-vis individual lending whenever $2H - m > 2$. This, however, is not the first best outcome though, as B_1 incurs a monitoring cost of m.

Proposition 1 Under 8.1 and 8.2:

1. Individual lending will lead to market failure, that is, no loan will be made.
2. Under group lending with joint liability, a loan to both borrowers can be sustained whenever $m < \min\{r, H - r\}$. Further, in this case both the borrowers will choose the efficient project, that is, project 1.

Remark 1 The preceding analysis draws on the ideas of Stiglitz (1990), Varian (1990), and Banerjee et al. (1994) on peer monitoring.

Joint Liability Lending in the Presence of Collusion

We then extend the analysis by allowing for the possibility of cheating by *both* the borrowers. Thus suppose now that even borrower 1 has the option of selecting either project 1 or project 2. Notice that this now introduces an interesting possibility, that of implicit collusion among the borrowers. Given that we are considering a situation where interlinked markets abound, and the borrowers are dependent on one another for various informal insurance schemes, it seems natural to allow for such collusive possibilities.

For ease of exposition, we assume that the project is not too productive, and, moreover, that monitoring is not too costly, that is:

$$H < 2r \text{ and } H - r - m > 0. \tag{8.3}$$

Now suppose that the MFI offers the same contract as before. Interestingly neither borrower may monitor in equilibrium. Suppose B_1 is not monitoring. Then B_2 has no incentive to monitor herself, as she can anyway invest in project 2, and obtain b herself. In fact there are two different equilibria, one where both borrowers monitor, and another where neither borrower monitors. Suppose B_1 monitors. Then if B_2 does not monitor, she will have an income of zero. This follows as she will have to invest in project 1, and with the other borrower defaulting, the whole of H will be taken away by the MFI. Whereas if she monitors, the other borrower will be investing in the good project herself, so that her own income is $H - r - m$, which is positive.

Thus, the monitoring game can have two different equilibria. Which one of these two equilibria is more 'natural'? From assumption 1, observe that from the point of view of borrowers, it is Pareto optimal if both of them decide not to monitor. In this scenario, it seems reasonable to argue that the borrowers will coordinate on this outcome. Given the typical context of micro-finance loans, that is, densely populated villages with villagers who are dependent on one another for mutual insurance, such coordination seems quite likely. Thus, in case the loan is given, the MFI will not recover its money if the borrowers reach the collusive outcome. Anticipating this, the MFI will not lend at all, and there will be market failure.

Proposition 2 Let 8.1–8.3 hold. In the presence of collusive possibilities, joint liability lending by itself may not lead to peer monitoring. If the MFI anticipates that this is going to happen, then it will not give a loan and there will be market failure.

Sequential Lending

We then argue that in the presence of sequential lending schemes, this market failure can be resolved. Suppose the scheme involves B_1 getting a loan initially, and in case B_1 repays her loan, B_2 is provided a loan. Thus, the scheme already incorporates elements of *dynamic* joint liability, in that the action of B_1 impacts B_2. Further, there is also *static* joint liability, in that in case a borrower fails to repay, her partner is supposed to repay for her.

In that situation note that B_2 is always going to monitor, otherwise B_1 will choose project 2, and B_1 will not even obtain a loan. Given that B_2 necessarily monitors, borrower 1 will invest in the good project. Would borrower 1 herself monitor? Note that unless she does so, borrower 2, who obtains the loan, will herself default, and borrower 1 will have to repay for her (given static joint liability). Thus, the outcome involves both borrowers monitoring, and both investing in the good project. Thus the MFI finds it feasible to give a loan.

Summarizing this discussion we have our next result.

Proposition 3 Let 8.1–8.3 hold. Consider a situation where the borrowers may potentially collude. Under sequential lending, however, the borrowers monitor each other and invest in the good project. Thus, it is optimal for the MFI to make the loan.

Remark 2 The analysis draws on Roy Chowdhury (2005). Varian (1990) and Kumar (2007) also emphasize the importance of sequential lending. Roy Chowdhury (2005) also shows that this framework can provide an economic justification for the weekly meetings common in many micro-finance schemes. The idea is that this helps the MFI to monitor, which in turn has a pump-priming effect in that it triggers further monitoring by the borrowers themselves. Of course weekly meetings may serve other purposes also, for example, inculcating discipline and bonding among different group members.

Assortative Matching

In this section, we explore the idea that group lending may encourage assortative matching whereby good borrowers group with good borrowers, and bad borrowers group with bad borrowers.

We now extend the basic framework to assume that there are two kinds of borrowers, good and bad. Let the total number of borrowers be normalized to 1. Good borrowers, λ in number, have only one kind of project, project 1. Whereas bad borrowers, $1 - \lambda$ in number, can either choose project 1 or project 2. We assume that neither the borrower, nor the MFI can monitor.

We first argue that under certain parameter configurations individual lending is not feasible. Suppose:

$$\lambda r - 1 < 0. \tag{8.4}$$

Under individual lending, the expected payoff of the MFI is $\lambda r - 1$, which given (8.4), is not feasible.

Joint Liability

We then consider group lending with joint liability. There can be three kinds of groups, GG, BB, and GB. We first consider the aggregate payoffs under the various groupings.

GG: In this case both borrowers invest in the good project, so that both have a payoff of $H - r$.

BB: In this case both the borrowers will default, so that both have a payoff of b.

GB: Note that while the bad borrower will invest in the bad project, obtaining a payoff of b, the good borrower will have to repay for her, ending up with a payoff of max $\{0, H - 2r\} = 0$.

For simplicity, suppose that transfers are not possible across borrowers. Consequently, in this framework while the bad borrowers are indifferent between having a good and a bad borrower as a partner, a good borrower will always prefer to have another good borrower as a partner when she has a payoff of $H - r$, rather than have a bad partner when her payoff is lower at $H - 2r$. Thus, there is positive assortative matching.

In fact, it can be argued that positive assortative matching occurs under transferable utility as well. Suppose there are four borrowers, two of each kind. Then there are two possible group alignments, GG and BB, or another alignment could be the formation of two GB groups. Given transferable utility, there is going to be positive assortative matching if the aggregate payoff under the GG and BB alignment exceeds that under the alternative alignment. Under the GG-BB alignment, the aggregate payoff of the borrowers will be $2(H - r) + 2b$, since the members of the GG groups will both repay, whereas that of the BB group will both default, obtaining b each. Next consider the outcome under the GB-GB alignment. Then the bad borrowers in both the groups will default, obtaining b each, whereas the good borrowers will have to repay for their partners, obtaining a payoff of zero. Clearly, the aggregate payoff under positive assortative matching is higher.

Depending on circumstances, either scenario can be natural. The transferable utility case, for example, is more natural whenever there is scope for mutual insurance among the villagers, or the scope for sharing implements, or capital assets. In general, of course, there will be some scope for transferring utilities, but not fully.

This, however, is not the end of the argument. Does assortative matching help MFIs to break even? Clearly, the expected payoff from making loans to all groups is $2[\lambda r - 2]$. Given (8.4), joint liability lending is not feasible.

Proposition 4 Under joint liability lending there will be positive assortative matching. However, MFIs will not find it feasible to give a loan.

Remark 3 We should clarify though that in Ghatak (2000), assortative matching can help resolve the feasibility issue. In Ghatak (2000) the good and the bad borrowers differ in terms of their ability, rather than in their project choices. In a framework with transferable utilities, Ghatak (2000) finds that the aggregate utility is higher with positive assortative matching, vis-à-vis negative assortative matching. Further, this allows the MFI to use a combination of the rate of interest and the extents of joint liability as a screening tool so as to weed out the group comprising bad borrowers, so that in his framework joint liability lending by itself can help restore feasibility. Another paper that utilizes the idea of screening is Tassel (1999).

Sequential Lending

We then argue that in such a scenario sequential lending is still going to work. To begin with note that under sequential lending also good borrowers will prefer to group with good borrowers, otherwise they may not obtain the loan at all.

The idea is simple. In this case the MFI can just lend to the groups that approach it. Suppose that the group is a GG group. Then, once the first loan is repaid, the MFI knows that the group is a good group, and can make the subsequent loan without any fear of further default. If, however, the MFI lends to a BB group, then once there is default, the MFI knows that the other borrower is also a bad borrower and need not lend to her. Consequently, the MFI can find out about the identity of the group as a whole, at the cost of lending to only one of the members. This is something that is not possible under joint liability lending. Hence, lending may be feasible in this scenario, while it is not possible under joint liability lending.

Given that lending is sequential, the buyer's expected payoff is:

$$2\lambda (r-1) - (1-\lambda). \tag{8.5}$$

Thus lending will be feasible whenever this expression is positive.

Proposition 5 Sequential lending leads to positive assortative matching. Further, the MFI finds it feasible to lend whenever $2\lambda (r-1) - (1-\lambda) < 0$.

Remark 4 Proposition 5 captures one of the central ideas in Roy Chowdhury (2007), that sequential lending helps the MFI to test for the type of a group relatively cheaply, that is, at the cost of lending to only one of the borrowers in a group. In Roy Chowdhury (2007), sequential lending also creates an additional incentive for assortative matching (over and above the incentives provided by joint liability alone).

Gradual Repayment

One feature that is typical to many micro-finance schemes is that of gradual repayments, whereby loans are repaid 'a-little-at-a-time'

(Jain and Mansuri 2003). Under Grameen I, for example, loans were repaid in small weekly instalments spread over a year.

There is a small but growing literature on schemes with early and frequent repayments. In Jain and Mansuri (2003), the requirement of early repayments forces borrowers to borrow from friends/local moneylenders who have better information about the creditworthiness of the borrowers. Thus, early repayment is a device for tapping into the information possessed by these agents.

In a couple of recent contributions, Fisher and Ghatak (2011, 2010) argue that present-biased preferences can provide an explanation for frequent instalments. Another related paper is by Chowdhury et al. (2010). Here the central idea is that with gradual repayments, the incentive to default at any point is not too large. This helps to keep default incentives in control.

* * *

We conclude this chapter by briefly discussing some of the salient papers in literature which have not been discussed so far because forcing them into the framework presented here might have caused some harm to the ideas developed in them.

One branch of literature deals with the issue of *ex post* moral hazard. In an important contribution, Besley and Coate (1995), argues that joint liability loans can help resolve *ex post* moral hazard problems when: (a) the MFI can impose a penalty on defaulters that is increasing in loan size, (b) and the project returns are reasonably large. In that case successful group members may have an incentive to repay for others. If the project size is not that large, however, then there may be group default, even though individually some members would have repaid. In a recent contribution, Sinn (2009) examines the effect of sequential lending in a framework with *ex post* moral hazard.

Next, turning to the role of social capital, Besley and Coate (1995) were the first to allow for social sanctions in a group lending context. They found that depending on the magnitude of social capital, group lending may, or may not lead to greater repayment as compared to individual lending. Other papers which examined the issue of social capital include Aghion (1999), Bhole and Ogden (2010) and Paal and Wiseman (2011).

Another branch examines the role of joint liability in mitigating adverse selection problems (among others, Aghion and Gollier (2000); Ghatak (1999, 2000); Laffont and N'Guessan (2000); Laffont and Rey (2003); Sadoulet (2000); Tassel (1999); and Varian (1990)). Other issues examined in literature include coordination failure (Bond and Rai 2009), cross-reporting by borrowers (Rai and Sjostorm 2004), and collusion (Laffont 2003).

References

Aghion, B.A. 1999. 'On the Design of a Credit Agreement with Peer Monitoring', *Journal of Development Economics*, 60: 79–104.
Aghion, B.A., and C. Gollier. 2000. 'Peer Group Formation in an Adverse Selection Model', *Economic Journal*, 110: 632–43.
Aghion, B.A., and J. Morduch. 2005. *The Economics of Micro-finance*. Cambridge, Massachusetts, London, England: MIT Press.
Banerjee, A., T. Besley, and T.W. Guinnane. 1994. 'Thy Neighbor's Keeper: the Design of a Credit Cooperative with Theory and a Test', *Quarterly Journal of Economics*, 109: 491–515.
Besley, T.J., and S. Coate. 1995. 'Group Lending, Repayment Incentives, and Social Collateral', *Journal of Development Economics*, 46(1): 1–18.
Bhole, B., and S. Ogden. 2010. 'Group Lending and Individual Lending with Strategic Default', *Journal of Development Economics*, 91: 348–63.
Bond, P., and A. Rai. 2009. 'Borrower Runs', *Journal of Development Economics*, 88: 185–91.
Chowdhury, S., P.R. Chowdhury, and K. Sengupta. 2010. 'Sequential Financing with Gradual Repayment in Micro-finance', mimeo, Indian Statistical Institute.
Christen, R., E. Rhyne, and R. Vogel. 1994. 'Maximizing the outreach of microenterprise finance: The emerging lessons of successful programs', mimeo, Washington, DC.
Fisher, G., and Ghatak, M., 2011. 'Spanning the Chasm: Uniting Theory and Empirics in Micro-finance Research', in B. Armendiariz and M. Labie (eds) *Handbook of Microfinance*, World Scientific.
———. 2010. 'Repayment Frequency in Micro-finance Contracts with Present-biased Borrowers', mimeo, London School of Economics.
Ghatak, M. 1999. 'Group Lending, Local Information and Peer Selection', *Journal of Development Economics*, 60: 27–50.
———. 2000. 'Screening by the Company you Keep: Joint Liability Lending and the Peer Selection Effect', *Economic Journal*, 110: 601–31.

Ghatak, M., and T.W. Guinnane. 1999. 'The Economics of Lending with Joint Liability: Theory and Practice', *Journal of Development Economics*, 60: 195–228.

Goldsmith, R.W. 1969. *Financial Structure and Development*. New Haven and London: Yale University Press.

Gurley, John G., and E.S. Shaw. 1955. 'Financial Aspects of Economic Development', *The American Economic Review*, 45(4): 515–38.

Hossein, M. 1988. 'Credit for the Alleviation of Rural Poverty: the Grameen Bank in Bangladesh', Research Report 65, IFPRI, February.

Jain, S., and G. Mansuri. 2003. 'A Little at a Time: The Use of Regularly Scheduled Repayments in Micro-finance', *Journal of Development Economics*, 72: 253–79.

Kumar, Aniket. 2007. 'Sequential Group-lending with Moral Hazard', ESE Discussion paper 136, Edinburgh School of Economics, University of Edinburgh.

Laffont, J.J. 2003. 'Collusion and Group-lending with Adverse Selection', *Journal of Development Economics*, 70: 329–48.

Laffont, J.J., and P. Rey. 2003. 'Moral Hazard, Collusion and Group-lending', IDEI Working Papers. Toulouse: IDEI.

Laffont, J.J., and T.T. N'Guessan. 2000. 'Group-lending with Adverse Selection', *European Economic Review*, 44: 773–84.

Levine, Ross. 1997. 'Financial Development and Economic Growth: Views and Agenda', *Journal of Economic Literature*, 35: 688–722.

Morduch, J. 1999. 'The Micro-finance Promise', *Journal of Economic Literature*, 37: 1569–614.

Paal, B., and T. Wiseman. 2011. 'Group Insurance and Lending with Endogenous Social Collateral', *Journal of Development Economics*, 94: 30–40.

Rai, A., and T. Sjostorm. 2004. 'Is Grameen Lending Efficient? Repayment Incentives and Insurance in Village Economies', *Review of Economic Studies*, 71: 217–34.

Roy Chowdhury, Indrani. 2010. 'Understanding the Grameen Miracle: Information and Organisational Innovation', *Economic and Political Weekly*, 45(6): 66–73.

Roy Chowdhury, P. 2005. 'Group-lending: Sequential Financing, Lender Monitoring and Joint liability', *Journal of Development Economics*, 77: 415–39.

Roy Chowdhury, P. 2007. 'Group-lending with Sequential Financing, Contingent Renewal and Social Capital', *Journal of Development Economics*, 84: 487–507.

Sadoulet, L. 2000. 'The Role of Mutual Insurance in Group-lending', working paper, ECARES/Free University of Brussels.

Sinn, M. 2009. 'Sequential Lending: A Mechanism to Raise Repayment Rates in Group Lending?', mimeo, London School of Economics.

Srinivasan, N. 2009. *Microfinance India, State of the Sector Report 2009*. New Delhi: Sage.

Stiglitz, J.E. 1990. 'Peer Monitoring and Credit Markets', *World Bank Economic Review*, 4: 351–66.

Tassel, E. van. 1999. 'Group-lending Under Asymmetric Information', *Journal of Development Economics*, 60: 3–25.

Udry, C. 1990. 'Credit markets in Northern Nigeria: Credit as Insurance in a Rural Economy', *World Bank Economic Review*, 4: 251–69.

Varian, H. 1990. 'Monitoring Agents with Other Agents', *Journal of Institutional and Theoretical Economics*, 146: 153–74.

SECTION IV

DEMOCRACY AND DEVELOPMENT

9

Democracy, Development, and the Informal Sector

Abhirup Sarkar[*]

This chapter is an attempt at understanding the relationship between democracy and economic development in the context of less-developed countries. There is substantial literature looking at the effect of democracy on economic performance. On the one hand, there are liberal thinkers who believe that economic freedom as provided by a free market and political freedom as facilitated by democracy are mutually reinforcing. In this view, an expansion of political rights fosters economic rights, curbs bad governance, and thereby tends to stimulate growth. This liberal tradition started with Adam Smith (1776) and found its flag bearers in later scholars such as Hayek (1944), Lipset (1959), Friedman (1962), Mises (1981),

---

[*] The author dedicates this paper to Professor Amitava Bose and Professor Dipankar Dasgupta. By doing so, he wishes to record his huge intellectual debt to them accumulated over a period of almost three decades.

Riker and Weimer (1993), and Feng (2003). On the other hand, there are scholars who find dysfunctional consequences of premature democracy on economic development and growth. In addition, it is argued that democracy, by redistributing too much to the poor, hinders savings, investment, and growth (Johnson 1964; Moore 1966; Gerschenkron 1962; O'Donnel 1973; Marsh 1979; Donnelly 1984). The rapid growth of some of the East Asian countries seems to support this view.

Barro (1996), in his extensive study on democracy and growth, found that the overall effect of democracy on growth is weakly negative. He also found some indication of a non-linear relation in which more democracy enhances growth at low levels of political freedom but depresses growth when a moderate level of political freedom has already been attained. His general conclusion is that property rights and free markets are more important than free political systems. For ensuring economic growth and prosperity, the importance of property rights for ordinary citizens has also been stressed by Olson (1993) and De Soto (2000). North (1990) argued that institutions or the rules of the game, both formal and informal, shape the structure of political, social, or economic incentives in human exchange which, in turn, determine the long-term performance of a society. Similarly, Acemoglu et al. (2001) find a link between the prevalence of property rights and other strong institutions in erstwhile colonies and their subsequent economic development. An excellent survey of literature on how property rights can affect efficiency and economic development can be found in Besley and Ghatak (2009).

Recent work by Keefer and Khemani (2004, 2005) raises doubts about the efficient functioning of democracy in a less-developed country. They ask why, in the less-developed economies, poverty has a tendency to persist and broad-based anti-poverty measures involving the provision of health and education are substituted by targeted public spending programmes. The authors argue that broad-based public goods provisions are less effective in winning elections as compared to providing employment, price subsidies, and other direct transfers. Therefore, even though broad-based policies are desirable from the point of view of long-term growth development and poverty alleviation, often they are not adopted.

This chapter raises doubts about the functioning of democracy in a less-developed country from a different standpoint. It illustrates yet another channel through which lack of property rights can affect economic efficiency. The chapter argues that if property rights are not well defined, or if the rule of law is not in place, a large chunk of the population will have to depend on political favours and this, coupled with universal franchise, will distort the incentives of the ruling party to adopt anti-development policies, which will keep the population poor. In other words, the chapter argues that if property rights are not secure and a rule of law is not in place, democracy and universal voting rights can be counterproductive for economic development. It also illustrates the role of informal institutions in determining political incentives and economic performance in a less-developed country in terms of a model of electoral competition.

The key element of the argument is the observation that in a less developed region for a significantly large number of people politics constitutes an integral part of their strategies for economic survival. As a result, they *cannot vote freely* according to their preferences. Chatterjee (2004) calls this a *political society* (see also Sarkar (2006)). People belonging to this society earn their bread in the informal sector where property rights are not well defined. They do not live by formal laws and norms. Some live illegally on government land and others encroach on city streets to sell their wares. A third group, owning shops or small businesses, is exposed to local thugs because it is too costly to get protection from the formal legal system. A fourth, earning its livelihood from the agricultural sector, crucially depends on political favours to get seeds, water, fertilizers, credit, and other inputs from local bodies. All these people need political protection, which is provided by the parties. Without political support from one of the parties, they cannot survive. If they were securely employed in the formal sector, they could have voted according to their free choice. But in the absence of secured formal sector jobs, they are compelled to sell their votes, the only endowment they have apart from labour, for economic survival.

The ruling party takes advantage of this dependence to secure votes in exchange for political favours. This, in turn, creates an incentive for the ruling government to maintain a large informal sector. As a result, universal franchise might prove inefficient for less developed countries. There is yet another way to view the present chapter. Development economists of the older generations had believed that the existence of informal sectors is a temporary phenomenon, which is going to dwindle away with development. History has proved otherwise. All over the developing world, informal sectors have retained their importance over the last 50 years or so. The present chapter tries to explain why.

The Environment

We consider a less-developed region where there is one formal and one informal sector. In the formal sector, output is produced with capital k and labour n. Capital is mobile nationally and internationally while labour is confined to the two sectors within the region. Due to free mobility, capital earns a fixed profit per unit which is given from outside. Again, the wage rate w in the formal sector is fixed institutionally and labour is always available at that wage. The reason is that the informal sector, which is the other source of employment, offers lower incomes and therefore the workers are always eager to switch from the informal to the formal sector. It is further assumed that the capital–labour ratio is fixed and each unit of capital employs l units of labour. Let π be the profit per unit of capital and s be the output per unit of capital. Then we have:

$$\pi = s - lw \qquad (9.1)$$

With capital mobility, π is given from outside. Since on the right-hand side lw is given, we observe from (9.1) that output per unit of capital, that is s is pegged. We postulate that the productivity of capital depends on two variables, total capital inflow k and the level of infrastructure I, that is:

$$s = s(k, I),\ s_k < 0,\ s_I > 0. \qquad (9.2)$$

Given infrastructure, as there is more inflow of capital, due to diminishing returns output per unit of capital goes down. Again, given k, an improvement in infrastructure leads to an increase in output per unit of capital. Now, we have already seen that s is pegged from (9.1). So (9.2) determines the level of capital inflow given infrastructure. If infrastructure improves, that is, I goes up, then k, the inflow of capital goes up in equilibrium. The capital–labour ratio being constant, employment in the formal sector is determined by capital inflow. Hence, as infrastructure improves and capital inflow goes up, there is an expansion of formal employment as well. The crucial variable is therefore the level of infrastructure which is determined by the ruling government and which, as we shall see later, is determined politically.

There are two identical political parties in the region and at any period, either of them is in power. Let p denote the probability that the ruling party wins the next elections and remains in power for one more period and let $(1 - p)$ denote that the opposition wins the next elections and comes to power in the next period. These transitional probabilities, to be determined endogenously, are assumed to remain constant over time. Moreover, since the two parties are identical, the probabilities are not dependent on which party is ruling and which is in the opposition.

We identify the informal sector as the political sector and the formal sector as the non-political sector. In the formal sector, production is carried on without any political patronage or support. More importantly, property rights are well defined in the formal sector. In the informal sector, on the other hand, political patronage is essential for production. There are, in fact, two common features of the people earning their bread in the informal sector. First and foremost, all of them are extremely vulnerable. They lack the security of formal sector jobs. Second, they do not always live by formal laws and norms. Some of them might be living on illegally encroached government or railway land. Others might illegally occupy pavements in the city streets to sell their wares. They become more vulnerable because they do not have any well-defined property rights within the formal legal framework. These people depend in a fundamental way on political parties for their livelihood. It is their vulnerability, which makes them dependent. A political party gives them protection and in return gets their support at the time of elections.

We, therefore, assume that an individual working in the informal sector has to get patronage from one of the two political parties. In exchange, he casts his vote in favour of his patron at the time of the elections. In other words, an informal sector worker sells his vote, apart from his labour, for his survival. Apart from political patronage, production in the informal sector requires only labour. In particular, one unit of labour produces a units of output in the informal sector and we assume that $a < w$, the last assumption guaranteeing that a worker employed in the informal sector earns less than a worker working in the formal sector.

There are two generations, young and old, coexisting in the economy. When young, an agent gets a job either in the informal sector or, if he is lucky, in the formal sector. In the latter case, he retires when old and lives on his savings and retirement benefits. In the former case, the agent continues to work in the informal sector when old. If an informal sector agent joins the ruling party, he gets a rent, in addition to his wage, in the current period. He continues to get a rent in the next period if that party, wins the elections and stays in power. Again, if an agent joins the party which is currently in opposition, he earns only the wage in the current period. He gets a rent in the next period if the opposition wins. Whichever party comes to power, there is a fixed amount of surplus Δ to be equally distributed among its young informal sector followers. Similarly, a surplus Δ' is kept for distribution among old followers. The surplus may be obtained through securing an important position in the government or in the party, which helps one to extract rents from the formal sector or in terms of getting exclusive favours from the government, for example, habitable land from the government at subsidized prices. It is reasonable to assume that $\Delta \leq \Delta'$ since old party followers have a higher grip over the party to extract more rent.

The population size of workers of each generation is normalized to unity and the agents are assumed to belong to the interval $[0,1]$. Of the total number of young people, n people work in the formal sector and $(1 - n)$ in the informal sector. In addition, a part of the old generation also works in the informal sector.

The sequence of events taking place in the economy is as follows. First, the party in power gets a fixed sum of money to spend on infrastructure. We assume that the region is a part of a larger country and gets the money from the central or federal government. If the entire money is spent on infrastructure, the resulting value of I is I^{max}. The party in power has an option of not spending the entire money.

The unspent money either goes back to the central government or is appropriated by the party bosses. In either case, it does not show up anywhere in the model. In the extreme case where the ruling party does not spend on infrastructure at all, the value of I is I^{min} with $I^{min} < I^{max}$.

Given I, capital inflow and employment in the formal sector are determined. The residual labour force is absorbed by the informal sector. Then in each sector output is produced. The relative price between these outputs is given by the rest of the world and we choose units in such a way that this relative price is unity. Also, choosing output as the numeraire, the absolute price is also taken to be equal to one. After output is produced in the formal sector, the young employed in that sector consume and save; the old who have retired from the formal sector consume their previous period's savings. Again, in the informal sector, the young and the old consume after they receive their income. We further assume that the old in both the sectors die after they consume and before they vote. This means that only the young are allowed to vote in our model. This assumption saves us from a lot of unnecessary algebraic complications. Finally, elections are held and a party is chosen for the next period.

Equilibrium

Let α denote the proportion of informal sector workers joining the ruling party. Since, at the margin, an agent must be indifferent between joining the ruling party and the opposition, we have:

$$\left(a + \frac{\Delta}{\alpha}\right) + p\left(a + \frac{\Delta'}{\alpha}\right) + (1-p)a = a + pa + (1-p)\left(a + \frac{\Delta'}{(1-\alpha)}\right) \tag{9.3}$$

The left-hand side of (9.3) represents the payoff from joining the ruling party and the right-hand side represents the payoff from joining the opposition. After some manipulation, (9.3) can be written as:

$$\alpha = \frac{\Delta}{\Delta + \Delta'} + \frac{p\Delta'}{\Delta + \Delta'} \tag{9.4}$$

Equation (9.4) expresses p as a function of α. It is a linear relationship with $p\left(\dfrac{\Delta}{\Delta+\Delta'}\right)=0$ and $p(1)=1$. Also, $p'(\alpha)=\dfrac{\Delta+\Delta'}{\Delta'}>1$.

We need one more relationship between p and α to determine them simultaneously. This is provided by the voting process. There are two types of voters in this model. Informal sector voters who are opportunistic and vote for their party and formal sector voters who are free to vote for any party they wish to. Each agent in the formal sector gets a private signal, which can take two values, good or bad. An agent votes for the ruling party if he gets a good signal and votes for the opposition if he gets a bad signal. Let π be the proportion of formal sector agents getting good signals and hence voting for the ruling party. We assume that π is a random variable with a distribution function: $F(x) = prob[\pi \leq x]$. Since p is the probability of winning for the ruling party, we have:

$$p = prob[\pi n + \alpha(1-n) > (1-\pi)n + (1-\alpha)(1-n)] \qquad (9.5)$$

After some manipulation, (9.5) can be written as:

$$p(\alpha, n) = 1 - F(x), \quad x \equiv \alpha + \frac{1-2\alpha}{2n} \qquad (9.6)$$

It is straightforward to verify that:

$$\frac{\partial p(\alpha, n)}{\partial \alpha} = -F'(x)\left\{1-\frac{1}{n}\right\} \geq 0, \quad \frac{\partial^2 p(\alpha, n)}{\partial \alpha^2} = -\left\{1-\frac{1}{n}\right\}^2 F''(x) \qquad (9.7)$$

$$p(0) = 1 - F\left(\frac{1}{2n}\right), \quad p(1) = 1 - F\left(1-\frac{1}{2n}\right) \qquad (9.8)$$

We make two assumptions at this point.

Assumption 1 The probability density function $f(x)$ corresponding to the distribution function $F(x)$ is single peaked at $x = x'$.

Assumption 2 The minimum size of the formal sector n^{min}, which corresponds to $I = I^{min}$, satisfies $n^{min} > \frac{1}{2}$.

For any given n, an equilibrium is a pair $\{p^*(n), \alpha^*(n)\}$ which simultaneously satisfies (9.4) and (9.6). As we argue later, under

Assumptions 1 and 2, an equilibrium exists, is interior (that is, $0 < p^*(n) < 1$, $0 < \alpha^*(n) < 1$) and is unique. The equilibrium is determined at the point of intersection of the graphs of (9.4) and (9.6). The graph of (9.4) is represented by the straight line AA in Figure 9.1.

Assumption 1 implies that for $x \leq x'$, $F''(x) \geq 0$ and for $x \geq x'$, $F''(x) \leq 0$ which, along with (9.7), imply that the graph of $p(\alpha, n)$ as a function of α is upward rising and (weakly) concave for $\alpha \leq \alpha'$ and (weakly) convex for $\alpha \geq \alpha'$, where α' corresponds to the value of α at $x = x'$. The graph of $p(\alpha, n)$ as a function of α is shown as the concave-convex upward rising curve BB in Figure 9.1 with a point of inflection at α'.

Assumption 2, along with (8), ensures $p(0) > 0$, $p(1) < 1$. It basically means that the informal sector by itself cannot decide the election outcome (if it could, the ruling party would stay in power with probability 1) and guarantees an interior intersection between the two graphs. Again, since there is a single point of inflection, the intersection point is unique.

All these arguments are put together in the following proposition:

Proposition 1 For any given n, under Assumptions 1 and 2 a unique equilibrium $\{p^*, \alpha^*\}$ exists where $0 < p^* < 1$, $0 < \alpha^* < 1$.

Next we consider the effect of a change in n. A straightforward differentiation of Equation (9.6) yields:

$$\frac{\partial p(\alpha, n)}{\partial n} = F'(x)\frac{1-2\alpha}{2n^2} \tag{9.9}$$

Clearly, the sign on the left-hand side depends on the sign of $(1-2\alpha)$. In other words, $\frac{\partial p}{\partial n}$ is positive, zero, or negative accordingly as α is less than, equal to, or greater than half. Therefore, as n increases, in Figure 9.1 the curve BB swings around $\alpha = \frac{1}{2}$ to curve CC.

The crucial question is: What happens to equilibrium p when n increases? A little reflection over Figure 9.1 will convince the reader that with an increase in n the probability of re-election decreases if and only if at the swing point $\alpha = \frac{1}{2}$, the value of p on AA is less than the value of p along BB (which does not change even when

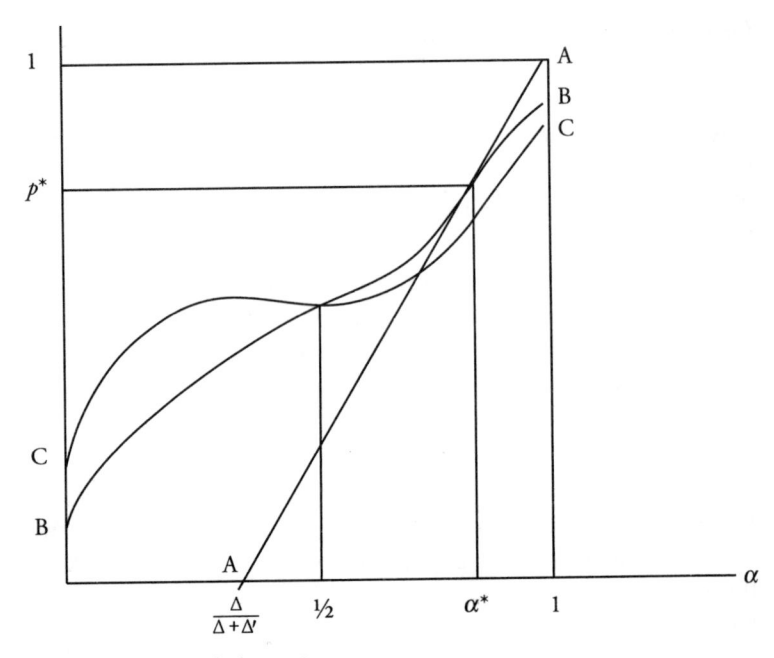

Figure 9.1 Effect of Change in *n* on *p*

n changes). From Equations (9.4) and (9.6) the required condition boils down to:

$$F\left(\frac{1}{2}\right) < \frac{\Delta}{\Delta'} \qquad (9.10)$$

This leads to the following proposition:

Proposition 2 An increase in the size of the formal sector leads to a fall in the probability of re-election of the ruling party if and only if $F\left(\frac{1}{2}\right) < \frac{\Delta}{\Delta'}$.

Condition (9.10) is intuitive. A low Δ' relative to Δ makes the expected payoff from joining the opposition relatively low and hence increases the probability of re-election when the informal sector is larger. On the other hand, a lower value of $F\left(\frac{1}{2}\right) = prob\left[\pi \leq \frac{1}{2}\right]$ clearly reduces the chance of re-election when the formal sector expands.

Government's Objective

If the ruling party's sole objective is to get re-elected, then Proposition 2 will imply that, provided condition (9.10) holds, infrastructural investment will be kept to a minimum to maximize the size of the informal sector. This will perpetuate underdevelopment. Two questions naturally come up. First, how likely is condition (9.10) to hold? Second, how should one modify the analysis to take into account a partially benevolent government, which has objectives other than re-election? We try to handle these questions in turn.

It is natural to assume that agents in the formal sector have a preference for infrastructure. Put differently, formal agents are more likely to get a good message about the performance of the ruling party if infrastructural investment is higher. Therefore, a higher n is likely to change the probability distribution function $F(x)$. Fortunately, we do not have to look at the change in the entire distribution. For our purpose, it will suffice to see how the value of $F(½)$ changes with a fall in n. We make the following reasonable assumption:

Assumption 3 An increase in n changes the probability distribution function and in particular reduces the value of $F(½)$.

Clearly, if the increase in n is large enough, condition (9.10) will be violated and there will be no incentive for the ruling party to lower infrastructural investment further. The optimal n will be determined where the two sides of (9.10) are just equal. This is shown in Figure 9.2.

Clearly, the equilibrium level of the informal sector will depend on how sensitive formal sector voters are to infrastructural investment. A more sensitive formal sector will shift the $F(½)$ curve to the right leading to an expansion of the formal sector.

In addition, the ruling government, apart from the objective of winning elections, may have a separate preference for development and an expanding formal sector. This may be captured by the following utility function of the government:

$$U(n) = V(n) + p(n), \quad V'(n) > 0 \qquad (9.11)$$

The first term on the right-hand side of (9.11) represents the ruling party's preference for an expanding formal sector while the

164 Emerging Issues in Economic Development

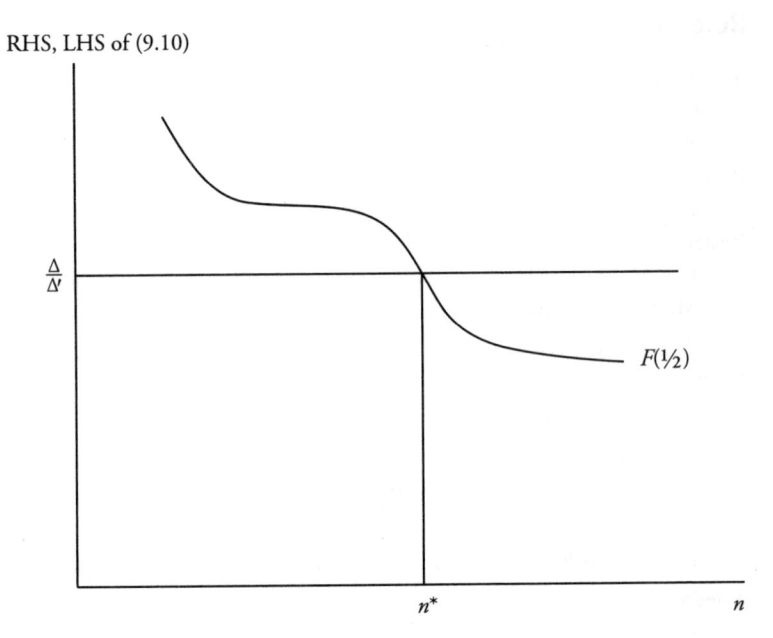

RHS, LHS of (9.10)

$\frac{\Delta}{\Delta'}$

$F(\tfrac{1}{2})$

n^* n

Figure 9.2 Determination of Optimal n

second term represents its preference for winning elections. This increases equilibrium n because at the previous optimum $n = n^*$, $U'(n) > 0$. The analysis of this section may be summarized in the following proposition:

Proposition 3 Even if the ruling government and voters in the formal sector have a preference for infrastructural investment, as long as the ruling government also cares for re-election, there is a possibility of suboptimal investment in infrastructure.

* * *

The chapter builds a simple theoretical model to argue that democracy and universal suffrage may lead to inefficiencies in less-developed economies with large informal sectors where property rights are not well defined. Because of ill-defined property rights, informal sector agents depend on political support for their survival, which is provided to them by the ruling political party. As a result, the ruling party has an incentive to keep the informal sector large which, in turn, affects economic development.

References

Acemoglu, D., S. Johnson, and James Robinson. 2001. 'The Colonial Origins of Comparative Development: An Empirical Investigation', *American Economic Review*, 91(5): 1369–401.

Barro, R. 1996. 'Democracy and Growth', *Journal of Economic Growth*, 1: 1–28.

Besley, T. and M. Ghatak. 2010. *Property Rights and Economic Development*, LSE STICERD Research Paper No. EOPP 006, in Dani Rodrik and Mark Rosenzweig (eds), *Handbook of Development Economics*, Volume 5, Chapter 68, pp. 4525–95. The Netherlands: North Holland.

Chatterjee, P. 2004. *Politics of the Governed*. New Delhi: Permanent Black.

De Soto, H. 2000. *Why Capitalism Triumphs in the West and Fails Everywhere Else*. New York: Basic Books.

Donnelly, Jack. 1984. 'Human Rights and Development: Complementary or Competing Concerns?', *World Politics*, 36: 255–83.

Feng, Yi. 2003. *Democracy, Governance, and Economic Performance*. Cambridge, Massachusetts: MIT Press.

Friedman, M. 1962. *Capitalism and Freedom*. Chicago: University of Chicago Press.

Gerschenkron, A. 1962. *Economic Backwardness in Historical Perspective: A Book of Essays*. Cambridge, Massachusetts: Harvard University Press.

Hayek, F.A. von. 1944. *The Road to Serfdom*. Chicago: University of Chicago Press.

Johnson, J. 1964. *The Military and Society in Latin America*. Stanford: Stanford University Press.

Keefer, P., and S. Khemani. 2004. 'Why Do the Poor Receive Poor Services', *Economic and Political Weekly*, 39(19): 935–43.

———. 2005. 'Democracy, Public Expenditure and the Poor: Understanding Political Incentives for Providing Public Services', *World Bank Research Observer*, 20(1): 1–27.

Lipset, S. 1959. 'Some Social Requisites of Democracy: Economic Development and Political Development', *American Political Science Review*, 53: 69–105.

Marsh, R. 1979. 'Does Democracy Hinder Economic Development in the Latecomer Developing Nations?', *Comparative Social Research*, 2: 148–215.

Mises, Ludwig von. 1981. *Socialism: An Economic and Sociological Analysis*. Indianapolis: Liberty Classics.

Moore, B. 1966. *Social Origins of Dictatorship and Democracy*. Boston: Little Brown.

North, D. 1990. *Institutions, Institutional Change, and Economic Performance*. Cambridge: Cambridge University Press.
O'Donnell, G. 1973. *Modernization and Bureaucratic-Authoritarianism: Studies in South American Politics*. Berkeley: Institute of International Studies, University of California.
Olson, M. 1993. 'Dictatorship, Democracy and Development', *American Political Science Review*, 87: 567–76.
Riker, W. and D. Weimer. 1993. 'The Economic and Political Liberalization of Socialism: The Fundamental Problem of Property Rights', *Social Philosophy and Policy*, 10: 79–102.
Sarkar, A. 2006. 'Political Economy of West Bengal: A Puzzle and a Hypothesis', *Economic and Political Weekly*, 41(9): 341–8.
Smith, Adam. 1776. *An Inquiry into the Nature and Causes of the Wealth of Nations*. London: Penguin Classics.

10

Efficient and Equilibrium Federation Structures with Externalities

Gordon Myers and Abhijit Sengupta

This chapter is concerned with developing a model of sovereign states voluntarily uniting to form a federation with the objective of securing greater efficiency through a coordination of policies. The history of many modern federations has been shaped in part, along with accidents of history and geography and exigencies of politics, by economic interests. The economic motive for a federation, at its most fundamental, is the potential for eliminating inefficiency—internalizing externalities—through a coordination of instruments: defence, tariffs, transportation, and immigration, among them. For example, in the United States, at the end of the revolutionary war, the clamour for a stronger central government that culminated in the Federal Convention of 1787 in Philadelphia was partly fuelled by acute problems with coordination: nine states had their own armies; several had their own navies; some had initiated independent international treaties; claims to land were overlapping and policies on tariffs inconsistent; there was a bewildering variety of coins in circulation; and a rapidly depreciating state and national paper bills. In Canada, the defence of British North America against the threat of annexation by the United States and the need for inter-provincial cooperation for building a transcontinental railway to overcome the barriers of distance contributed to the ultimate confederation. In Australia, barriers to inter-colonial trade were a constant source of frustration and friction in the six colonies; not only were there tariffs to pay and customs to clear, but each colony even had its own railway gauge. In the still-evolving story of the European Union, economic incentives have been the driving force from the outset. The Schuman Declaration of 1950, which laid the foundation, was especially concerned with the pooling of coal and steel resources.

The setting for our chapter concerns a set of sovereign states, each with control over a set of instruments, where appropriately coordinating the instruments among the set of all states is efficient. We suppose that any group of states can choose to form a federation. Forming a federation is entering into a binding agreement to behave cooperatively with other members of the federation. Specifically, it entails setting instruments jointly with a view to maximizing the federation's aggregate payoff at a Nash equilibrium against other federations and to split the aggregate payoff by a sharing rule that has been pre-set (in a separate game to be described in the next section). In this setting, we think of each state formulating a partnership plan specifying what other states it wishes to join in a federation. How each profile of partnership plan is reconciled into a federation structure is described by a rule, and we impose structure on the rule. This allows us to regard the formation of a federation structure as an outcome of a well-defined game, and we consider two notions of an equilibrium federation structure.

One objective of the chapter is developing a framework for constructing an equilibrium model of the formation of a federation that is flexible enough to adapt to applications in specific contexts. A second objective is identifying conditions under which the efficient federation structure—in this case, the formation of the grand federation, with the federation consisting of all of the states—can be supported as an equilibrium structure. To this end, we first demonstrate that the grand federation structure need not be efficient and then derive results that characterize conditions under which the grand federation is an equilibrium structure for each of the two notions of equilibrium that we consider. The characterizations we provide are computationally simple to apply, in that they involve checking only a system of linear inequalities.

From the point of view of game theory, our study is a particular model of coalition formation set in a context in which there are externalities across coalitions. Although a formal analysis of coalitions dates back to the very birth of game theory in von Neumann and Morgenstern (1944) and has received intensive scrutiny almost continuously since then, an analysis of coalition formation under externalities is of startlingly recent vintage. However, we now have a masterly state-of-the-art book-length survey of the field in Ray (2007). We therefore dispense with a literature review and urge the interested reader to consult the relevant parts of Ray (2007), especially, chapters 2, 3, 11, and 12. The papers that are most relevant to our study are Hart and Kurz (1983), Burbidge et al. (1997), Ray and Vohra (1997), and Diamantoudi and Xue (2007). Here we extend the ideas of the first two of these papers; the latter two take complementary approaches, in many ways more abstract and general but more difficult to apply to our context.

The Context

The context of our study concerns a set of $N = \{1,..., n\}$ *states*, where each state $i \in N$ has a set of instruments at its disposal and there is scope for large efficiency gains from appropriately coordinating the instruments among the states. Let $A_i \subset \Re^{l_i}$ be the set of *actions* available to state $i \in N$, acting alone in setting its l_i instruments. Each state is affected by the choice of instruments by all the states. The *gross payoff function* of state i is given by[1] $h_i: \prod_{i \in N} A_i \to \Re$. This defines a game among the set of states that we will call the *underlying game*.

Two characteristics of the environment are particularly relevant for our study. First, *before* the play of the underlying game, any subset of states has the opportunity to decide to act as a unit and form a federation. We define a *federation* to be any non-empty group of

---

[1] We use the term gross payoff to distinguish from the net payoff of a state which may include transfers that are discussed later in the chapter.

states that make a binding commitment to cooperate by coordinating actions in the underlying game. Let A_S denote $\prod_{i \in S} A_i$ for any non-empty subset S of N. A_S is the set of coordinated actions available to a federation S in the underlying game. Second, transfers can be made freely within a federation but not across federations.[2]

Given a profile of actions in the underlying game, one for each state in N, $a = (a_1,..., a_n) \in A_N$, the *aggregate payoff* of a federation S is given by $\sum_{i \in S} h_i(a)$.

A *federation structure* $F = \{S_1,..., S_m\}$ is an alignment of the states into mutually exclusive and collectively exhaustive federations. That is, it is a partition of the set of states N. The set of all possible federation structures will be denoted by F.

We suppose that commitments cannot be enforced across federations so that the interaction among federations is non-cooperative. In particular, we suppose that competition among federations in the federation structure F leads to a Nash equilibrium of the underlying game in which the players are the federations in F, federation S has available the set of actions in A_S and its payoff function is $\sum_{i \in S} h_i(a)$. Given a federation structure F, we call such a Nash equilibrium profile of actions, $a^* \in A_N$, an *equilibrium relative to the federation structure F*.

Remark 1 A standard result on the existence of Nash equilibria implies that if A_i is non-empty, convex, and compact and h_i is continuous and quasi-concave for each $i \in N$, then there exists an equilibrium relative to each federation structure.

In what follows, we restrict attention to those environments that generate a unique equilibrium for every federation structure.

Given a federation structure $F = \{S_1,..., S_m\}$ and an equilibrium profile $a^* \in A_N$ relative to the structure F, the aggregate payoff of the federation S_j for the structure F is given by the *partition function* defined by:

$$w_{S_j}(F) = \sum_{i \in S_j} h_i(a^*). \tag{10.1}$$

---

[2] Transfer of resources among member states within a federation is normal practice, and even trade agreements often include transfer or compensation mechanisms. In particular, that transfers are used to promote a federation or prevent secession seems beyond doubt.

Remark 2 An obvious but important point to note is that the aggregate equilibrium payoff of a federation S_j depends on the action profile of all the states in N and thus the entire federation structure F: different alignments of complementary federations will give rise to different payoffs for S_j. It is in this sense that there are *externalities across federations*. This merely reflects that, in general, there are externalities across players in any strategic form game: the payoff to a player depends on the actions of all other players.

Our objective is to delineate the boundaries of cooperation as they arise endogenously through states non-cooperatively choosing federation partners before the play of the underlying game. We are especially interested in characterizing the conditions under which an endogenously determined federation structure is efficient for the underlying environment.

We therefore need a model of how a federation structure is determined as a result of states choosing partners to join in coordinating actions in the underlying game. Each state, however, is only interested in its own payoff. We therefore also need to specify how a federation will divide its aggregate payoff defined in (10.1) among its members. The decision of a given state on which other states will join in a federation will obviously depend both on that federation's aggregate payoff in the underlying game and the state's share in the federation's aggregate payoff.

In the framework we present, events unfold in three stages. First, for every (potential) federation structure $F = \{S_1,\ldots, S_m\}$ and each federation S_j in F, an assignment of the shares of the federation's aggregate payoff to the member states is determined. We call such an allocation a *sharing rule*:

$$cs_j(F) = \left(c_{s_j,1}(F),\ldots, c_{sj,|sj|}(F)\right) \qquad (10.2)$$

for federation S_j under the structure F.[3] The sharing rule is set in a game that is described in the section 'Sharing Rules.'

Second, knowing this, states choose which other states to join in a federation and a federation structure F is determined. This stage is described in the section 'Federation Formation'.

[3] For any federation S, $|S|$ will denote the cardinality of F.

Finally, states within a federation coordinate actions in the underlying game and play non-cooperatively against outsiders, as already described. The payoff of a state is given by the state's share of the federation's aggregate payoff, as prescribed in the federation's sharing rule.

Federation Formation

Partnership Plans and Federation Structure Rules

We now describe the stage in which the states, taking as given the sharing rule for each federation in every federation structure and in cognizance of the underlying game to be played, have an opportunity to choose which other states to join in a federation. To form a federation is to enter into a binding agreement to coordinate actions in the ensuing underlying game, in the manner described in the section 'The Context', and to abide by the sharing rule of the federation.

We think of each state formulating a plan (possibly after extensive non-binding pre-play communication that we do not model) for joining a set of other states in a federation. A *partnership plan* of a state $i \in N$ is a choice of a federation to which i wants to belong: formally, it is a subset S_i of N with the property that $i \in S_i$. A *profile of partnership plans* is an n-tuple of partnership plans, $\sigma = (S_1,..., S_n)$, one for each state. The set of all possible partnership plans for player i will be denoted by S_i. The set of all possible profile of partnership plans will be denoted by S, that is:

$$S = \prod_{i \in N} S_i$$

A question immediately confronts us. How does a profile of partnership plans get reconciled into a resultant federation structure, especially if the plans in the profile are mutually incompatible? We suppose that the states have a commonly held and correct conjecture summarized by a function, $\psi : S \to F$, that associates with each profile of partnership plans $\sigma \in S$ a federation structure $\psi(\sigma) = F$. We call the function ψ the *federation structure conjecture* or, since it is assumed to be correct, the *federation structure rule*.

What would be a sensible modelling choice for the function ψ? Ideally, a fully satisfactory model will endogenously determine the federation structure rule by building a theory of consistent conjectures. At this point, we are not aware of any extant theory that is entirely natural in the present context and we are not ready to propose one. Instead, we choose a middle course in which we impose desiderata on the federation structure rule, in the spirit of axioms. This is taken up in the subsection 'Restrictions on Federation Structure Rules.'

We note that we now have a well-defined game to describe the federation formation stage. The set of actions available to each state $i \in N$ consists of the set of possible partnership plans for i; every profile of partnership plans σ induces a federation structure $\psi(\sigma)$; the equilibrium of the ensuing underlying game among the federations will give rise to an aggregate payoff $w_{\psi_i(\sigma)}(\psi(\sigma))$, as defined in (10.1); the sharing rule for $\psi_i(\sigma)$, already given at this stage, then determines the payoff of each state i in $\psi_i(\sigma)$ defined by:

$$u_i(\sigma) = c_{\psi_i}(\sigma)_i (\psi(\sigma)) \left[w_{\psi_i(\sigma)}(\psi(\sigma)) \right]. \tag{10.3}$$

We refer to this game as the federation formation game.

Equilibrium Federation Structures

We want to identify a federation structure S as an 'equilibrium' structure if $S = \psi(\sigma)$ for an 'equilibrium' profile of partnership plans σ for the federation formation game. The question now is: What would be an appropriate equilibrium concept for the game?

For our purpose, Nash equilibrium is too weak a solution concept. The profile of partnership plans $\sigma = (S_1, ..., S_n)$ with $S_i = \{i\}$, for every $i \in N$, is a Nash equilibrium of the federation formation game for any federation structure conjecture ψ that satisfies either the unanimity principle or the non-coercion principle, regardless of what the underlying game is or what the constitutions for the federations are. No state i, taking as given the partnership plans of the other $n-1$ states, can affect the resultant federation structure, given by $\psi(\sigma) = \{\{1\}, ..., \{n\}\}$, and hence its payoff. Therefore, the singleton federation structure $\{\{1\}, ..., \{n\}\}$ is always a Nash equilibrium structure.

For a model of federation formation such as this one, it is natural to allow a group of states to coordinate on a joint deviation if such a deviation were to make each deviating state better off. We are thus led to a subset of Nash equilibria such that equilibrium profiles are immune to unilateral as well as multilaterally coordinated deviations. The standard solution concepts in this class are variants of a strong Nash equilibrium, proposed by Aumann (1959). In this chapter, the solution concepts that we study are the strong Nash equilibrium and another appealing refinement in this class, due to Bernheim et al. (1987), called the coalition proof Nash equilibrium.

A profile of actions is a *strong Nash equilibrium* (SNE) if no subset of players, taking the actions of its complement as fixed, can fashion a profitable deviation for each of its members. Note that an action profile is ruled out as a SNE if there is any profitable multilateral deviation at all. A *coalition proof Nash equilibrium* (CPNE) embeds a consistency requirement: an action profile is ruled out as an equilibrium only if it is vulnerable to a 'credible' deviation. Roughly, a profile of actions is coalition proof if no set of players, taking the actions of its complement as fixed, can fashion a profitable deviation for each of its members that is itself immune to further deviations by subsets of the deviating coalition. We refer readers to Bernheim et al. (1987) for a formal definition.

It is worth remarking on two advantages of adding a stage with an explicit model of federation formation to the underlying game. First, it permits us to consider any multilateral deviation. In particular, we are able to handle cases in which a deviation by a federation from an existing federation structure may lead to a coarser structure. For example, consider the deviation from an arbitrary profile $\tilde{\sigma}$ by the set of all players to the profile σ in which $S_i = N$ for every $i \in N$. By the unanimity principle, we must have $\psi(\sigma) = \{N\}$, a coarser structure than can result from $\psi(\tilde{\sigma})$. Second, although we use SNE or CPNE as a solution concept for the federation formation game—so that a deviating federation takes the actions of its complement as fixed— we are able to accommodate arbitrary resultant federation structures by virtue of the flexibility built into the federation structure rule. In particular, we do not need to assume that following a deviation by a federation S, the actions taken by the complementary federations *in the underlying game* remain fixed.

Restrictions on Federation Structure Rules

We now impose some restrictions on the class of federation structure rules that we will consider. The hope is to identify some subclasses that appear natural in particular contexts.

Let us say that a group of states S has a *unanimous* partnership plan if $S_i = S$ for every $i \in S$. Thus, unanimity among a group requires not only that states in the group have an identical plan, but also that the plan calls for each member in the group to join the other members in the group and no one else. A minimal property we demand of any federation structure is that it respects unanimity: should a group of S states be unanimous on a partnership plan, federation S indeed forms.

Formally, a federation structure conjecture ψ satisfies *unanimity principle* if:

(U) for any $\sigma = (S_1,..., S_n) \in S$ and any $S \subset N$, $S_i = S$ for every $i \in S$ implies that $S \in \psi(\sigma)$.

A second property we impose is a type of separability axiom that is useful in considerations of deviations from the grand federation. To motivate it, suppose we start with the profile of partnership plans in which $S_i = \{N\}$ for every $i \in N$; denote this profile by σ^N. Under any federation structure rule ψ that satisfies (U), $\psi(\sigma) = N$ under σ^N. Now consider the profile in which $S_i = S$ for every $i \in S$ and $S_i = N$ for every $i \in N \setminus S$. This can be interpreted as a profile in which a federation F has made a *unanimous joint deviation* from the profile σ^N. Let us denote such a profile by d^S.

By the unanimity principle, we must have $\psi_i(d^S) = S$ for every $i \in S$. Thus, the resultant federation structure at the profile d^S must be an $N \setminus S$-refinement[4] (in the weak sense) of the structure $\{S, N\setminus S\}$. Condition (U) does not impose any restriction on how the players in $N \setminus S$ are to be aligned at d^S. Although in contemplating the consequences of a deviation, a federation S takes the participation plans of players in $N \setminus S$ as fixed, that does not mean that the federation $N \setminus S$

---

[4] Given any federation structure $F = \{S_1,..., S_m\}$, by a S_j-*refinement* of F, we mean a partition F' that consists of the sets $S_k \in F$, $k \neq j$, and some partition of S_j.

will remain intact following a deviation by S. The next condition we impose goes some way towards disciplining the federation structures that such profiles can give rise to.

Suppose a set of I players has maintained an identical participation plan shared by its members across two profiles σ and σ', and that no player in a set J shared this plan either in the profile σ or σ'. Then, we require that the federations to which members of I belong according to the rule ψ not change across the two profiles—even if there has been a change in the plans of some members of J between σ and σ'.

Formally, we say that a federation structure rule ψ satisfies the *separation principle* if the following condition is met:

(SEP) For any $\sigma = (S_1,..., S_n)$ and $\sigma' = (S'_1,...,S'_n)$ in S, such that there is a set of I players with $S'_i = S_i = T$, for some $T \subset N$, for every $i \in I$ and that there is a set of J players with $S_j = T$ and $S'_j \neq T, j \in J$. Then, $\psi_i(\sigma) = \psi_i(\sigma')$ for all $i \in I$.

Two particular federation structure rules satisfying (U) and (SEP) are somewhat natural candidates for special attention: the ones that generate the finest and the coarsest structures under d^S.

Call the federation structure rule $\psi^*: S \to F$, the *strict consensus rule* if for any $\sigma = (S_1,..., S_n) \in S$ and any $i \in N$:

$$\psi_i^*(\sigma) = \begin{cases} S_i \text{ if } S_j = S_i \text{ for every } j \in S_i \\ \{i\} \text{ otherwise.} \end{cases}$$

Thus, under the strict consensus rule, a multiplayer federation forms only on the basis of a unanimous partnership plan by its members; players who fail to achieve unanimity with respect to a partnership plan are in singleton federations. In particular, at the profile d^S, the federation $N \setminus S$ breaks up into singletons under ψ^*.

Call the federation structure rule $\hat{\psi}: S \to F$, the *weak consensus rule* if for any $\sigma \in S$ and any $i \in N$:

$$\hat{\psi}_i(\sigma) = \{j \in N | S_i = S_j\}.$$

Thus, under the weak consensus rule, every set of players with the same partnership plan are in a federation. In effect, we are interpreting a player's partnership plan as the largest set of partners it is willing to be associated with in a federation. In particular, at the profile d^S, the federation $N \setminus S$ remains intact under $\hat{\psi}$.

It is clear that the strict consensus rule and the weak consensus rule respectively generate the finest and the coarsest partitions of any federation structure rule satisfying the unanimity principle and the separation principle. The strict consensus rule first appeared in von Neumann and Morgenstern (1944) and the weak consensus rule was featured in Hart and Kurz (1983), although in both cases in the context of coalitional games without externalities. They also appear to be plausible natural candidates to consider under some contexts of actual federation formation.

Sharing Rules

We are now at the stage in which the sharing rule for each federation S for every federation structure F containing S is determined. For a federation S, the sharing rule stipulates an allocation of the shares of the federation's aggregate payoff to the members of the federation. We allow the sharing rule of a given federation S to depend on the structure F. Formally, a *sharing rule for a federation S* embedded in the structure F is a function c_S that associates with each federation $S \in F$ an element of $[0,1]^{|s|}$ with the property that $\sum_{i \in S} c_{si}(F) = 1$. By a *profile of sharing rules* we mean a list of sharing rules, c, one for each federation S, for every structure F containing S.

To determine an 'equilibrium' profile of sharing rules, we introduce, in addition to the 'regular' players, a set of players whom we call potential *founders* of federations. Each federation has a founder; the sole object of the founder of federation S is to bring the federation into being. The set of actions available to the founder of S is the set of sharing rules $cs\,(F)$ for each structure F containing S. Clearly, a federation's sharing rule affects the payoffs of players joining the federation and thus affects the behaviour of players in the federation formation game.

Now, consider the game in strategic form in which the players are the founders, the set of actions of the founder of federation S is the set of all possible sharing rules for S for each structure F containing S, and the payoff of the founder of S is 1 if federation S forms and zero otherwise. We call this game the *founders' game*. A profile of sharing rules, one for each founder, is called an *equilibrium* if it is a Nash equilibrium of the founders' game.

Since our introduction of a new set of players—potential founders—is unorthodox, some clarification is in order. First, in our view, there are many contexts in which it is not at all far-fetched to take the notion of founders of federations quite literally. Many federations in history have had identifiable founders. Second, the founders may alternatively be thought of as 'meta-players', a theoretical construct somewhat like the notion of the Walrasian auctioneer. It is a convenient modelling device for formally determining an equilibrium profile of sharing rules in some ways like the notion of the Walrasian auctioneer has been used in history as a device for formally determining an equilibrium price vector.

We now define an equilibrium for the overall game. An *equilibrium* for the game is a profile of sharing rules, c^*, in the founders' game, a profile of partnership plans, $\sigma^*(c^*)$, in the federation formation game, and an action profile, $\alpha^*(\sigma^*(c^*), c^*)$ in the underlying game such that c^* is a Nash equilibrium of the founders' game, $\sigma^*(c^*)$ is a SNE (or a CPNE) of the federational formation game and $\alpha^*(\sigma^*(c^*)\ c^*)$ is an equilibrium relative to the structure $\psi(\sigma^*(c^*))$ of the underlying game. In particular, we refer to a federation structure associated with an equilibrium as a *strong equilibrium* or a *coalition-proof equilibrium* structure, depending on whether SNE or CPNE is used as the solution concept for the federation formation game.

Equilibrium and Efficiency

The focus of this chapter is a class of environments (that is, underlying games) for which efficiency entails coordinating actions of all the states. Thus, in this section, we make assumptions on the underlying game to ensure that the grand federation is the unique efficient structure. We then want to derive conditions under which it arises as an equilibrium structure.

We begin with a preliminary result to establish that, in general, the grand federation, even if a unique efficient structure, need not be a strong or even a coalition-proof equilibrium structure, and it is possible that the only equilibrium coalition-proof structure is inefficient. Analogous results have been derived in literature in some form or another, for example, in Burbidge et al. (1997) and in Ray and Vohra (1997), among others. The proofs of all the results are gathered in Appendix A10.

Proposition 1 Let the underlying game be such that the grand federation is the unique efficient structure and let the federation structure rule be the weak consensus rule. The grand federation may not be a coalition-proof (hence strong) equilibrium structure. Moreover, an inefficient federation structure of the form may be the unique coalition proof equilibrium structure.

At first glance, each part of the proposition may seem somewhat puzzling. After all, by assumption, full efficiency gains are only achieved by the grand federation; forming federations is not costly and efficiency gains can be shared through transfers within the federation. Thus, the grand federation always admits payoff profiles that Pareto dominate all payoff profiles obtainable from any alternative federation structure. When there are more than two states, however, there are multiple alternate federation structures and there is no guarantee that payoffs in the grand federation will *simultaneously* Pareto dominate the payoffs from all alternate structures.[5] How can an inefficient structure be an equilibrium structure? It is true that the grand federation can always coordinate a profitable deviation from an inefficient structure—so that the inefficient structure cannot be a strong equilibrium structure—but there is no guarantee that the grand federation can coordinate a *credible* profitable deviation immune to further deviations from within. Therefore, inefficient structures may be coalition-proof.

In view of Proposition 1, our objective is to give conditions under which the grand federation structure can be supported as an equilibrium structure. To this end, we provide two characterization results, one for the grand federation to be a strong equilibrium and another for it to be a coalition-proof equilibrium structure. The

---

[5] When there are only two states, there is only one alternative structure to the grand federation: the singleton structure. And it follows immediately that the grand federation is the unique strong equilibrium structure when $N = \{1, 2\}$.

characterizations involve the core of a game in coalitional form, derived from the partition function generated by the underlying game. In the next subsection, after some general preliminary remarks on games in coalitional form, we construct the coalitional game.

The ψ-Coalitional Form

Ever since the publication of the classic treatise by von Neumann and Morgenstern (1944), the main tool for analysing games in which players can make binding commitments, often called *cooperative games,* has been the coalitional form. Recall that a *game in coalitional form* is a pair (N, v) where $N = \{1,..., N\}$ is a finite set of players and the function v, called the *coalition function,* or the *characteristic function,* associates with every coalition S a real number $v(S)$, interpreted as the *worth* of the coalition S. A standard analysis of coalitional games treats the coalitional form as a primitive. Thus, by definition, externalities across coalitions are assumed away: the coalition's worth does not depend on any aspects of the complementary coalitions. In the context of federation formation—indeed, in many other economic contexts—this is a severe limitation. A fundamental reason why game theory has proved to be such a fruitful tool in economics is its explicit recognition of the dependence of a player's payoff on the actions of other players. To recognize strategic linkages at the level of individuals but to assume it away at the level of coalitions is difficult to justify.[6]

If a coalitional game is explicitly derived from an underlying game in strategic form at all, typically one of two conversions, suggested by Aumann (1961), is used: the α-coalitional form or the β-coalitional form. Both are based on extremely pessimistic conjectures on the behaviour of complementary coalitions, conjectures that are patently

---

[6] We recognize that the general competitive equilibrium theory for economies with no externalities or public goods is an area in which the assumption of absence of externalities is sensible and the study of coalitional games has led to remarkable new insights: most prominently, the celebrated 'core-equivalence theorems'.

unreasonable in most economic contexts.[7] The point we have been making in this subsection so far is by no means new but still of surprisingly recent vintage. However, Ray (2007) eloquently discusses this point, and we can do no better than refer to it for further elaborations.

We introduce a particular coalitional form that we call the ψ-*coalitional form*, which will be useful for our study of the conditions under which the grand federation is an equilibrium structure.

To define the ψ-coalitional form, we start with the profile σ^N, that is, the profile of partnership plans in which $S_i = \{N\}$ for every $i \in N$. Now consider the profile d^s in which a coalition S has made a unanimous joint deviation from the profile σ^N: that is, the profile in which $S_i = S$ for every $i \in S$ and $S_i = N$ for every $i \in N \setminus S$.

The ψ-*coalitional form* is a pair (N, v_ψ), where N is the set of states and ψ is a federation structure rule satisfying (U) and (SEP), and v_ψ is a function that associates with each non-empty $S \subset N$ the real number $v_\psi(S)$ defined by:

$$v_\psi(S) = w_S\left(\psi(d^S)\right). \quad (10.4)$$

Thus, for any federation S, it gives the aggregate payoff to the federation at an equilibrium relative to the structure in which the members of S are together in a federation and any state $j \in N \setminus S$ is allied according to the prescription $\psi_j(d^s)$. Intuitively, it may be thought of as the *conjectured* coalitional form under conjecture ψ.

Remark 3 It should be emphasized that given any federation structure rule ψ, (N, v_ψ) is a well-defined standard game in a coalitional form. Thus, one can apply the standard solution concepts for coalitional games—such as the core or the Shapley value—to the ψ-coalitional form.

---

[7] In the α-conversion, the worth of a coalition S is taken to be what it can guarantee itself regardless of the choice of actions of players outside the coalition; in the β-conversion, the worth of a coalition S is taken to be what it cannot be prevented from getting by the players in $N \setminus S$. That is, for the α-coalitional form, $v_\alpha(S) = \min_{a_{N \setminus S}} \max_{a_S} w_s(a)$; for the β-coalitional form, $v_\beta(S) = \max_{a_S} \min_{a_{N \setminus S}} w_s(a)$.

We use the core of the ψ-coalitional form to characterize games in which the grand federation is an equilibrium structure. Recall that for any game in coalitional form (N, v), the *core* of the game, $C(N, v)$, is the set of all payoff vectors $x = (x_1,..., x_n) \in \Re^n$ such that $\sum_{i \in S} x_i \geq v(S)$ for every coalition S. That is, a payoff vector is in the core of a coalitional game if no coalition can improve upon it.

Grand Federation as Equilibrium Structures: Characterization Results

Recall that, given a federation structure $F = \{S_1,..., S_m\}$, the interaction among federations in the underlying game generates a partition function, as defined in (10.1). For the characterization results, we consider underlying games that generate a partition function with the following *superadditivity* property:

$$(SUP) \quad w_{S \cup S'}\left(B \setminus \{S, S'\} \cup \{S \cup S'\}\right) \geq w_S(F) + w_{S'}(F)$$

$\forall B$ and $\forall S, S'$ in B.

Remark 4 It is clear that the grand federation is always an efficient structure under (SUP).

The first of our two main results is a characterization of games in which the grand federation is a strong equilibrium structure.

Proposition 2 Let the federation structure rule ψ be any rule satisfying the unanimity principle (U) and the separation principle (SEP) and let the underlying game be such that (SUP) is satisfied. The grand federation structure $\{N\}$ can be supported as a strong equilibrium structure if and only if the core of the game in ψ-coalitional form, (N, v_ψ), is non-empty. Moreover, if $\{N\}$ is a strong equilibrium structure, then the equilibrium share profile, c^*_N, generates payoff vectors belonging to the core of (N, v_ψ).

Computing the core is simple: it involves checking a system of linear inequalities. Therefore, the proposition provides a simple tool for verifying whether the grand federation is a strong equilibrium structure and calculating the associated payoffs of the states.

The notion of a SNE has been criticized as embodying too strong a criterion of stability: a profile of actions is ruled out as an equilibrium if it admits any profitable multilateral deviation at all, even if the deviation itself would have been vulnerable to further deviations. The concept of a CPNE was designed to partially address this criticism: only deviations that are themselves immune to further deviations by sub-coalitions of a deviating coalition are entertained.

In our view, more than an insistence on theoretical consistency is involved in this critique. The issue is relevant for many a real-world federation formation problem. To take but one example, an important consideration for the pro-separatist movement in Quebec has always been the response of the non-French communities within Quebec should Quebec secede from the rest of Canada.

We now investigate the conditions under which the grand federation structure is a coalition-proof structure. Since a SNE is also a CPNE, if the core of the ψ-coalitional form is non-empty, the grand federation is a coalition-proof structure under the conditions of the previous proposition. However, a non-empty core of the ψ-coalitional form is *not* a necessary condition for the grand federation to be a coalition-proof structure, as the following remark establishes.

Remark 5 Let the federation structure rule ψ be the weak consensus rule and let the underlying game be such that (SEP) is satisfied. The grand federation structure may be a coalition-proof structure even if the ψ-coalitional form has an empty core.

Our second main result is a characterization of the games for the grand federation to be a coalition-proof structure in the special case of the strict consensus rule.

Proposition 3 Let the federation structure rule ψ be the strict consensus rule and let (SUP) be satisfied. The grand federation structure $\{N\}$ can be supported as a coalition-proof structure if and only if the core of the game in ψ-coalitional form, (N, v_{ψ}), is non-empty. Moreover, if $\{N\}$ is a coalition-proof structure, then the equilibrium share profile generates payoff vectors belonging to the core of the game (N, v_{ψ}).

In order that the grand federation be an equilibrium outcome the gains from the federation must be sufficiently large for it to be incentive compatible. The condition that the core of the ψ-coalitional form be non-empty provides in effect lower bounds on how large the gains from the federation will have to be. However, intuition and lessons of history suggest that for cooperation to be viable the parties must also feel that the gains have been 'fairly' shared. It is well-known that often sharing schemes that are regarded as fair do not belong to the core. Thus, the characterization results hint at possible conflicts between achieving efficient cooperation and sharing the gains from efficiency fairly. The next remark makes this point.

Remark 6 Let $N = \{1, 2, 3\}$, the federation structure rule the weak consensus rule, and let the underlying game be such as to generate the following aggregate payoffs:[8]

$$w_i(i, j, k) = 0, \quad i = 1, 2, \quad w_3(i, j, k) = 3/8, \tag{10.5}$$

$$w_i(i, jk) = 0, \quad w_{jk}(i, jk) = 3/4, \quad w_N(N) = 1. \tag{10.6}$$

Note that in every federation of which state 3 is a member, it makes at least as high a marginal contribution (and sometimes strictly higher contribution) as any other partner state. Here the grand federation structure can be supported as a coalition-proof structure. Yet equilibrium constitution profiles supporting the grand federation as a coalition-proof structure lead to zero payoff for state 3 while the other states receive a positive payoff!

Discussion

The results in Propositions 2 and 3 that relate the notions of equilibrium and efficiency of the grand federation offer complete characterizations (under the hypothesis of the propositions) in that they identify necessary and sufficient conditions. However, a key point of view that has guided our study makes us emphasize the necessary conditions: we view the results as demonstrating the difficulty of supporting the efficient structure as an equilibrium. It is worth elaborating on the point of view. Many of our modelling choices are of course open to criticisms. For example, we have not modelled coalition formation as a dynamic game—as real coalition formation

---

[8] In the interest of brevity, we start from the aggregate payoffs. It is easy to construct an underlying game involving public good provision in strategic form that would give rise to this numerical example.

no doubt is and as is also more common in literature. This is because any extensive form of coalition formation one writes down is bound to be somewhat arbitrary and equilibria of dynamic games are notoriously sensitive to the extensive form. However, as Hart and Kurz (1983) had noted, if the solution of the dynamic game converges at all, a necessary condition would seem to be that the outcome is also an 'equilibrium' of the static game. To the extent that our primary interest is in the necessary conditions for supporting an efficient structure as an equilibrium, not pursuing a dynamic theory is less of a handicap.

The device of the federation structure rule can be a flexible way of distilling our intuition about the underlying dynamics for a particular applied context in a 'reduced form'. For example, during the formative years of the European Union (EU), the federation structure rule was explicitly the strict consensus rule. Now that the EU is already in existence, and as of this writing in 2011, fundamental constitutional changes are being contemplated, if one country such as the UK refuses to fall in line, the others are likely to remain together, that is, the weak consensus rule seems indicated. Moreover, the framework presented in this chapter can be adapted to analyse some questions of topical interest. For example, if a change in some aspect of the constitution requires ratification by the population of each member country, what further constraints does it impose such that the grand federation can be sustained as an equilibrium?

Appendix A10

Proof of Proposition 1

An example suffices for the proof. Let $N = \{1, 2, 3\}$ and consider the following example (it should be clear that one could easily specify an underlying game that generates it, as in Burbidge et al. (1997); we refrain from doing so to economize on space):

$$w_i(i, j, k) = 0, \quad i = 1, 2, \quad w_3(i, j, k) = 3/8, \tag{A10.1}$$

$$w_i(i, jk) = 0, \quad w_{jk}(i, jk) = 3/4, \quad i \in N, \{j, k\} \subset N, \quad w_N(N) = 1. \tag{A10.2}$$

For any c_N there must be at least one state, say, i, with:

$$c_{N,i}(\{N\})\,[u_N(\{N\})] < u_{\{i\}}[(\{h,j\},\{i\})]$$

because:

$$u_N(\{N\}) < 3u_{\{i\}}[(\{h,j\},\{i\})].$$

Then, there is a unilateral and profitable deviation for state i from $S_i = N$ to $S_i = \{i\}$. Therefore, there is no c_N for which σ^N is a NE and since the set of CPNE and SNE action profiles are subsets of the set of NE there is no c_N for which σ^N is a CPNE or a SNE at the federation formation stage. Since any share profile c leads to the same result, if there is a CPNE or SNE federation structure, it is not the efficient grand federation.

Now, consider σ' with $S_i = \{i\}$ and $S_h = S_j = \{h,j\}$ which leads to $\{\{h,j\}\{i\}\}$ by (U). There are c_N which lead to allocations which strictly Pareto dominate any set of payoffs in this federation structure so with such a c_N, a joint deviation by all states to σ^N is individually profitable (thus σ' is not SNE). But this deviation is not credible because for any c_N there must be at least one state, say h (a subset of the original deviators), with an individually profitable deviation to $S_h = \{h\}$. Given the example, there is no $c_{\{k,i\}}$ for $k = h, j \neq i$ that could lead to a profitable deviation by i and this is required for either $\{k,i\}$ to form given $S_i = \{i\} \in \sigma'$ and (SEP). Given the example, there are also no profitable deviations by h or j which would lead to the singleton federation structure. Thus, for any profile c, σ' is a CPNE of the federation formation stage. Because this holds for any c, there are no unilaterally profitable deviations at the founders' game for the founder of any federation. So $\{\{h,j\}\{i\}\}$ is a CPNE equilibrium structure and all $c_{\{h,j\}}$ are $c^*_{\{h,j\}}$.

Proof of Proposition 2

We first establish two lemma used in the proof of Proposition 2.

Lemma 1 Let the federation structure rule ψ satisfy the unanimity principle (U) and the separation principle (SEP) and let σ be a profile of participation plans resulting from a deviation by some federation S from the profile σ^N. The federation structure $\psi(\sigma)$ is an S-refinement of $\psi(d^s)$, the structure at the profile resulting from a unanimous deviation by S.

Proof of Lemma 1 We need to show that:

$$\text{for all } i \in N \setminus S, \psi_i(\sigma) = \psi_i(d^S) \quad (A) \tag{A10.3}$$

$$\text{for all } i \in S, \psi_i(\sigma) \subseteq \psi_i(d^S) \quad (B) \tag{A10.4}$$

(A) Since $S'_i = S_i$ for all $i \in N$ such that $S_i = N$ in σ or d^S and $S'_j \neq N$ for all $j \in N$ such that $S_j \neq N$ in σ and d^S then $\psi_i(\sigma) = \psi_i(d^S)$ for all $i \in N$ such that $S_i = N$ by letting $T = N$, and $\sigma' = d^S$ in the definition of (SEP).

(B) Suppose for some $i \in S$, $\psi_i(d^S) \subset \psi_i(\sigma)$. Since $S_i = S$ for all $i \in S$ in d^S then $\psi_i(d^S) = \{S\}$ for all $i \in S$ by U. Then for $\psi_i(d^S) = \{S\} \subset \psi_i(\sigma)$ for some $i \in S$ who we denote h, there must exist some $i \in N \setminus S$, which we denote k, with $\psi_k(\sigma) = \psi^h(\sigma)$. But then $\psi_h(\sigma) = \psi_k(\sigma) = \psi_k(d^S)$ the latter equality by (A) and thus $h \in \psi_k(d^S)$ and $k \in \psi_h(d^S) = \{S\}$—a contradiction.

Lemma 2 Let the underlying game be such that (SUP) is satisfied and let the federation structure rule ψ satisfy (U) and (SEP). Given a c'_N, if there is not a profitable fully coordinated joint deviation from σ^N for any $c_S[\psi(d^S)]$, then there is also not a profitable partially coordinated joint deviation for any c with c'_N.

Proof of Lemma 2 Any partially coordinated joint deviation by S leads to a S-refinement of $\psi(d^s)$ by Lemma 1. Thus, a partially coordinated deviation by S cannot be profitable by superadditivity and the premise that a fully coordinated joint deviation by S is not profitable.

Proof of Proposition 2 (Necessity) Consider a share profile c such that the grand federation's profile c'_N leads to a payoff configuration $u(N)$ that does not belong to core of (N, v_ψ). Then, by definition, there exists a federation S such that $v_\psi(S) > \sum_{i \in S} u_i(N)$. By the definition of $v_\psi(S)$, there exists a $u_S(\psi(d^s)) > \sum_{i \in S} u_i(N)$. Thus, there exists a sharing rule $c_S(\psi(d^s))$ in the founders' game which instigates a fully coordinated joint deviation in the federation formation game that leads to the federation structure $(\psi(d^s))$ and is thus profitable for the founder of S in $F = (\psi(d^s))$.

(Sufficiency) Now consider a share profile c such that the grand federation's profile c'_N leads to a $u(N)$ that does belong to the core of (N, v_ψ). Thus, for every $S \subset N$, $\sum_{i \in S} u_i(N) \geq v_\psi(S)$. This means that no federation S can have a profitable fully coordinated deviation irrespective of the founder of S in $F = \psi(d^S)$'s sharing rule. Then, by Lemma 2, there is also no profitable partially coordinated deviation by any $S \subset N$ for any c with c'_N.

Proof of Proposition 3

Sufficiency has already been established via the proof of Proposition 2.

(**Necessity**) Suppose c'_N leads to a $u(N)$ that does not belong to the core of (N, v_ψ). Then there is at least one federation that can improve upon $u(N)$ with a fully coordinated joint deviation. Since N is a finite set, there is a smallest federation (under the operation of set inclusion) which can improve upon it. Let S^* be a smallest federation. By definition, then:

$$v_{\psi^*}(S^*) > \sum_{i \in S^*} u_i(N) \tag{A10.5}$$

and

$$v_{\psi^*}(S) \leq \sum_{i \in S} u_i(N) \text{ for each } S \subset S^*. \tag{A10.6}$$

We now argue that the founder of S^* in $F = \psi^*(d^{s*})$ can instigate a fully coordinated, profitable, and credible joint deviation.

Clearly by (A10.5), the founder of S^* in $F = \psi^*(d^{s*})$ can propose a $c_S^*(\psi^*(d^{s*}))$ that leads to a vector $(y_i)_{i \in S}^*$ with:

$$y_i > u_i(N) \; \forall i \in S^*.$$

This makes the joint deviation by S^* to d^{s*} profitable.

Now suppose this is not a credible deviation due to a proper subset S' of S^* having a profitable fully coordinated deviation from d^{s*}. Under strict consensus, the complement of S^* is splintered into singletons in $\psi^*(d^{s*})$ and the complement of S' is splintered into singletons in $\psi^*(d^{s\prime})$ and thus, the aggregate consumption available to S' is $v_\psi^*(S')$. Therefore, we must have:

$$v_\psi(S') > \sum_{i \in S'} y_i > \sum_{i \in S'} u_i(N)$$

which contradicts (A10.6). Further, since a partially coordinated joint deviation by S' leads to a refinement of $\psi^*(d^s)$ under strict consensus then by superadditivity there are no partially coordinated profitable deviations by any proper subset of S^*. Finally, since a partially coordinated deviation by S^* from d^{s*} leads to a refinement of $\psi^*(d^{s*})$ then by superadditivity, there are no partially coordinated profitable deviations by S^* either. Therefore, σ^N is not a CPNE of the federation formation game if c'_N leads to a $u(N)$ that does not belong to the core of (N, v_ψ).

References

Aumann, R.J. 1959. 'Acceptable Points in Cooperative n-Person Games', *Annals of Mathematics Studies*, 40: 287–324.

———. 1961. 'The Core of a Cooperative Game without Sidepayments', *Transactions of the American Mathematical Society*, 98: 539–52.

Bernheim, D.B., B. Peleg, and M. Whinston. 1987. 'Coalition-Proof Nash Equilibria I: Concepts', *Journal of Economic Theory*, 42: 1–12.

Burbidge, J.B., J.A. DePater, G.M. Myers, and A. Sengupta. 1997. 'A Coalition-Formation Approach to Equilibrium Federations and Trading Blocs', *American Economic Review*, 87: 940–56.

Diamantoudi, E., and L. Xue. 2007. 'Coalitions, Agreements and Efficiency', *Journal of Economic Theory*, 136: 105–25.

Hart, S., and M. Kurz. 1983. 'Endogenous Formation of Coalitions', *Econometrica*, 51:1047–64.

Ray, D. 2007. *A Game-Theoretic Perspective on Coalition Formation*. New York: Oxford University Press.

Ray, D., and R. Vohra. 1997. 'Equilibrium Binding Agreements', *Journal of Economic Theory*, 73: 30–78.

von Neumann, J., and O. Morgenstern. 1944. *A Game-Theoretic Perspective on Coalition Formation*. Princeton: Princeton University Press.

SECTION V

BARGAINING, TECHNOLOGY TRANSFER, AND DETERRENCE

11

Markets with Bilateral Bargaining and Incomplete Information

Kalyan Chatterjee and Bhaskar Dutta[*]

One fruitful way of modelling the microstructure of markets has been to conceive of them as the results of pair-wise meetings between economic agents, with the market outcome being determined by the various agreements concluded by those pairs who agree to trade. This approach goes back a long way (see, for example, the housing market example in Shubik (1982)); the modern interest in it dates back to the papers of Rubinstein and Wolinsky (1985), Gale (1986), and Binmore and Herrero (1988) and the ensuing debate on the nature and properties of the equilibria generated.

These papers were concerned with random matching in large markets. Rubinstein and Wolinsky (1990) discussed markets with small numbers of buyers and sellers and their work was followed up

---

[*] Bhaskar Dutta gratefully acknowledges support from ESRC Grant RES-000-22-0341. We thank Kaustav Das and Tomas Sjostrom for comments on this draft.

by Hendon and Tranaes (1991) and Chatterjee and Dutta (1998) among others. Chatterjee and Dutta (1998) considered a model of a market in which sellers competed for heterogeneous buyers in a setting that has some features of auction-like competition and of bilateral bargaining. They showed that in general one cannot obtain uniform prices across pairs or efficient (immediate) trade in this setting.

All the models mentioned here have assumed *complete information*. As is well-known, a literature on bilateral bargaining under incomplete information also developed around the same time.[1] However, possibly because of the general perception of the difficulty in obtaining determinate results in this literature without using equilibrium refinements, there has been no work that we know of that addresses small markets with some incomplete information and with the features of competition for bargaining partners that occur in some of the complete information papers.

This chapter attempts to make a start in studying the relationship between bargaining and competition with incomplete information, using as our basis a simplified version of a model of bilateral bargaining with two types that appears as a sub-model in Chatterjee and Samuelson (1988). Our purpose here, of course, is not just to fill a perceived gap in the literature. The interaction of competition and incomplete information has potentially interesting implications for the value of outside options and how this changes with incomplete information, a problem studied in a different setting by Fudenberg et al. (1987) and Samuelson (1992). In the first model only a single seller has the ability to switch among buyers and would do so in the event of a rejection from a buyer signalling that the buyer is of a recalcitrant type. We discuss the incentive to switch in this way, but like Chatterjee and Dutta (1998), add competition among sellers as well as a finite number of players on both sides of the market.

Our basic setup is as follows (a more formal description appears in the next section): There are two buyers and two sellers.[2] One of the sellers has a privately-known reservation price, which can either be

---

[1] See the illuminating survey by Ausubel et al. (2002), and the references cited there.

[2] We discuss extensions to more buyers and sellers in the last section.

Low or *High* with commonly-known probabilities. The other seller has no private information, and her reservation price is commonly known to be *in between* the Low and High values of the privately informed seller. The two buyers have the same commonly-known value, which is greater than the High seller reservation price. The buyers move in sequence and make offers with the second buyer observing the offer made by the first buyer. The sellers respond simultaneously[3] and accept or reject the offers made. Any acceptance leads to the trading pair leaving the market. In the next period, buyers again make offers and sellers accept or reject them. Future payoffs are discounted with the common discount factor being δ.

What would intuition suggest about a market of this nature? One might expect, first, competition among buyers to equalize equilibrium expected payoffs for the buyers (in which case the order in which they move will not matter in equilibrium). One might also expect that if the probability is high that the privately informed seller is of a *Low* type, that seller will reap the benefits of buyer competition with the opposite being true if the informed seller is more likely to be a *High* type, so that the weakness could be a strength. One might also surmise that the reservation price of the known seller will play a crucial role in determining prices in the first case and the reservation price of the *High* type in the second.[4]

It turns out there are two types of (perfect Bayes) equilibrium, one in which the intuition about equal expected payoffs of the buyers is satisfied and the other in which the second buyer to move does better. More surprisingly, if we consider the first kind of equilibrium, the price received by the known seller is entirely driven by the payoffs in the two-player incomplete information game, so that no switch occurs as described in the previous paragraph.

Moreover, we demonstrate through an example that when *both* the sellers are privately informed, even though their reservation prices are independent draws, the first kind of equilibrium with payoffs to buyers being order-independent need not exist.

---

[3] We also consider what will happen if the sellers move in the order in which they are named by the buyers (if only one seller receives offers only that seller moves).

[4] These were our own initial intuitions about this problem.

It seems natural to compare our results to Shubik's discussion (Shubik 1982) of the housing market, especially the attainment of the core allocation. The incomplete information of course leads to potential inefficiency through delay, so there is no hope of achieving the complete-information core. However, the equality in expected payoffs between the buyers seems a good proxy for the core, as in some loose sense we have equality in expectations of prices. However, this is not true in general if there is 'too much' private information.

The outline of the rest of the chapter is as follows: The next section introduces the notation and the explicit description of the model. The section that follows considers the complete information benchmark, in there are no privately informed sellers. The next section describes the two-player bargaining game with incomplete information and is based on Chatterjee and Samuelson (1988). The next section contains the basic analysis of the four-player game with the section following it giving an example with two privately informed sellers. The next section discusses markets with more sellers and buyers in addition to providing concluding remarks.

The Model and the Notation

There are *two* identical buyers B_1 and B_2. Each buyer has one unit demand for an indivisible good. The buyers' common and commonly-known valuation for the good is $v > 0$. There are also two sellers. Each seller owns one unit of the good. The first seller, to be denoted S_M, has a reservation value of M for the good, and this is common knowledge. The second seller's reservation value is private information with the seller. However, it is common knowledge that her reservation value is either H with probability π or L with probability $1 - \pi$, where $v > H > M \geq L$. In what follows, we simplify the notation by setting $L = 0$. We will sometimes refer to the second seller as the *informed* seller, and denote her as S_I.

We consider the following infinite horizon bargaining game in which only buyers make offers. In each period, the two buyers make offers to the sellers *sequentially*, the order of offers being random. An offer is simply a price p at which the buyer is willing to buy one unit of the good. The offer is targeted at a particular seller, since they are not identical. After both offers are on the table, the sellers decide whether to accept at most one of the offers.[5]

Matched pairs, if any, leave the market. If some pair is left unmatched, then the bargaining proceeds to the next period, in which the unmatched buyer(s) again make price offers to the unmatched seller(s). All players have the same discount factor $\delta \in (0,1)$. All players are risk neutral.

We adopt the terminology of Fudenberg and Tirole (1991) and denote each period as a 'stage' in this game, to avoid the use of 'subgames' in a game of incomplete information. We also use their equilibrium concept of 'Perfect Bayes' Equilibrium', namely sequential rationality at every stage given beliefs at that stage and beliefs being compatible with Bayes' theorem on and, wherever possible, off the equilibrium path.

Note that a stage in which a buyer and S_I have left the market and the other players remain begins a complete-information subgame (with a trivial solution). If a buyer and seller S_M have traded and left the market, the ensuing game is a two-player bargaining game of one-sided incomplete information with two types. This too has a determinate sequential equilibrium, to be discussed in the next section. We essentially adopt part of the Chatterjee and Samuelson's (1988) paper for this part. In that paper, there is a one-sided incomplete information 'subgame' with two-sided offers. However, the informed player's offers are always rejected in the equilibrium constructed there except possibly in the last stage. The game with the uninformed player being the sole proposer therefore has an easily derived equilibrium.[6]

The specification in which the buyers move in sequence might need some comment. We specify the model in this way rather than

---

[5] Our results do not depend qualitatively on whether sellers move simultaneously or sequentially, though some details differ as pointed out later.

[6] See, for instance, Deneckere and Liang (2001). The game with a continuum of types was solved by Sobel and Takahashi (1983) and Fudenberg et al. (1985) and there is no substantive difference in the results. So, we do not claim any novelty for our reformulation of the relevant part of Chatterjee and Samuelson (1988).

having buyers make simultaneous targeted offers, as in Chatterjee and Dutta (1998), mainly for analytical tractability. However, one can think of buyers moving in continuous time and extraneous irrelevant factors determining who moves first in a particular stage. This rules out strategically choosing whether to move first or second; such a restriction does not matter if the order of moves is payoff-irrelevant in equilibrium.

The Complete Information Game

In this section we briefly describe the nature of equilibrium payoffs when seller valuations are also commonly known. The main purpose of this section is to act as a benchmark for the case when one of the sellers is privately informed about his reservation value; the case that is of principal interest in this chapter.

We consider the case where seller reservation values are publicly known to be M and L. What will be the nature of equilibrium payoffs in this case? Intuition suggests that there should be competition for S_L, and this competition 'should' drive up the price offered by the Low seller to M, which is also offered to S_M. Hence, in this equilibrium, buyer payoffs will be equalized at $v - M$.

Indeed, this will be one set of equilibrium payoffs. However, there is also another set of equilibrium payoffs. Suppose buyer B_1 is the first to make offers. Then, B_1 'knows' that if she offers a price $p < M$ to seller S_L, then B_2 will win over S_L with a slightly higher price p'. Hence, B_1 knows that her payoff cannot exceed $v - M$. On the other hand, she can always ensure herself a payoff of $v - M$ by offering a price M to S_M. Notice, however, that if B_1 does make this offer to S_M, then B_2 can trade with S_L at the Low price of L.

Hence, this suggests that there will be a second set of equilibrium payoffs where buyer payoffs are not equalized because B_1 essentially drops out of a contest she cannot win.[7]

The proposition below summarizes this discussion.

---

[7] Of course, this equilibrium arises due to the fact that buyers make offers sequentially.

Proposition 1 The following constitute the only sets of equilibrium payoffs in the bargaining game when seller valuations are commonly known to be M and L.

1. Both buyers buy at the common price of $p = M$ giving rise to buyer payoffs of $v - M$. Seller S_M has zero payoff while seller S_L derives a payoff of $M - L$.
2. Buyer B_1 (the first buyer to make an offer in the initial period), has a payoff of $v - M$, while B_2 has a payoff of $v - L$. Both sellers get zero payoff.

Proof We first describe equilibrium strategies which give rise to these payoffs.[8] The following strategies support the first set of payoffs:

(a) Buyer B_1 offers a price of M to S_L in the initial period.
(b.1) If B_1 has offered a price of at least M to S_L, then B_2 offers M to S_M.
(b.2) If B_1 has offered $p < M$ to S_L, then B_2 offers $p' = \max(p, L)$ to S_L.
(b.3) If B_1 has made an offer to M, then B_2 offers L to S_L.
(c) If S_L receives only one offer p, then she accepts this offer if $p \geq L$. If she receives two offers, then she accepts the higher of the two offers if this is at least as high as L. If both buyers offer the same price $p \geq L$, then she accepts the offer from B_2.
(d) If S_M receives only one offer p, then she accepts this offer if $p \geq M$. If she receives two offers, then she accepts the higher of the two offers if this is at least as high as M. She uses any tie-breaking rule if both buyers offer the same $p \geq M$.

In subsequent periods, if only one pair is unmatched, then the players play the unique equilibrium of the two-player game, where the buyer offers a price exactly equal to the reservation value of the remaining seller. If both pairs are unmatched, then all players play the equilibrium strategies corresponding to the second set of equilibrium payoffs which are now described.

In the second equilibrium buyer B_1 offers M to S_M, instead of to S_L. All other strategies are as described earlier.

---
[8] We do not claim that there are only two sets of equilibrium strategies.

We leave it to the reader to check whether these indeed constitute equilibrium strategy profiles.

To verify that these are the only equilibrium payoffs possible, simply note that B_1 cannot obtain a payoff higher than $v - M$. For if she did, then she must be trading with S_L at a price $p < M$. Since B_2 makes her offer after B_1, she can make a slightly higher payoff and win over S_L.

The Two-player Game with Incomplete Information

Play of the four-player game may lead to a two-player 'subgame' involving the informed seller and one of the buyers. In fact, as we show in the next section, this continuation game will be reached with positive probability along the equilibrium path when S_M accepts the targeted offer made to her while S_I rejects the offer made to her with some probability. In this section, we briefly review the results on the equilibrium of this two-player game.

Since the subgame has only one buyer and one seller, we simplify the notation by denoting the buyer as B and the (informed) seller as S. Suppose the subgame starts in period t', and let $\pi_{t'}$ be the initial probability that the seller's reservation value is L. We describe the *unique* equilibrium which is essentially the one described in Chatterjee and Samuelson (1988) and Deneckere and Liang (2001).[9]

It is convenient to count time 'backwards'. That is, period t means that the game will end t periods from now. Of course, this assumes that the game ends in finite time. Fortunately, it turns out that for any $\delta < 1$, the game ends in a finite number of periods $N(\delta)$. Moreover, as δ tends to one, $N(\delta)$ is *uniformly bounded*.[10]

Construct an *increasing* sequence of probabilities $\{0, q_1, ..., q_t, ...\}$. Recall that π^0 is the initial probability that S_I is of the Low type, and define $p_t \equiv \delta^t H$ for all $t = 1, ..., N(\delta)$. The nature of the equilibrium

---

[9] There is a small difference in our description of the equilibrium from that of Chatterjee and Samuelson (1988). They specify an alternating offers extensive form so that buyers make offers every two periods. Since B makes an offer in every period in our model, there is a difference in the rate of discounting.

[10] This is shown in Deneckere and Liang (2001).

path is the following. Suppose that in period t, the play of the game so far and Bayes Rule implies that $\pi_t \in (q_t, q_{t+1})$ is the updated probability that the seller is the Low type. Then, B offers p_t. The High seller rejects this offer with probability 1, while the Low seller accepts this with a probability which implies through Bayes Rule that the updated probability π_{t-1} equals q_{t-1}. If $\pi_t < q_1$, then B offers H. This offer is accepted by both types of S.

The cut-off points, q_t, are chosen such that the buyer is indifferent between making the offer $\delta^t H$ and ending the game in t periods or offering $\delta^{t-1} H$ and ending the game one period earlier. So, at q_1, B is indifferent between offering H and δH. The latter offer is accepted with probability 1 by L. Hence, B's expected payoff from the offer δH is $q_1 (v - \delta H) + (1 - q_1) \delta (v - H)$. Equating this to $v - H$, we get:

$$q_1 = \frac{v - H}{v}$$

It is trivial to check that the Low type seller's behaviour is optimal given B's specified strategy. For suppose, he receives the offer p_t. If he rejects this offer, her payoff in the next period is p_{t-1}. Since $\delta p_{t-1} = p_t$, he is indifferent between rejecting and accepting this offer.

It is also easy to show that the two-player game has a unique equilibrium. Clearly, after every history of the game, equilibrium must be unique if $\pi_t < q_1$ as this essentially becomes a two-player complete information game. A form of 'backward induction' argument can be used to establish uniqueness.

The Four-player Game with Incomplete Information

In this section, we consider the four-player game described in the section 'The Model and the Notation'.

We use the cut-offs, q_t, derived in the previous section. Recall that if π is below q_1, the two-player game essentially becomes a complete information game with the high offer made to the seller and if π is between q_1 and q_2, the two-player game will last at most for two periods. We first consider the four-player game in these ranges of values of π as an example of what happens in equilibrium in this game. We then extend the analysis to all values of π.

Let $\pi^0 \in (q_1, q_2)$ be the initial probability of type L. Define $\bar{p}_1^M$ and p_t^M as follows:

1. $v - \bar{p}_1^M = \pi^0(v - \delta H) + (1 - \pi^0)\delta(v - H)$ and
2. $p_1^M = M + (1 - \pi^0)\delta(H - M)$.

Note that the q_t are functions of δ.

Example 1 Without loss of generality (WLOG), let B_1 move first as the outcome of the random draw. The following is an equilibrium of the game for sufficiently high δ.

B_1 offers $\bar{p}_t^M$ to S_M. B_2's offers depend on the offers made by B_1, and are:

1. If B_1 offers a price $p \geq \bar{p}_t^M$ to S_M, then B_2 offers $p_1 = \delta H$ to S_I.
2. If B_1 offers a price $p < \bar{p}_t^M$ to S_M, then B_2 offers $p + \epsilon$ also to S_M.
3. If B_1 offers H or higher to S_I, then B_2 offers M to S_M.
4. If B_1 makes an offer $p \in (\delta H, H)$ to S_I, then B_2 makes an offer p_t^{M1} to S_M.
5. If B_1 makes an offer $p \in (\delta^2 H, \delta H)$ to S_I, then B_2 offers $\bar{p}_1^M = M + (1 - \pi^0 \alpha)\delta(H - M)$ to S_M where α is as defined in the response for type L below.
6. Finally, if B_1 makes an offer $\rho \leq \delta^2 H$ to S_I, then B_2 makes an offer $M + \delta(\bar{p}_1^M - M)$ to M.

Seller S_I, type L accepts all offers $\rho \geq \delta H$, rejects all offers $\rho \leq \delta^2 H$ and accepts offers in $(\delta^2 H, \delta H)$ with probability α such that

$$q_1 = \frac{\pi^0(1-\alpha)}{\pi^0(1-\alpha) + 1 - \pi^0}.$$ Type H accepts all offers $\rho \geq H$ and rejects all offers below H; and S_M accepts any offer greater than her expected continuation payoff, which could be either p_t^M or $\bar{p}_t^M$, depending on the offer made to S_I.[11]

---

[11] We have not set down details of possible deviations by B_2: They do not affect the sellers' response strategies.

If the initial offers are rejected, the game goes into the following period with all four players and with π either unchanged ($=\pi^0$), $\pi = q_1$ or $\pi = 0$. If $\pi = \pi^0$, the strategies above are played. If $\pi = q_1$, the offer to S_I randomises between δH and H. An analogue of (1) then determines the offer made to S_M. If $\pi = 0$, the complete information strategies described in the section, 'The Complete Information Game', are used, that is, H is offered to both sellers. Thus, the equilibrium outcome path is: B_1 offers $\bar{p}_t^M$ to S_M and B_2 offers δH to S_I, S_M and type L accept and in the next period, B_2 offers H to S_I who accepts.

If S_I accepts and S_M rejects, the buyer remaining offers S_M a price of M in the following period. If S_M accepts and S_I rejects, the ensuing game is a two-player game of incomplete information and the strategies are as described in the previous section.

Proof The argument constructs two prices for seller S_M, her continuation payoff, given in (2), and the price obtained by competition among the buyers as given in (1). We shall show that, in fact, the second is strictly higher than the first, so S_M always finds it optimal to accept $\bar{p}_t^M$. Seller S_I here plays the two-player game of the previous section with one of the buyers, so the two-player analysis carries over. The buyers follow strategies that equalize their expected payoffs.

We check deviations. If B_1 deviates and offers $p = \bar{p}_t^M$ to S_M, S_M accepts and B_1 is worse off. If B_1 offers $P < \bar{p}_t^M$, B_2 offers a higher price which S_M accepts, thus giving B_1 the two-player expected payoff with S_I but one period later. This makes him strictly worse off. If B_1 deviates and offers to S_I, the best resulting expected payoff is exactly equal to that obtained by offering $\bar{p}_t^M$ to S_M and therefore no gain is realized. If B_1 does not make a serious offer or makes a rejected offer, B_2 induces acceptance by making an offer to S_M of $M + \delta(\bar{p}_1^M - M)$, thus making B_1 worse off. Deviations by B_2 can be shown similarly to be unprofitable.

For the sellers, S_M will accept $\bar{p}_t^M$, since this is strictly greater than her continuation payoff, p_t^M. To see this, we explicitly calculate:

$$\bar{p}_1^M - p_1^M = (v-M)(1-\delta) + \delta\pi^0 H - \pi^0 v + \delta\pi^0(v-M) \quad (11.1)$$

$$= v(1-\delta)(1-\pi^0) + \delta\pi^0(H-M) - M(1-\delta) \quad (11.2)$$

As long as δ has been chosen sufficiently close to 1, the first and the third terms are close to zero and the second term is positive.[12]

We can similarly check that the rest of her strategy is optimal for S_M, namely to accept anything at least as high as her continuation payoff. The response strategy of S_I is the same as in the corresponding two-player game with one buyer. This is optimal because S_M finds it optimal to accept the equilibrium offer, and so S_I faces a two-player continuation game. If the offers are such that S_M will reject but S_I type L is supposed to accept, a rejection by L signals he is a H type. But he can only obtain the H offer in the following period. The offer is such that L is indifferent between accepting and rejecting and getting the high offer in the next period.

Remark 1 Note that if the sellers were to respond in the order they were named rather than simultaneously, there would be no change as long as S_M moves first. If S_I moves first, S_M's continuation payoff will depend on whether S_I accepted or rejected. This will not make a difference on the equilibrium path because B_1 will still be indifferent between making an offer of $\bar{p}_t^M$ to S_M or p_1 to S_I and thus will not gain by deviating. So in fact S_M will move first. But if S_I were chosen by B_1, the offer from B_2 to S_M can be either M or $M + \delta(H - M)$, depending on B_2's belief about S_I's probability of accepting.

One would expect the (high) price needed to obtain a trade with type L of S_I when the probability of L is small to drive buyer competition for S_M. What happens when this probability is high? Suppose for instance that S_I is 'almost certainly' of the low type. Surely, the buyers should be competing to trade with S_I? The next lemma shows, surprisingly, that for sufficiently high δ, the competition is always over S_M.

Define the following sequences of prices for all $t = 1,\ldots$, with $a_t = \pi_t \alpha_t$ the equilibrium acceptance probability for such an offer in the two-player incomplete information game.

(i) $p_t^I = \delta^t H$

(ii) $p_t^M = M + \delta(1 - a_t)(\bar{p}_{t-1}^M - M)$

---

[12] If $\delta = 0$ and π_0 is close to q_1, then the expression is positive. However, when π_0 is close to q_2, the expression is negative (with $\delta = 0, p_1^M = M$).

(iii) $\bar{p}_t^M = v - \left[(v - p_t^I)a_t + (1 - a_t)\delta(v - \bar{p}_{t-1}^M)\right]$

(iv) $\hat{p}_t^M = \max(p_t^M, \bar{p}_t^M)$

We now prove a lemma, which we shall refer to as the 'competition lemma'.

Lemma 1 For all $t = 1,\ldots$, there exists $\bar{\delta}(t)$ such that for all $\delta \geq \tilde{\delta}(t), \hat{p}_t^M = \bar{p}_t^M$.

Proof: We show that for all $t \geq 1$ and for sufficiently high $\delta, \bar{p}_t^M \geq p_t^M$:

$$\bar{p}_t^M - p_t^M = v - \left[(v - p_t^I)a_t + (1 - a_t)\delta(v - \bar{p}_{t-1}^M)\right] -$$
$$M - \delta(1 - a_t)(\bar{p}_{t-1}^M - M)$$
$$= (v - M)(1 - \delta + \delta a_t) - a_t(v - p_t^I)$$
$$= (1 - \delta)(v - M) + a_t(\delta v - \delta M - v + \delta^t H)$$
$$= (1 - \delta)(v - M) + a_t(\delta^t H - \delta M - (1 - \delta)v).$$

We have remarked earlier that for all $\delta < 1$, the equilibrium duration of the two-player incomplete information game is uniformly bounded by say T^*. Fix $t = T^*$. It is sufficient to show that the second term (the coefficient of a_t) is non-negative for some $\bar{\delta}$. Note that this is increasing in δ; at $\delta = 1$, it is clearly positive. Therefore, there exists a $\bar{\delta} < 1$ such that for $\delta > \bar{\delta}$, the second term is positive. If this is true for $t = T^*$, it is clearly true for smaller values of t. Therefore, $\bar{p}_1^M$ and p_t^M whenever $\delta \geq \tilde{\delta}$.

We now construct the equilibrium for $\delta > \tilde{\delta}$ such that the expected payoff to the buyer does not depend on the order in which the offers are made. We utilize four sequences, one of probabilities and three of prices, $\{q_t\}, \{p_t^I\}, \{\bar{p}_t^M\}, \{p_t^M\}$. The interesting feature here is that competition results in S_M getting more than her continuation game expected payoff. This is because S_M's continuation payoff is the combination of two terms. If S_I accepts, S_M is at the mercy of the other buyer who gives him M in the next period. If S_I rejects, she is more likely to be a H type and gets a higher equilibrium payoff. This drives up S_M's payoff in the following period as buyers potentially compete for her good. The driving force in the competition is the incomplete information in the game.

Proposition 2 Define sequences $p_t^I, \bar{p}_t^M, p_t^M$ from conditions (i)–(iii) in the preceding lemma. Let q_t be defined as in the two-player game with incomplete information. Let p_{ikt}[13] represent the offer made by buyer i to seller S_k when $\pi \in [q_t, q_{t+1}]$; let B_1, without loss of generality, be the first mover in each period. Let $\delta \geq \tilde{\delta}$, where $\tilde{\delta}$ has been defined in the competition lemma. There is one equilibrium in which the buyers obtain the same expected payoffs u_i. The common expected payoff, $u = u_1 = u_2$, is the expected buyer payoff in the two-player incomplete information game with the given value of π^0, which we denote by $V_B(\pi^0)$.

The stationary[14] strategies that sustain these equilibrium payoffs are:

1. B_1 chooses $p_{1Mt} = \bar{p}_t^M$ and does not make an offer to S_I.
2. If $p_{1Mt} \geq \bar{p}_t^M$, B_2 chooses $p_{2It} = p_t^I$; S_M accepts, S_I of type L accepts with a probability sufficient to make $\pi = q_{t-1}$ in the next period, S_I of type H rejects any offer less than H.
3. If $p_{1Mt} < \bar{p}_t^M$, B_2 chooses $p_{2Mt} = p_{1Mt} + \epsilon$ such that $p_{2Mt} \leq \bar{p}_t^M$ and $p_{2Mt} \geq M + \delta(\bar{p}_t^M - M)$, S_M accepts p_{2Mt}, S_I has no move.
4. If $p_{1It} \geq p_t^I$ and B_1 does not make an offer to S_M, B_2 offers p_t^M to S_M, S_M accepts, S_I of type L uses the same acceptance strategy a_t as in the two-player incomplete information game.
5. If $p_{1It} \in [p_{t-1}^I, p_t^I)$, $p_{2Mt} = p_t^M(\bar{a}_t)$, where $\bar{a}_t$ is the equilibrium acceptance probability of the corresponding two-player incomplete information game, player S_M accepts. Player S_I's (L type) acceptance decision implies that $\bar{a}_t$ is the acceptance probability.
6. If B_2 deviates from (2), S_I of type L responds according to the two-player game equilibrium strategy, S_M accepts if $\bar{p}_t^M$ is at least as high as her continuation payoff given the acceptance probability for S_I.

---

[13] Each buyer can choose only a single value of *pikt* in this game.
[14] By 'stationary' we mean independent of history apart from the updated value of π and of the set of players remaining in the game.

7. If $p_{2Mt} > 0$, S_M accepts any $p_{2Mt} \geq p_t^M(a_t)$, S_M's continuation payoff given an acceptance probability of a_t by the L type of S_I. The response behaviour of S_I (L type) follows that of the seller in the two-person incomplete information game with an uninformed buyer.

Proof Consider deviations by B_1. If he chooses $p_{1Mt} > \overline{p}_t^M$, he is worse off because (a) S_M accepts any offer greater than her expected continuation payoff, p_t^M and, by the competition lemma, $\overline{p}_t^M > p_t^M$, and (b) B_2 is better off making an offer to S_I than choosing, so B_2 will not offer such a price to S_M. If $p_{1Mt} < \overline{p}_t^M$, B_2 raises the offer by (3), S_M accepts p_{2Mt}, and B_1 gets an expected payoff equal to the discounted buyer payoff in the incomplete information game with S_I. From the definition of $\overline{p}_t^M$, this is strictly less than $v - \overline{p}_t^M$. If B_1 chooses to make an offer to S_I, S_I will respond as in the two-player incomplete information game and, again by the definition of $\overline{p}_t^M$, B_1 will not be strictly better off with the optimal p_{1IT}. B_2 moves second. If she deviates (a) by not following (2), she is worse off since p_t^I is the equilibrium offer in the ensuing two-player incomplete information continuation game (since S_M will accept); (b) by not following (3), she is clearly worse off by the definition of $\overline{p}_t^M$; (c) by not following (4), she is worse off because S_M accepts any offer at least as high as her continuation payoff for which p_t^M is an upper bound and $v - p_t^M > v - \overline{p}_t^M$, by definition. The responses of the sellers are clearly optimal from the two-player continuation games and the four-player game with the updated value of π.

Remark 2 Out-of-equilibrium beliefs do not play a significant role here because buyers make offers. Their deviations (and deviations by S_M) cannot signal anything about S_I's type by the requirement of 'no signalling what you don't know'. Player S_I always has a positive probability of accepting or rejecting and deviations in these probabilities are not observable. The sole exception is if the offer to S_I is $p \geq H$. In this case, a rejection does not change beliefs.

Remark 3 The comment after the first example in this section about the order of responses holds more generally.

As a complete information analysis of the section 'The Complete Information Game', will suggest, this is not the only equilibrium in stationary strategies. There is another equilibrium in which the first mover in each period makes an offer to S_I and the second proposer offers S_M that seller's continuation payoff. We write this as a proposition (we are again restricting our attention to sufficiently high values of δ).

Proposition 3 There exists an equilibrium in stationary strategies where the first buyer to move, B_1 obtains an expected payoff $u'_1 = v_B(\pi^0)$, B_2 obtains $u'_2 = v - M$ and $u'_2 > u'_1$.

Proof The strategies that sustain these as equilibrium payoffs are obtained from (4) to (7) of the previous proposition. B_1 chooses $p_{1It} > 0$, making the equilibrium offer in the two-player incomplete information bargaining game for the given value of π. A deviation to making an offer to S_M will not increase this payoff from the previous proposition. If B_1 makes an offer to S_I, B_2 offers M to S_M, who accepts any offer $p \geq M$. The continuation payoff for S_M is 0. If $\pi < q_1$, B_1 makes an offer of H to S_I, who accepts with probability 1. S_M will then accept any offer $p \geq M$. Since, in each period, B_2 makes an offer p_{2Mt} equal to the continuation payoff of S_M, backward induction shows that the continuation payoff must be zero in each period. S_I responds as in her equilibrium strategy in the two-player, incomplete information game.

If B_1 makes an offer to S_M, the response from B_2 follows (2) and (3) from the previous proposition. This ensures B_1 does not gain by deviating. It is clear that B_2, S_I will not gain by deviating.

These two are equilibria in stationary strategies. One can think of the second as essentially a decomposition into two separate two-player games, one with incomplete information and one with complete information. The first equilibrium shows that putting the four players together can give rise to competition and to outcomes different from the two-player game for some of the players.

We can clearly combine the two equilibria to obtain others. For example, take the second equilibrium discussed earlier. Suppose that if there is no agreement in the first period, the players switch to the first equilibrium (in which the first proposer makes an offer to S_M). In this case, the first-period offer by B_2 to S_M will be $p_t^M > M$, since S_M has a continuation payoff greater than 0. However, we can identify the following properties of all equilibria.

Proposition 4 In all equilibria of the four-player game, after every history, the following hold.

1. The offer to the informed player S_I as well as her response is identical to that of the two-player game with a single buyer.
2. The first proposer B_1 obtains an expected payoff $v_B(\pi)$.
3. The payoff to S_M varies between 0 and $\overline{p}_t^M - M$.

Proof To prove the first point, consider the first period t where $\pi_t \leq q_1$. An offer of H is optimal for a buyer in the two-player game and is accepted by S_I with probability 1. Clearly a higher offer is not optimal in the four-player game since even the type H seller will accept an offer of H with probability 1. A lower offer is not optimal because the type H seller will reject this, and the definition of q_1 implies that it is better to offer H instead. So, in the four-player game S_I will get the same offer for $\pi_t \leq q_1$. Now consider type L of S_I playing a pure strategy in equilibrium at some period τ in the four-player game. In equilibrium, the pure strategy cannot be to reject with probability 1, because no updating takes place and the buyer will increase her offer. Suppose the pure strategy is to accept with probability 1. Then, in period $\tau - 1$, $\pi_{\tau-1} = 0$, and the buyer must offer H. But, incentive compatibility for the Low type implies the offer that is accepted is δH and optimality for the buyer implies $\pi_\tau \leq q_2$.

For other values of type π_t, S_I must be playing a non-degenerate mixed strategy. Let t' be the first period (counting backwards) in which S_I in the four-player game gets an offer $p_{t'}^I$, strictly greater than the equilibrium offer in the two-player game for $\pi_{t'}$ (a strictly lower offer will clearly not occur in equilibrium). If S_I, type L, plays a randomized behavioural strategy, he must be indifferent between accepting $p_{t'}^I$ or rejecting and accepting the two-player equilibrium offer in period $t'-1$. Therefore $p_{t'}^I = \delta p_{t'+1}^I$. But this is exactly the equilibrium offer in the two-player game, contradicting our hypothesis.

For the second and third parts, note that the first buyer to make a proposal can choose either S_I or S_M. If she chooses S_I, she has to offer the two-player game offer and gets a payoff of $v_B(\pi_t)$. If she chooses S_M she has to offer a price that cannot be bid up by the buyer following $\overline{p}_t^M$. This shows point 2 of the proposition. If B_1

being indifferent between S_I and S_M randomizes in period $t-1$, the continuation payoff for S_M in period t will depend on the sequence of such randomizations employed by the first proposer in periods $t-1$ onwards. The minimum continuation payoff for S_M will be obtained if the first proposer always makes an offer to S_I – a payoff of 0. The highest payoff will be obtained if B_1 always chooses S_M, a payoff of $\overline{p}_t^M - M$.

Remark 4 It is not possible to rule out rejection with probability 1 by S_M. This could happen, for example, if the randomization chosen by B_1 in periods $t-1$ onwards depended on the offer made by B_2 in period t.

The preceding discussion was based on the protocol where the order of proposers is chosen randomly at the beginning of the game. Suppose, alternatively, that each buyer is chosen as first proposer with equal probability in each period. Clearly, there is no difference in the first equilibrium in which the buyers have the same expected payoffs. The second equilibrium also survives. Suppose B_1 and B_2 have been chosen in that order in a particular period. B_1 might consider making a non-serious offer so as to wait for the chance to make an offer to S_M in the following period. However, a non-serious offer to S_I will (a) not result in any updating of π, and (b) S_M will accept the equilibrium offer from B_2, so that B_1 will not have S_M available in the next period. If B_1 makes an offer to S_M, the optimal offer does not increase her payoff beyond $v_B(\pi)$ Therefore, a change in the protocol does not affect the equilibrium.

Extensions

In this section we consider some extensions of the basic model considered earlier.

Many Buyers and Sellers

The results of the basic model extend easily to the case when there are 'many' buyers and sellers, provided only one seller has private information. Suppose there are $n > 2$ buyers and sellers, with each buyer's valuation being v, while sellers $1,\ldots, n-1$ have known reservation values $M_1 \geq \ldots \geq M_{n-1} \geq 0$. Seller n is the informed seller, and her valuation is either H with probability $1 - \pi_0$ or $L = 0$ with probability π_0, where:

$$v > H > M_1$$

Suppose δ is sufficiently high. Then, there is an equilibrium in which all buyers get the same expected payoff $u(\pi_0)$, where $u(\pi_0)$ is the expected buyer payoff in the two-person game where π_0 is the initial probability that the informed seller is of the low type.

We describe informally the strategies which sustain this equilibrium. WLOG, let $B_1, ..., B_n$ be the order in which buyers make offers. Then, each buyer B_i, $i < n$ offers $\bar{p}_t^M$ [15] to some seller S_i, $i < n$ so that each seller receives only one offer. Seller B_n makes the equilibrium offer of the two-person bargaining game with an informed seller. Sellers $1, ..., n-1$ accept their offers, while S_n's response mimics that of the informed seller in the two-person game. B_n has no incentive to deviate because she is essentially playing the two-person game with an informed seller. If some other buyer B_i offers a lower price $p < \bar{p}_t^M$ to seller $i < n$, then this does not help because buyer B_n then offers $p + \epsilon$ to the same seller, who obviously accepts the higher offer. Thus, deviation results in B_i tarding with B_n one period later.

As before, there is also an equilibrium in which buyers who make offers later in the sequence get higher payoffs.[16]

Two Privately-informed Sellers

Suppose now that both sellers are privately informed. If both sellers are ex ante identical, that is, both sellers have an identical probability of being the low type then the four-person market essentially splits up into two two-person markets. The interesting case is when the two sellers are not ex ante identical. In particular, will there still be an equilibrium in which both buyers obtain the same expected payoffs?

---

[15] As before, the price $\bar{p}_t^M$ is such that $v - \bar{p}_t^M = u(\pi_0)$.

[16] The inequality in buyer payoffs will be strict if the reservation values $M_1, ..., M_{n-1}$ are all distinct.

We construct an example in which there is no equilibrium with both buyers obtaining the same expected payoffs.

Let $v = 5$, $H = 4$, $\delta = \dfrac{3}{4}$, $\pi_0^1 = \dfrac{1}{2}$, $\pi_0^2 = \dfrac{4}{7}$, where π_0^1, π_0^2 are the initial probabilities that sellers 1 and 2 are of the low type.

We first calculate the cut-offs q_1, q_2, q_3.

If the probability of the low type is q_1, the buyer (in the two-player game) is indifferent between offering H and δH, the latter being accepted with probability 1 by the low type. This immediately yields:

$$q_1 = \frac{v - H}{v} = \frac{1}{5}$$

Similarly, the buyer is indifferent between offering δH and $\delta^2 H$ when $\pi_0 = q_2$. An offer of δH is accepted with probability 1 by the low type. Let the probability of acceptance of $\delta^2 H$ be α_{21}. So:

$$(v - \delta H)q_2 + (1 - q_2)\delta(v_H) = (v - \delta^2 H)q_2\alpha_{21} + (1 - q_2\alpha_{21})\delta(v - H)$$

Hence:

$$\alpha_{21} = \frac{5}{8}$$

Also, from Bayes Rule:

$$q_2 = \frac{q_1}{1 - \alpha_{21}(1 - q_1)} = \frac{2}{5}$$

When $\pi_0 = q_3$, the buyer is indifferent between offering $\delta^2 H$ and $\delta^3 H$. Let $V_B(\delta^3 H)$ and $V_B(q_2)$ denote the buyer's expected payoff from the offer $\delta^3 H$ and the equilibrium payoff when $\pi_0 = q2$. Then:

$$V_B(\delta^3 H) = (v - \delta^3 H)q_3\alpha_{32} + (1 - q_3\alpha_{32})\delta V_B(q_2) \quad (11.3)$$

where α_{32} is the probability of acceptance which along with Bayes Rule implies that the updated probability of the seller being the Low type is q_2. Now:

$$V_B(q_2) = (v - \delta H)q_2 + (1 - q_2)\delta(v - H) = \frac{5}{4}$$

Substituting in Equation (11.3), we get:

$$V_B(\delta^3 H) = \frac{53}{16} q_3 \alpha_{32} + (1 - q_3 \alpha_{32}) \frac{15}{16}$$

Also:

$$V_B(\delta^2 H) = (v - \delta^2 H) q_3 \alpha_{31} + (1 - q_3 \alpha_{31}) \delta(v - H)$$
$$= \frac{11}{4} q_3 \alpha_{31} + (1 - q_3 \alpha_{31}) \frac{3}{4}$$

where α_{31} is the probabbility of acceptance by the low type which results in an updated probability of $\pi = q_1$.

Equating $V_B(\delta^2 H)$ and $V_B(\delta^2 H)$ yields:

$$16 a_{31} - 19 a_{32} = \frac{3}{2} \qquad (11.4)$$

where $a_{ik} = q_i \alpha_{ik}$.

Since $(1 - a_{31}) = (1 - a_{32})(1 - a_{21})$, substitution in Equation (11.4) yields $a_{32} = \frac{5}{14}$. Finally, since $q_3 = q_2(1 - a_{32}) + a_{32}$, we have:

$$q_3 = \frac{43}{70}$$

So, $q_1 = \frac{1}{5}$, $q_2 = \frac{2}{5}$, $q_3 = \frac{43}{70}$

Let B_1 make the offer to S_1. We first calculate the expected payoff of B_1.

The offer to S_1 must be $\delta^2 H = \frac{9}{4}$. If a denotes the probability of acceptance by the low type, then the updated probability, after rejection, is q_1. Hence:

$$q_1 = \frac{\pi_0^1 - a}{1 - a}$$

This yields:

$$a = \frac{3}{8}$$

When the updated probability that S_1 is the low type is q_1, the buyer is indifferent between offering H and δH. So, the expected payoff of B_1 is:

$$E(B_1) = (v - \delta^2 H)a + (1-a)\delta(v-H) = \frac{3}{2}$$

So, we need to check whether there is an equilibrium in the four-player game where $E(B_2) = \frac{3}{2}$. First, there cannot be such an equilibrium where S_2 accepts the price offer with probability 1. For suppose there is indeed such an equilibrium. Then, since rejection will imply that the seller is of type H, the price offer p must be at least $\delta H = 3$. But if $p \geq 3$, then:

$$E(B_2) \leq (v-3)\pi_0^2 + (1-\pi_0^2)\delta(v-H) = \frac{41}{28} < \frac{3}{2}$$

Suppose that an offer of p brings forth a mixed response from the low type of S_2. Since S_2 is indifferent between accepting and rejecting p, p must equal the discounted value of the seller's expected payoff if he rejects p. The latter is calculated as follows. With probability $a = \frac{3}{8}$, the other seller has accepted the offer, and so this is the probability with which S_2 will be involved in a two-player game in the next period. The next period is a four-player game with residual probability. In this game, the equilibrium offer (to S_1) is $\delta H = 3$. Letting $\hat{\pi}$ denote the updated probability that S_2 is of the Low type, we get:

$$p = \delta\left[aV_S(\hat{\pi}) + (1-a)\delta H\right] \tag{11.5}$$

where $V_S(\hat{\pi})$ is the equilibrium offer to S in the two-player game when the initial probability of the Low, type is $\hat{\pi}$.

Case 1 $\hat{\pi} > q_2$. Then, $V_S(\hat{\pi}) = \delta^2 H = \frac{9}{4}$. Substituting in Equation (11.5), we get:

$$p = \frac{261}{128}$$

We now calculate the expected payoff to B_2. Let $\hat{a}$ denote the probability with which p is accepted by B_2. Since $\hat{a}$ results in the updated probability of $\hat{\pi}$ (from π_0^2):

$$\hat{a} = \frac{\pi_0^2 - \hat{\pi}}{1 - \hat{\pi}}$$

Also, let $V_B(\hat{\pi})$ denote the expected payoff to the buyer in the two-person game when the initial probability that the seller is of the low type is $\hat{\pi}$. Then:

$$V_B(\hat{\pi}) = (v - \delta^2 H)\frac{\hat{\pi} - \frac{1}{5}}{1 - \frac{1}{5}} + \frac{1 - \hat{\pi}}{1 - \frac{1}{5}}\delta(v - H)$$

$$= \frac{1}{4}(10\hat{\pi} + 1)$$

So:

$$E(B_2) = (v - p)\hat{a} + (1 - \hat{a})\delta(aV_B)(\hat{\pi}) + (1 - a)(v - H)$$

$$= \left(5 - \frac{261}{128}\right)\frac{\left(\frac{4}{7} - \hat{\pi}\right)}{(1 - \hat{\pi})} + \frac{\frac{3}{7}}{(1 - \hat{\pi})}\frac{3}{4}\left(\frac{3}{8}\frac{1}{4}\{10\hat{\pi} + 1\} + \frac{5}{8}\right)$$

$$= \frac{379}{128}\left(\frac{4 - 7\hat{\pi}}{7(1 - \hat{\pi})}\right) + \frac{9}{28(1 - \hat{\pi})}\left(\frac{15\hat{\pi}}{16} + \frac{23}{32}\right)$$

$$\frac{1723 - 2383\hat{\pi}}{896(1 - \hat{\pi})}$$

Equating this to $E(B_1) = \frac{3}{2}$ yields:

$$\hat{\pi} = \frac{379}{1039} < 0.4 = q_2$$

Hence, Case 1 cannot occur.

Case 2 Suppose $\hat{\pi} \in (q_1, q_2)$.

Then, $V(\hat{\pi}) = \delta H = 3$.

Substituting in Equation (12.5), we get:

$$p = \frac{9}{4}$$

Then, the expected payoff to B_2 is:

$$E(B_2) = \left(5 - \frac{9}{4}\right) \frac{\frac{4}{7} - \hat{\pi}}{1 - \hat{\pi}} + \frac{\frac{3}{7}}{(1-\hat{\pi})} \frac{3}{4} \left(\frac{3}{8}\left\{\frac{5}{4}\hat{\pi} + \frac{3}{4}\right\} + \frac{5}{8}\right)$$

$$= \frac{44 - 77\hat{\pi}}{28(1-\hat{\pi})} + \frac{9}{28(1-\hat{\pi}_2)} \left(\frac{15}{32}\hat{\pi} + \frac{29}{32}\right)$$

Equating this to $E(B_1) = \frac{3}{2}$ yields $\hat{\pi} > 1$, which is clearly not possible.

This shows that there cannot be an equilibrium in which both buyers get equal expected payoffs.

Remark 5 However, there will be an equilibrium in which B_1 (the first buyer to make an offer) and B_2 both offer $\delta^2 H$ to S_1 and S_2 respectively. The seller-responses are identical to that in the equilibria of the two-person games. In this equilibrium, $E(B_2) > E(B_1)$.

* * *

This chapter attempted to model competition among small numbers of market participants with incomplete information. The small numbers make random matching less desirable as a model and we consider players making targeted offers to particular individuals on the other side. All offers are made by buyers, so as to keep the bargaining-theoretic complexity to a minimum. We find that there are equilibria in which buyers' expected payoffs are equalized in equilibrium if only one of the sellers has private information (adding more buyers and sellers with complete information does not matter). However, if an additional privately informed seller is present, such an equilibrium need not exist and the second buyer to move has an advantage. Surprisingly the competition is always driven by incomplete information and not by the values of the complete information sellers, in contrast to the complete information model.

References

Ausubel, Lawrence M., Peter Cramton, and Raymond Deneckere. 2002. 'Bargaining with Incomplete Information', in Robert J. Aumann and Sergiu Hart (eds), *Handbook of Game Theory*, Vol. 3. Amsterdam: Elsevier Science B.V.: Chapter 50, 1897–945.

Binmore, Kenneth G., and Maria Herrero. 1988. 'Matching and Bargaining in Dynamic Markets', *Review of Economic Studies*, 55: 17–32.

Chatterjee, Kalyan, and Bhaskar Dutta. 1998. 'Rubinstein Auctions: On Competition for Bargaining Partners', *Games and Economic Behavior*, 23(2): 119–45.

Chatterjee, Kalyan, and Larry Samuelson. 1988. 'Bargaining under Two-sided Incomplete Information: The Unrestricted Offers Case', *Operations Research*, 36(4): 605–18.

Deneckere, Raymond, and Meng-Yu Liang. 2001. 'Bargaining with Interdependent Values', Working Paper 20017, UWO Department of Economics.

Fudenberg, Drew, David Levine, and Jean Tirole. 1985. 'Infinite Horizon Models of Bargaining with Incomplete Information', in Alvin E. Roth (ed.), *Game-Theoretic Models of Bargaining*. Cambridge and New York: Cambridge University Press, 73–98.

———. 1987. 'Incomplete Information Bargaining with Outside Opportunities', *Quarterly Journal of Economics*, 102(1): 37–50.

Fudenberg, Drew, and Jean Tirole. 1991. *Game Theory*. Cambridge, MA: MIT Press.

Gale, Douglas. 1986. 'Bargaining and Competition: Part 1, Characterization', *Econometrica*, 54: 785–806.

Hendon, Ebbs, and Torben Tranaes. 1991. 'Sequential Bargaining in a Market with One Seller and Two Different Buyers', *Games and Economic Behavior*, 3(4): 453–66.

Rubinstein, Ariel, and Asher Wolinsky. 1985. 'Equilibrium in a Market with Sequential Bargaining', *Econometrica*, 53: 1133–50.

———. 1990. 'Decentralised Trading, Strategic Behaviour and the Walrasian Outcome', *Review of Economic Studies*, 57: 63–78.

Samuelson, Larry. 1992. 'Disagreement in Markets with Matching and Bargaining', *Review of Economic Studies*, 59: 177–86.

Shubik, Martin. 1982. *Game Theory in the Social Sciences*, Vol. 1, Concepts and Solutions. Cambridge, MA: MIT Press.

Sobel, Joel, and Ichiro Takahashi. 1983. 'A Multistage Model of Bargaining', *Review of Economic Studies*, 50: 411–26.

12

Technology Transfer as a Means to Combat Global Warming

Vivekananda Mukherjee, Dirk T.G. Rübbelke, and Tilak Sanyal

In the run-up to the decisive rounds of negotiations concerning a post-Kyoto agreement, there is much dispute about aspired emission reduction levels as well as about the adequate policies to mitigate greenhouse gas (GHG) emissions. Concerning the latter, one main controversial subject is the procedure for integrating developing countries in the international climate protection architecture.

The question regarding emission reduction targets is only blurredly addressed by the UN Framework Convention on Climate Change (UNFCCC) which was the groundwork for the Kyoto Protocol. The Convention stipulates in Article 2 that the ultimate objective of this Convention is to achieve the stabilization of GHG concentrations in the atmosphere at a level that would prevent dangerous anthropogenic interference with the climate system.

Concerning the adequate policies to mitigate GHG emissions, UNFCCC assigned the main responsibility for combating climate change to the North. A way considered for also involving developing countries in the international abatement efforts is the transfer of cleaner technologies from industrialized towards developing countries.[1] The application of such technologies in developing countries tends to reduce GHG emissions and, due to the public good property of climate protection,[2] to raise global welfare.

Technology transfer (see, for example, Schelling (1992); IPCC (2007); OECD (2011)) as well as R&D (see, for example, Stern (2007)), are regularly regarded as important strategies to combat global warming. Barrett (2006: 22) stresses that 'R&D is especially needed to bring about substantial, long-term reductions in atmospheric concentrations of greenhouse gases'. And Hoel and de Zeeuw (2008: 396) state that the international debate on climate protection agreements 'circles to some extent around the question whether international treaties should focus on technology development rather than on emission reduction.' Benedick (2001) proposes a portfolio of elements for a post-Kyoto plan, which draws heavily on the diffusion of technology. The included elements are emission reduction policies, governmental research development, technology standards, and technology transfer.

IPCC (2000: 58) points to the fact that one salient feature of technology transfer related to global climate change is that of scale. 'Essentially all countries of the world could be involved in the process, and the number of technologies could easily run into the thousands'.

Some strand of scientific literature addresses questions of how environmental policy influences the diffusion of cleaner technology. As Jaffe et al. (2002) point out: 'the long term nature of policy challenges such as that posed by the threat of global climate change makes it all the more important that we improve our understanding of the effects of environmental policy on innovation and diffusion of new technology'.

The flexible clean development mechanism (CDM) of the Kyoto scheme is seen as one important option to push the transfer of

[1] In contrast, Rive and Rübbelke (2010) consider effects of monetary transfers towards developing countries on environmental quality and poverty. They specifically regard transfers channelled via the clean development mechanism.

[2] Put it inversely, 'global climate change is a public good (bad) par excellence' (Arrow 2007: 3).

cleaner technologies. Haites et al. (2006) note that although CDM has no explicit technology transfer mandate, roughly one-third of all CDM-projects involve technology transfer. Dechezleprêtre et al. (2008) even find that 43 per cent of the 644 CDM projects they investigated involved technology transfer and these projects were responsible for 84 per cent of the expected annual CO_2 emission reductions. However, the host countries are very heterogeneous in their capability to attract technology transfer (Dechezleprêtre et al. 2008). Furthermore, Dechezleprêtre et al. (2008) discovered that technology transfers are more likely in large projects and that the probability of technology transfer is 50 per cent higher when the project is developed in a subsidiary of an Annex 1 company; having an official credit buyer in the project also exerts a positive effect on transfer likeliness.

Aslam (2001) investigated the role that CDM could play in enhancing the effectiveness of North-South technology transfer. Millock (2002), in turn, argues that technology transfer can improve incentives for cost-effective emission reductions under bilateral CDM contracts when there is asymmetric information between the investor and the project-hosting party. Glachant and Ménière (2007) evaluated the ability of CDM to yield the optimal diffusion path when firms can adopt a cleaner technology simultaneously or sequentially. Since adaptation involves fixed cost endogenously decreasing with previous adaptation, inefficiencies are created and these are not properly addressed by CDM. Due to these inefficiencies, Glachant and Ménière (2007) propose design improvements.

In contrast to this literature, in this chapter, we do not confine the analysis to a specific (technology) transfer scheme like CDM, although the considered transfers could—in principle—be provided via CDM projects. We analyse costless transfers of technology from industrialized countries towards the developing world in a general equilibrium framework.[3] The focus of the analysis is on the role that

---

[3] Neary (2006) reviews and extends three approaches to trade and environmental policies: competitive general equilibrium, oligopoly, and monopolistic competition. He finds that competitive general equilibrium and oligopoly competition have surprisingly similar implications.

international trade plays with respect to the effects of technology transfer on global environmental protection. The role of trade in international technology transfer is a vivid field of research, as Saggi (2002) illustrates in his survey. Our interest is focused on environmental protection technologies. More precisely, in our analysis we investigate and answer the following research question: Can technology transfer serve as an effective instrument to stabilize global GHG emissions at a level that prevents dangerous anthropogenic interference with the climate system, as claimed by UNFCCC?

Within our analytical framework we regard two different scenarios: (1) the no-trade ('autarkic') situation, and (2) the setting where trade in two commodities takes place. Thus, the basic setting is similar to that proposed by Mukherjee and Rübbelke (2006) but in contrast to their study, we include an immobile polluting input factor into the analysis which can be traded in none of the two scenarios. This polluting input can be regarded to be an 'electric power', whose production causes emissions of the GHG CO_2.

The technology transfer that we regard in our Ricardian model causes a mitigation of GHG emissions per production-output unit. Beladi et al. (1997) as well as Itoh and Tawada (2003) also employ a Ricardian approach to analyse technology transfer. Yet, Beladi et al. (1997) deal only with the transfer of production technologies and do not consider the change in the pollution level associated with the change in the production structure as an effect of trade. Therefore, in their framework, technology transfer from the North to the South is always beneficial. Itoh and Tawada's (2003) study—which adopts the framework of Copeland and Taylor (1999)—investigating the technology transfer issue and its interaction with pollution differs to ours due to differences in the assumptions about abatement commitments. Yang (1999) also considers the pollution-mitigating effect of technology transfers towards the South, but ignores what Copeland and Taylor (2004, 2005) call the 'scale effect', that is, the expansion of the polluting industry. In contrast to our approach, in their analysis of endogenous technical change, Copeland and Taylor (2005) as well as Takarada (2005) do not employ a Ricardian but a Heckscher-Ohlin framework and they do not address the technology transfer issue.

In our study we find a similar set of conditions for the effectiveness of technology transfers in stabilizing global pollution at the desired level and for which the technology transfer offer is accepted by the South as Mukherjee and Rübbelke (2006). The source of pollution is not important in determining the scope of technology transfer and in equilibrium a partial transfer of technology is possible.

The chapter is structured as follows: In the following section, we describe the basic model, while, in the next section, we introduce the policy instrument of technology transfer both in the no-trade and the free-trade scenarios. We elaborate the conditions for which the technology transfer becomes effective in stabilizing global pollution at the desired level and determine the conditions for which it is desirable for the South to accept the offered technology transfer. In the next section, the results from the previous section are discussed and conclusions are drawn.

The Model

Preliminary Remarks

In our framework we assume—in line with Article 4 of UNFCCC—that the main responsibility for combating climate change is assigned to the industrialized world. In this spirit we regard an international climate protection agreement aiming at the stabilization of the global climate which commits only industrialized countries to pursue climate protection policies.[4] Hence, due to these predetermined rules, the issue of strategic interaction about international commitments does not arise in the context analysed here (strategic interactions concerning the countries' negotiations of the rules are disregarded and are assumed to have taken place already at an earlier stage).

Production of Goods

We assume that there are two countries, one is a developed country designated as North (N) and the other is an underdeveloped country

---

[4] Thus, there are similarities to the Kyoto Protocol which also assigned obligations for reducing GHG emissions only to industrialized countries.

designated as South (S). Each country produces two distinct private goods X_1 and X_2 which are used for final consumption. These goods are produced with the help of the primary input labour and an intermediate input X_3. X_3 is again produced by labour only, but the production of X_3 causes pollution by emitting CO_2. For simplicity, we assume that one unit of X_3 production emits one unit of CO_2. Thus X_3 is an impure public commodity as it has private good properties along with a public bad property by creating a negative externality all over the world (for the concept of 'impure public goods' see, for example, Cornes and Sandler (1996)). Suppose both the countries have the technology to abate pollution but the North has a better technology than the South. We assume that the ith country abates the fraction ψ^i of CO_2 emissions per unit of X_3 production using labour, where $\psi^i \in (0, 1)$. So the final emission of CO_2 in the ith country becomes $\phi^i = 1 - \psi^i$ per unit of X_3 production.

Let us suppose that the labour endowment of the ith country is L^i; $L^i \neq L^j$, $\forall i \neq j$. Both countries have full employment of labour such that we obtain the following equations for the ith country:

$$L^i = a_1^i X_1^i + a_2^i X_2^i + a_3^i X_3^i + a_4^i \psi^i X_3^i \tag{12.1}$$

and

$$X_3^i = a_{31}^i X_1^i + a_{32}^i X_2^i . \tag{12.2}$$

Here a_j^i is the labour coefficient for the jth good in the ith country. It represents the amount of labour required to produce one unit of the jth good in the ith country, $\forall j = 1, 2, 3$, and $\forall i = N, S$. a_4^i is the amount of labour required to abate the fraction ψ^i of one unit of CO_2 in the ith country. And a_{3k}^i is the amount of X_3 required as intermediate input to produce one unit of the kth good in the ith country, $\forall k = 1, 2$.

By substituting the value of X_3^i from (12.2) into (12.1) we derive the equation of the production possibility frontier (PPF) for the ith country:

$$L^i = [a_1^i + (a_3^i + a_4^i \psi^i) a_{31}^i] X_1^i + [a_2^i + (a_3^i + a_4^i \psi^i) a_{32}^i] X_2^i . \tag{12.3}$$

We assume that the North is more efficient in the production of X_1, X_2, and X_3 and also in the abatement process than the South. So, all the labour coefficients of the North are lower than the corresponding labour coefficients of the South.

Assumption 1 In either country X_1 is relatively more pollution-intensive in production.

Assumption 1 implies: $\dfrac{a_{31}^i}{a_1^i + (a_3^i + a_4^i \psi^i) a_{31}^i} > \dfrac{a_{32}^i}{a_2^i + (a_3^i + a_4^i \psi^i) a_{32}^i}$
for all $i = N, S$.

Let us call the pollution intensity gap of the ith country as χ^i. So
$$\chi^i = \dfrac{a_{31}^i}{a_1^i + (a_3^i + a_4^i \psi^i) a_{31}^i} - \dfrac{a_{32}^i}{a_2^i + (a_3^i + a_4^i \psi^i) a_{32}^i}.$$

Utility Functions

Each country receives a positive utility from consuming X_1 and X_2. Yet the consumption of these goods inflicts a negative external effect on the other country. This is because consumption of these goods demands production of X_3 which gives rise to global pollution. Thus, in the process of consumption of X_1 and X_2, the society also has a disutility arising out of pollution. Accordingly we write the welfare function of the ith country as:

$$U^i = U(X_1^i, X_2^i) - v(R). \qquad (12.4)$$

In (12.4), R represents the global pollution level. Thus, it holds:

$$R = \phi^N X_3^N + \phi^S X_3^S. \qquad (12.5)$$

We consider $U(X_1^i, X_2^i)$ as being a continuous, twice differentiable, and strictly quasi-concave function over the domain $X_1^i, X_2^i \geq 0$. It also has the following properties: $U_1, U_2, U_{12} = U_{21} > 0$ and $U_{11}, U_{22} < 0$. We assume that the environmental disutility function $v(R)$ is a strictly increasing and convex function over the domain $X_1^i, X_2^i \geq 0$ that $v'(R) > 0$ and $v''(R) > 0$.

Assumption 2 $U_j > v'$ for $j = 1, 2$.

Assumption 2 implies that either of the countries attaches higher weight to consumption of the commodities rather than to the emission generated in their production. So, even if the countries have pollution concerns, they prefer to produce on their PPF than inside it and always maintain full employment. In other words, Assumption 2 implies that the ith country's production plan must satisfy (12.3).

Substituting the value of X_3^i from (12.2) in (12.5) we get:

$$R = \phi^N(a_{31}^N X_1^N + a_{32}^N X_2^N) + \phi^S(a_{31}^S X_1^S + a_{32}^S X_2^S). \tag{12.6}$$

The Equilibrium without Commitment

In the absence of a global planner and any commitments concerning the control of global GHG emissions, individual countries decide about their production plans strategically without coordination. The global pollution level is determined by the Nash behaviour of individual countries.

In the Nash equilibrium, the ith country maximizes its welfare function in (12.4) subject to the equation of the PPF in (12.3). Thus, the maximization problem for the ith country is:

$$\underset{\{X_1^i > 0, X_2^i > 0\}}{\text{Max}} \quad U^i = U(X_1^i, X_2^i) - v(R)$$

subject to $L^i = [a_1^i + (a_3^i + a_4^i \psi^i)a_{31}^i]X_1^i + [a_2^i + (a_3^i + a_4^i \psi^i)a_{32}^i]X_2^i,$

where $R = \phi^N(a_{31}^N X_1^N + a_{32}^N X_2^N) + \phi^S(a_{31}^S X_1^S + a_{32}^S X_2^S).$

Substituting $X_2^i = \dfrac{L^i - [a_1^i + (a_3^i + a_4^i \psi^i)a_{31}^i]X_1^i}{[a_2^i + (a_3^i + a_4^i \psi^i)a_{32}^i]}$ and

$X_2^j = \dfrac{L^j - [a_1^j + (a_3^j + a_4^j \psi^j)a_{31}^j]X_1^j}{[a_2^j + (a_3^j + a_4^j \psi^j)a_{32}^j]} \quad \forall i, j = N, S; i \neq j$ in the objective function, the utility maximization problem of the ith country becomes:

$$\text{Max } U^i = U\left(X_1^i, \frac{L^i - [a_1^i + (a_3^i + a_4^i \psi^i)a_{31}^i]X_1^i}{[a_2^i + (a_3^i + a_4^i \psi^i)a_{32}^i]}\right)$$

$$-v\left\{\phi^i\left(a_{31}^i X_1^i + a_{32}^i \frac{L^i - [a_1^i + (a_3^i + a_4^i \psi^i)a_{31}^i]X_1^i}{[a_2^i + (a_3^i + a_4^i \psi^i)a_{32}^i]}\right)\right.$$

$$\left.+\phi^j\left(a_{31}^j X_1^j + a_{32}^j \frac{L^j - [a_1^j + (a_3^j + a_4^j \psi^j)a_{31}^j]X_1^j}{[a_2^j + (a_3^j + a_4^j \psi^j)a_{32}^j]}\right)\right\}. \quad (12.7)$$

Maximizing U^i as given in (12.7), with respect to $X_1^i > 0$, yields the following first order condition:

$$U_1 - U_2\left(\frac{[a_1^i + (a_3^i + a_4^i \psi^i)a_{31}^i]}{[a_2^i + (a_3^i + a_4^i \psi^i)a_{32}^i]}\right) - v'$$

$$\left[\phi^i a_{31}^i - \phi^i a_{32}^i\left(\frac{[a_1^i + (a_3^i + a_4^i \psi^i)a_{31}^i]}{[a_2^i + (a_3^i + a_4^i \psi^i)a_{32}^i]}\right)\right] = 0. \quad (12.8)$$

Since $U(X_1^i, X_2^i)$ is strictly quasi-concave and $v(R)$ is strictly convex, the entire welfare function is strictly quasi-concave. This implies that the second-order condition for this constrained maximization problem is also satisfied.

Equation (12.8) yields $X_1^i = f^i(X_1^j)$ which is the reaction function of the ith country with respect to j's choice of X_1. If X_1^j rises by one unit the global pollution level also rises. This increases the disutility of the ith country and reduces its welfare. In order to increase its welfare to the maximum level the ith country internalizes the negative externality by reducing its own output of X_1. Hence, we have $\frac{dX_1^i}{dX_1^j} < 0, \forall i \neq j$. Consequently, the reaction function of the ith country $\forall i = 1, 2$ has a negative slope. The Nash equilibrium (X_1^{N*}, X_1^{S*}) satisfies the reaction functions of both North and South. We assume that a unique interior Nash equilibrium exists of the game described earlier. The stability of the Nash equilibrium demands that the slope of the reaction function of the North ($A_N B_N$) must be steeper than the slope of the reaction function of the South ($A_S B_S$). In Figure 12.1, point E represents the Nash equilibrium.

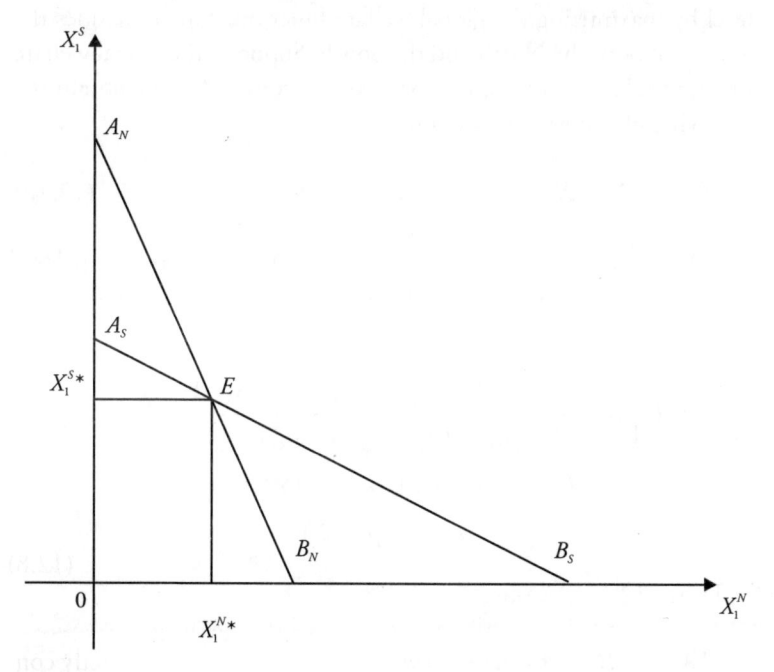

Figure 12.1 The Nash equilibrium

Substituting the value of X_1^{i*} in (12.3), X_2^{i*} is obtained. Substituting these values of X_1^{i*} and X_2^{i*} in Equation (12.2), we derive the optimum production of the polluting good in the ith country as X_3^{i*}. Thus, the pollution caused by the ith country is $\phi^i X_3^{i*}$. Hence, the global pollution level at Nash equilibrium becomes:

$$R^* = \phi^N X_3^{N*} + \phi^S X_3^{S*}. \tag{12.9}$$

Here, the global pollution level is determined through independent actions of the North and the South. Neither of them cares about the negative externality it imposes on the other country when choosing its production plans. In the next subsection we show that R^* overshoots the globally desired pollution level.

Globally Desired Level and the Overshooting of Nash Pollution Level

If there were a global planner, she would choose the global emission level by maximizing the global welfare function, which includes the welfare of both the North and the South. Suppose, the global welfare function takes the utilitarian form, then, from (12.4) we obtain the following global welfare function:

$$W = U(X_1^N, X_2^N) + U(X_1^S, X_2^S) - 2v(R). \qquad (12.10)$$

Substituting the value of X_2^i from (12.3) into the respective country's utility function, the global welfare function can be written as:

$$W = U\left(X_1^N, \frac{L^N - [a_1^N + (a_3^N + a_4^N \psi^N)a_{31}^N]X_1^N}{[a_2^N + (a_3^N + a_4^N \psi^N)a_{32}^N]}\right) + U\left(X_1^S, \frac{L^S - [a_1^S + (a_3^S + a_4^S \psi^S)a_{31}^S]X_1^S}{[a_2^S + (a_3^S + a_4^S \psi^S)a_{32}^S]}\right) - 2v(R). \qquad (12.11)$$

From (12.11) we observe:

$$\frac{\partial W}{\partial X_1^i} = \left(\frac{\partial U}{\partial X_1^i} - \frac{\partial v(R)}{\partial X_1^i}\right) - \frac{\partial v}{\partial X_1^i} \quad \forall i = N, S. \qquad (12.12)$$

The global planner chooses $(\bar{X}_1^N, \bar{X}_1^S)$ by setting $\frac{\partial W}{\partial X_1^i} = 0$ $\forall i = N, S$. The choice stands in contrast to the Nash equilibrium choice made by each of the countries without any regard to the negative externality $\frac{\partial v(R)}{\partial X_1^i} > 0$ they impose on each other. At (X_1^{N*}, X_1^{S*}) the ith country sets $\left(\frac{\partial U}{\partial X_1^i} - \frac{\partial v(R)}{\partial X_1^i}\right) = 0$. Since $\frac{\partial v(R)}{\partial X_1^i} > 0$ and $\frac{\partial^2 W}{\partial X_1^{i2}} < 0$, it must be $\bar{X}_1^N < X_1^{N*}$ and $\bar{X}_1^S < X_1^{S*}$.

So the desired level of global pollution becomes:

$$\bar{R} = \phi^N \bar{X}_3^N + \phi^S \bar{X}_3^S. \qquad (12.13)$$

Since $\overline{X}_1^N < X_1^{N*}$ and $\overline{X}_1^S < X_1^{S*}$ clearly $R^* > \overline{R}$: the Nash equilibrium pollution level overshoots the global optimum due to lack of coordination between the countries.

Now let us assume that for solving the coordination problem the North commits to an international protocol which aims to stabilize the global emission levels at $\overline{R}$, while the South does not make any such commitment. Since X_1 is more pollution-intensive than X_2, North chooses to reduce the output of X_1 to keep its commitment. Then, given the stock of technology, the North will produce an amount $(X_1^N < X_1^{N*}, X_2^N > X_2^{N*})$ which requires X_3^N amount of the intermediate input such that the following equality holds:

$$\phi^N X_3^N + \phi^S X_3^{S*} = \overline{R}. \tag{12.14}$$

Yet, the North also realizes that corresponding to any of its choice of $X_1^N < X_1^{N*}$, there is a best response output of the South given by $f^S(X_1^N)$. Since X_1^N and X_1^S are strategic substitutes of each other, it holds that $f^S(X_1^N) > X_1^{S*}$. Because of the rebound effect it will be impossible for the North to keep its commitment unless it reduces its output of commodity 1 further. However, the South will respond to the change by choosing a still higher value of compared to its previous choice, forcing the North to make a further cut. This process continues until an equilibrium is reached where the North stops producing commodity 1. In Figure 12.1, the new equilibrium is represented by the point A_S, where $X_1^{NI} = 0$, $X_1^{SI} > 0$. Although $X_1^{NI} = 0$, the North still produces some amount of $X_2^{NI} > 0$ to maintain full employment of labour (this follows from Assumption 2). Moreover, since $X_1^{SI} > X_1^{S*}$, there is no guarantee that (12.14) is satisfied. If (12.14) is satisfied, then the North's sacrifice serves the purpose. Otherwise, North's sacrifice fails to meet the objective. Hence, there arises a case for transfer of abatement technology from the North to the South. In the next section, we check if the North can do better in fulfilling its objective by transferring its abatement technology to the South.

Technology Transfer

Technology Transfer under Autarky

Suppose the abatement technology available in the North is divisible. So it can choose to transfer either the entire technology or a part of it to the South. For example, the different parts of a technology include its blueprint, technical knowledge and expertise, maintenance, operating and servicing knowledge, and so on. Let the North chooses to transfer $\theta \in \left[\dfrac{\psi^S}{\psi^N}, 1\right]$ proportion of its better abatement technology ψ^N to the South free of charge. If θ^* represents the optimal choice by the North, then $\theta^* = \dfrac{\psi^S}{\psi^N}$ implies 'no technology transfer'. This is because the South's technology remains unchanged at ψ^S. On the other hand, $\theta^* = 1$ implies 'complete transfer of technology' as the South's technology changes to ψ^N. Any value of $\theta^* \in \left(\dfrac{\psi^S}{\psi^N}, 1\right)$ represents 'partial technology transfer'. In this case South's technology changes to $\theta^* \psi^N$.

If the North transfers its technology to the South, the South's reaction function shifts in the outward direction. Hence, from Figure 12.1 the new Nash equilibrium point shifts in the north-west direction of E. Clearly, after the transfer of technology takes place, the North produces less of good 1 as compared to the pre-transfer situation, that is, $\breve{X}_1^N(\theta^*) < X_1^{N*}$. On the other hand, the South's production of good 1 increases. Thus, it holds that $\breve{X}_1^S(\theta^*) < X_1^{S*}$.

From (12.6) we get the value of the global emission level in the new equilibrium as:

$$R(\theta^*) = \phi^N(a_{31}^N \breve{X}_1^N + a_{32}^N \breve{X}_2^N)$$
$$+ (1 - \theta^* \psi^N)(a_{31}^S \breve{X}_1^S + a_{32}^S \breve{X}_2^S). \qquad (12.15)$$

Let us denote the labour coefficients of X_1^i and X_2^i in (12.3) as α^i and β^i respectively, $\forall i = N, S$. Observe that after receiving the technology from North, the labour coefficients of the South become $\alpha^S(\theta^*)$ and $\beta^S(\theta^*)$. Substituting $\breve{X}_2^i = \dfrac{L^i - \alpha^i \breve{X}_1^i}{\beta^i}$

from (12.3) in (12.15), we can rewrite the amount of global emissions as:

$$R(\theta^*) = \phi^N \left[a_{31}^N \breve{X}_1^N + a_{32}^N \left(\frac{L^N - \alpha^N \breve{X}_1^N}{\beta^N} \right) \right] + (1 - \theta^* \psi^N)$$
$$\left[a_{31}^S \breve{X}_1^S + a_{32}^S \left(\frac{L^S - \alpha^S (\theta^*)}{\beta^S (\theta^*)} \right) \right]. \quad (12.16)$$

If no technology is transferred, that is, $\theta^* = \frac{\psi^S}{\psi^N}$, then $R\left(\frac{\psi^S}{\psi^N}\right) = R^* > \bar{R}$. So for achieving $R^* = \bar{R}$, the necessary condition requires that $\frac{dR}{d\theta} < 0$ for all values of $\theta^* \in \left(\frac{\psi^S}{\psi^N}, 1\right)$. Let us define $\varepsilon_1^N = -\frac{dX_1^N}{d\theta} \times \frac{\theta}{X_1^N}$ and $\varepsilon_1^S = \frac{dX_1^S}{d\theta} \times \frac{\theta}{X_1^S}$ where ε_1^i is the elasticity of output of good 1 of the ith country in response to a change in the extent of technology transfer. Observe $\frac{dR}{d\theta} < 0$ holds if the following condition is satisfied:

$$\varepsilon_1^S < \frac{\theta^*}{(1 - \theta^* \psi^N) \alpha^S (\theta^*) \chi^S \breve{X}_1^S} \left[\psi^N \breve{X}_3^S + \frac{\phi^N \alpha^N \chi^N \breve{X}_1^N}{\theta^*} \varepsilon_1^N \right.$$
$$\left. + (1 - \theta^* \psi^N) \frac{a_{32}^S}{\beta^S (\theta^*)} \left(\alpha^{S\prime} \breve{X}_1^S + \beta^{S\prime} \breve{X}_2^S \right) \right]. \quad (12.17)$$

We have already argued earlier that $R\left(\frac{\psi^S}{\psi^N}\right) = R^* > \bar{R}$, and thus, if $R(1) < \bar{R}$, then there exists a value of $\theta = \theta^* \in \left(\frac{\psi^S}{\psi^N}, 1\right)$ for which $R(\theta^*) = \bar{R}$. A partial technology transfer can achieve the global optimum. Similarly, if $R(1) = \bar{R}$, then we also have $\theta^* = 1$. In this case only the complete technology transfer achieves the global optimum. But if $R(1) > \bar{R}$, then no amount of technology transfer can bring about the global optimum.

After having looked at the necessary and sufficient condition for technology transfer to bring about the global optimum, we still have to address the question whether the South would accept the technology offers of the North. This question is important because even if the transfer of technology achieves the global optimum, it can only do so if the South is willing to accept the offer. If the technology transfer adversely affects the South, then it will decline the offer and hence the North's initiative to stabilize the level of CO_2 in the atmosphere will fail even though inequality (12.17) holds.

The South chooses the value of $\breve{X}_1^S$ to maximize its utility function given as:

$$U^S = U\left(\breve{X}_1^S, \frac{L^S - \alpha^S(\theta^*)\breve{X}_1^S}{\beta^S(\theta^*)}\right) - v[R(\theta^*)].$$

The South accepts the technology offer of the North only when $\frac{dU^S}{d\theta} \geq 0, \forall \theta^* \in \left[\frac{\psi^S}{\psi^N}, 1\right]$. Defining $\xi = -\frac{dR}{d\theta} \times \frac{\theta^*}{R}$, the necessary condition for the South to accept the technology offer becomes:

$$\varepsilon_1^S \geq \frac{\theta^* \beta^S(\theta^*)}{\breve{X}_1^S[\beta^S(\theta^*)U_1 - \alpha^S(\theta^*)U_2]}$$
$$\left[\frac{v'R}{\theta^*}\xi + \frac{U_2}{\beta^S(\theta^*)}\left(\alpha^{S\prime}\breve{X}_1^S + \beta^{S\prime}\breve{X}_2^S\right)\right]. \quad (12.18)$$

Combining (12.17) and (12.18), we get the first proposition.
Proposition 1 If the necessary condition given by:

$$\frac{\theta^* \beta^S(\theta^*)}{\breve{X}_1^S[\beta^S(\theta^*)U_1 - \alpha^S(\theta^*)U_2]}\left[\frac{v'R}{\theta^*}\xi + \frac{U_2}{\beta^S(\theta^*)}\left(\alpha^{S\prime}\breve{X}_1^S + \beta^{S\prime}\breve{X}_2^S\right)\right]$$
$$\leq \varepsilon_1^S < \frac{\theta^*}{(1-\theta^*\psi^N)\alpha^S(\theta^*)\chi^S \breve{X}_1^S}$$
$$\left[\psi^N \breve{X}_3^S + \frac{\phi^N \alpha^N \chi^N \breve{X}_1^N}{\theta^*}\varepsilon_1^N + (1-\theta^*\psi^N)\frac{a_{32}^S}{\beta^S(\theta^*)}\left(\alpha^{S\prime}\breve{X}_1^S + \beta^{S\prime}\breve{X}_2^S\right)\right]$$

holds, the North's choice of technology transfer $\theta^* \in \left[\dfrac{\psi_S}{\psi_N}, 1\right]$ is capable to stabilize the global emission level at the global optimum.

Proof The discussion earlier.

In the next section we observe how the North strives for fulfilment of its commitment under free trade.

Technology Transfer under Free Trade

We assume that the North has comparative advantage in the production of relatively less pollution-intensive good 2 and the South has comparative advantage in the production of relatively more pollution-intensive good 1. This pattern of comparative advantage determines the pattern of production specialization by the countries in the trading equilibrium. We denote the relative price of good 2 in the free trade equilibrium $\dfrac{p_2}{p_1}$ by p. The value of p is determined by the forces of demand and supply in the international market. Thus, at the trading equilibrium the following inequality holds:

$$\frac{a_1^N + (a_3^N + a_4^N \psi^N) a_{31}^N}{a_2^N + (a_3^N + a_4^N \psi^N) a_{32}^N} \geq \frac{1}{p} \geq \frac{a_1^S + (a_3^S + a_4^S \psi^S) a_{31}^S}{a_2^S + (a_3^S + a_4^S \psi^S) a_{32}^S}. \qquad (12.19)$$

Whatever the value of p determined at the international market, each country takes it as given.

Case 1 $\quad \dfrac{a_1^N + (a_3^N + a_4^N \psi^N) a_{31}^N}{a_2^N + (a_3^N + a_4^N \psi^N) a_{32}^N} > \dfrac{1}{p} > \dfrac{a_1^S + (a_3^S + a_4^S \psi^S) a_{31}^S}{a_2^S + (a_3^S + a_4^S \psi^S) a_{32}^S}$

In this case, according to the pattern of comparative advantage as prevailing in the Ricardian model of trade, the North completely specializes in the production of commodity 2 and the South completely specializes in the production of commodity 1. So in the trading equilibrium, the North produces $\left(\hat{X}_1^N = 0, \hat{X}_2^N = \dfrac{L^N}{\alpha^N}\right)$ while the South produces $\left(\hat{X}_1^S = \dfrac{L^S}{\alpha^S}, \hat{X}_2^S = 0\right)$. Yet, both countries consume both of the goods at international prices p_1 and p_2. The consumption levels in each country are determined in the equilibrium by maximization of (12.4), subject to their respective budget constraints.

Suppose $\left(\tilde{X}_1^N, \tilde{X}_2^N\right)$ represent the consumption levels of the North in the equilibrium. So its budget constraint becomes:

$$\tilde{X}_1^N + p\tilde{X}_2^N = p\frac{L^N}{\alpha^N}. \tag{12.20}$$

Similarly, if we consider the equilibrium consumption levels of the South as $\left(\tilde{X}_1^S, \tilde{X}_2^S\right)$, its budget constraint becomes:

$$\tilde{X}_1^S + p\tilde{X}_2^S = \frac{L^S}{\alpha^S}. \tag{12.21}$$

The value of p is determined by the world market clearing condition of good 1:

$$\tilde{X}_1^N(p) + \tilde{X}_1^S(p) = \frac{L^S}{\alpha^S}. \tag{12.22}$$

The extent of global pollution in the trading equilibrium is given by:

$$R = \phi^N a_{32}^N \hat{X}_2^N + \phi^S a_{31}^S \hat{X}_1^S. \tag{12.23}$$

Observation 1 $R > \bar{R}$.

Proof The complete specialization in production leads to a more efficient production pattern compared to the autarkic situation. Thus, we have $\hat{X}_2^N > X_2^{N*} + X_2^{S*}$. Similarly we can also argue that $\hat{X}_1^S > X_1^{N*} + X_1^{S*}$.

Multiplying both sides of $\hat{X}_2^N > X_2^{N*} + X_2^{S*}$ by $\phi^N a_{32}^N$ yields $\phi^N a_{32}^N \hat{X}_2^N > \phi^N a_{32}^N X_2^{N*} + \phi^N a_{32}^N X_2^{S*}$. Note that $\phi^N < \phi^S$ and $a_{32}^N < a_{32}^S$. Hence, we get $\phi^N a_{32}^N X_2^{N*} + \phi^N a_{32}^N X_2^{S*} < \phi^N a_{32}^N X_2^{N*} + \phi^S a_{32}^S X_2^{S*}$. Consequently, we arrive at $\phi^N a_{32}^N \hat{X}_2^N \gtrless \phi^N a_{32}^N X_2^{N*} + \phi^S a_{32}^S X_2^{S*}$.

Again multiplying both sides of $\hat{X}_1^S > X_1^{N*} + X_1^{S*}$ by $\phi^S a_{31}^S$ yields $\phi^S a_{31}^S \hat{X}_1^S > \phi^S a_{31}^S X_1^{N*} + \phi^S a_{31}^S X_1^{S*}$ As before we face $a_{31}^N < a_{31}^S$. Hence, we observe that $\phi^S a_{31}^S X_1^{N*} + \phi^S a_{31}^S X_1^{S*} > \phi^N a_{31}^N X_1^{N*} + \phi^S a_{31}^S X_1^{S*}$. Finally, we obtain $\phi^S a_{31}^S \hat{X}_1^S > \phi^N a_{31}^N X_1^{N*} + \phi^S a_{31}^S X_1^{S*}$.

So far we have $\phi^N a_{32}^N \hat{X}_2^N + \phi^S a_{31}^S \hat{X}_1^S \gtreqless \phi^N a_{32}^N X_2^{N*} + \phi^S a_{32}^S X_2^{S*} + \phi^N a_{31}^N X_1^{N*} + \phi^S a_{31}^S X_1^{S*}$, i.e. $R \gtreqless \overline{R}$.

If $\phi^N a_{32}^N \hat{X}_2^N \geq \phi^N a_{32}^N X_2^{N*} + \phi^S a_{32}^S X_2^{S*}$, then we can conclude that $R > \overline{R}$. Yet, even if $\phi^N a_{32}^N \hat{X}_2^N < \phi^N a_{32}^N X_2^{N*} + \phi^S a_{32}^S X_2^{S*}$, the fact that production of one unit of commodity 1 creates more pollution than the production of one unit of commodity 2 implies that $(\phi^S a_{31}^S \hat{X}_1^S - \phi^N a_{31}^N X_1^{N*} - \phi^S a_{31}^S X_1^{S*}) > (\phi^N a_{32}^N X_2^{N*} + \phi^S a_{32}^S X_2^{S*} - \phi^N a_{32}^N \hat{X}_2^N)$. Hence, it follows that $R > \overline{R}$.

This completes the proof.

This observation creates scope for technology transfer from the North to the South in the present situation.

As the North transfers its abatement technology to the South the PPF of the South shifts in the outward direction. Since it specializes completely in the production of commodity 1, its respective production increases. Furthermore, the better technology reduces the extent of pollution per unit of output. So there is no guarantee that the global pollution level R will decline to $\overline{R}$. In this situation the important question is: Should the North also adjust its output of commodity 2 to ensure $R > \overline{R}$? Note that Assumption 2 ensures that the countries always produce on their PPF. Now if the North reduces its output of commodity 2 as a part of the adjustment mechanism, then it will have to increase the output of commodity 1 to maintain full employment of labour. This implies it must specialize incompletely in equilibrium. However, an increase in output of good 1 by one unit raises emissions to a much higher extent than the reduction of output of good 2 by one unit mitigates emissions. Thus, it is clear that such adjustment by the North cannot stabilize the global pollution level at $\overline{R}$. Since it is the commitment of the North to stabilize the global pollution level at $\overline{R}$, it will never reduce its production of commodity 2. Consequently, the North will choose the extent of technology transfer in such a way that the reduction in the emission effect outweighs the scale effect in the South.

The global emission level in the post technology transfer equilibrium is given as:

$$R(\theta^*) = \phi^N a_{32}^N \hat{X}_2^N + (1 - \theta^* \psi^N) a_{31}^S \hat{X}_1^S.$$

If no technology is transferred, that is, $\theta^* = \dfrac{\psi^S}{\psi^N}$, then $R\left(\dfrac{\psi^S}{\psi^N}\right) > \bar{R}$. Thus, for achieving $R^* = \bar{R}$ it is necessary that $R(\theta^*)$ shrinks to $\bar{R}$ as the higher values of θ^* are chosen, that is, it requires $\dfrac{dR}{d\theta} < 0 \ \forall \ \theta^* \in \left(\dfrac{\psi^S}{\psi^N}, 1\right)$. $\dfrac{dR}{d\theta} < 0$ in turn requires:

$$\varepsilon_1^S < \frac{\theta^* \psi^N}{1 - \theta^* \psi^N}. \tag{12.24}$$

$\dfrac{dR}{d\theta} < 0$ ensures that $R(\theta^*)$ is a monotonically decreasing function over the domain $\theta^* \in \left[\dfrac{\psi^S}{\psi^N}, 1\right]$. Since we have already argued earlier that $R\left(\dfrac{\psi^S}{\psi^N}\right) > \bar{R}$, if $R(1) < \bar{R}$ as well, there exists a value of $\theta = \bar{\theta} \in \left(\dfrac{\psi^S}{\psi^N}, 1\right)$ such that $R(\theta^*) = \bar{R}$. A partial technology transfer by the North is capable of achieving the global optimum. By a similar argument it follows that if $R(1) = \bar{R}$, it must hold that $\theta^* = 1$. In this case, only the complete technology transfer by the North achieves the global optimum. If $R(1) > \bar{R}$, no amount of technology transfer is capable of achieving the global optimum.

Next, we look at the condition for which the technology transfer is accepted by the South.

The indirect welfare of the South in the post transfer equilibrium is given by:

$$U^S = U\left(\tilde{X}_1^S, \tilde{X}_2^S\right) - v\left[R(\theta^*)\right].$$

The South accepts the technology transfer offer of the North only when $\frac{dU^S}{d\theta} \geq 0, \forall \theta^* \in \left[\frac{\psi^S}{\psi^N}, 1\right]$. Since the South chooses $\left(\tilde{X}_1^S, \tilde{X}_2^S\right)$ to maximize its utility subject to its budget constraint $\tilde{X}_1^S + p\tilde{X}_2^S = \frac{L^S}{\alpha^S(\theta^*)}$, by applying the envelope theorem we obtain the condition for $\frac{dU^S}{d\theta} \geq 0$ as:

$$\varepsilon_1^S \geq \frac{1}{U_1 \hat{X}_1^S}\left[U_1 \tilde{X}_2^S \eta p - v' R \xi\right]. \tag{12.25}$$

Here, $\eta = \frac{dp}{d\theta}\frac{\theta^*}{p}$ measures the elasticity of terms of trade as a response to a change in the extent of technology transfer. Note that if the North increases the extent of technology transfer, it induces the South to produce more of good 1. Since the supply of good 1 rises in the international market, its relative price falls in the trading equilibrium. In other words, the relative price of good 2, that is, p, increases. Thus, we have $\frac{dp}{d\theta} > 0$.

Combining (12.24) and (12.25), we state the next proposition of the chapter as follows.

Proposition 2 If the necessary condition given by $\frac{1}{U_1 \hat{X}_1^S}\left[U_1 \tilde{X}_2^S \eta p - v' R \xi\right] \leq \varepsilon_1^S < \frac{\theta^* \psi^N}{1 - \theta^* \psi^N}$ holds, the North's choice of technology transfer $\theta^* \in \left(\frac{\psi^S}{\psi^N}, 1\right)$ is capable of stabilizing the global emission level at the global optimum.

Proof The earlier discussion.

Case 2 $\dfrac{a_1^N + (a_3^N + a_4^N \psi^N)a_{31}^N}{a_2^N + (a_3^N + a_4^N \psi^N)a_{32}^N} = \dfrac{1}{p}$

In this case the North specializes incompletely in the production of both the goods while the South specializes completely in the production of commodity 1. Hence, at the trading equilibrium, the South produces $\left(\hat{X}_1^S = \frac{L^S}{\alpha^S}, \hat{X}_2^S = 0\right)$. It exports $\left(\hat{X}_1^S - \tilde{X}_1^S\right)$ to the North and imports $\tilde{X}_2^S$ from it. The North produces $(\hat{X}_1'^N > 0, \hat{X}_2'^N > 0)$ where $\hat{X}_2'^N = \frac{L^N - \alpha^N \hat{X}_1'^N}{\beta^N}$. Both countries consume both the goods at the international prices p_1 and p_2. The global emission level is given by:

$$R' = \phi^N \left(a_{31}^N \hat{X}_1'^N + a_{32}^N \hat{X}_2'^N\right) + \phi^S a_{31}^S \hat{X}_1^S.$$

The South produces the same amount of product 1 as it produced in Case 1. So the emission level in the South remains unchanged (as compared to Case 1). For the North, $\hat{X}_2'^N < \hat{X}_2^N$ but $\hat{X}_1'^N > 0 = \hat{X}_1^N$. In comparison to Case 1, the pollution in the North due to the production of commodity 2 decreases but the pollution arising from the production of commodity 1 increases. Since product 1 is more pollution-intensive than product 2, overall emissions in the North will rise. Consequently, we get: $R' > R > \bar{R}$. This creates scope for technology transfer from the North to the South in this situation too.

After transferring $\theta^* \in \left(\frac{\psi^S}{\psi^N}, 1\right)$ from the North to the South the global emission level becomes:

$$R(\theta^*) = \phi^N \left(a_{31}^N \hat{X}_1'^N + a_{32}^N \hat{X}_2'^N\right) + \left(1 - \theta^* \psi^N\right) a_{31}^S \hat{X}_1^S.$$

If $\theta^* = \frac{\psi^S}{\psi^N}$, then $R\left(\frac{\psi^S}{\psi^N}\right) = R' > \bar{R}$. To make the technology transfer effective in reducing the pollution level we require $\frac{dR}{d\theta} < 0$ for $\theta^* \in \left[\frac{\psi_S}{\psi_N}, 1\right]$. $\frac{dR}{d\theta} < 0$ holds if the following condition is satisfied:

$$\varepsilon_1^S < \frac{\theta^*}{(1 - \theta^* \psi^N) \alpha^S (\theta^*) \chi^S \hat{X}_1^S} \left[\psi^N \hat{X}_3^S + \frac{\phi^N \alpha^N \chi^N \hat{X}_1^N}{\theta^*} \varepsilon_1^N\right].$$

(12.26)

As we have already argued earlier, $R\left(\dfrac{\psi^S}{\psi^N}\right) > \bar{R}$, if $R(1) < \bar{R}$ as well, there exists a value of $\theta = \theta^* \in \left(\dfrac{\psi^S}{\psi^N}, 1\right)$ such that $R(\theta^*) = \bar{R}$. A partial technology transfer by the North is capable of achieving the global optimum. By a similar argument it follows that if $R(1) = \bar{R}$, it must hold that $\theta^* = 1$. In this case, only the complete technology transfer by the North achieves the global optimum. If $R(1) > \bar{R}$, no amount of technology transfer is capable of achieving the global optimum.

Next, we look at the condition for which the technology transfer is accepted by the South.

The indirect welfare of the South in the post transfer equilibrium is given by:

$$U^S = U(\tilde{X}_1^S, \tilde{X}_2^S) - v[R(\theta^*)].$$

The South accepts the technology offer of the North only when $\dfrac{dU^S}{d\theta} \geq 0$, $\forall \theta^* \in \left[\dfrac{\psi^S}{\psi^N}, 1\right]$. Since the South chooses $(\tilde{X}_1^S, \tilde{X}_2^S)$ to maximize its utility subject to its budget constraint $\tilde{X}_1^S + p\tilde{X}_2^S = \dfrac{L^S}{\alpha^S(\theta^*)}$, we get:

$$\dfrac{dU^S}{d\theta} = U_1 \dfrac{dX_1^S}{d\theta} - v' \dfrac{dR}{d\theta}. \tag{12.27}$$

Observe that $U_1, v', \dfrac{dX_1^S}{d\theta} > 0$ and $\dfrac{dR}{d\theta} < 0$ $\forall \theta^* \in \left[\dfrac{\psi^S}{\psi^N}, 1\right]$ from which it follows that $\dfrac{dU^S}{d\theta} > 0$ $\forall \theta^* \in \left[\dfrac{\psi^S}{\psi^N}, 1\right]$.

From (12.26) and (12.27) we get the next proposition.

Proposition 3 If the necessary condition given by $0 \leq \varepsilon_1^S < \dfrac{\theta^*}{(1-\theta^*\psi^N)\alpha^S(\theta^*)\chi^S \hat{X}_1^S}\left[\psi^N \hat{X}_3^S + \dfrac{\phi^N \alpha^N \chi^N \hat{X}_1^N}{\theta^*}\varepsilon_1^N\right]$ holds, the

North's choice of technology transfer $\theta^* \in \left(\dfrac{\psi^S}{\psi^N}, 1\right)$ is capable of stabilizing the global emission levels at the global optimum.

Proof The earlier discussion.

Case 3 $\dfrac{a_1^S + (a_3^S + a_4^S \psi^S)a_{31}^S}{a_2^S + (a_3^S + a_4^S \psi^S)a_{32}^S} = \dfrac{1}{p}$

In this case the South specializes incompletely in the production of both the goods while the North specializes completely in the production of good 2. Thus, at the trading equilibrium, the North produces $\left(\hat{X}_1^N = 0, \hat{X}_2^N = \dfrac{L^N}{\alpha^N}\right)$. It exports $\left(\hat{X}_2^N - \tilde{X}_2^N\right)$ to the South and imports $\tilde{X}_1^N$ from it. The South produces $(\hat{X}_1^{\prime\prime S} > 0, \hat{X}_2^{\prime\prime S} > 0)$ where $\hat{X}_2^{\prime\prime S} = \dfrac{L^S - \alpha^S \hat{X}_1^{\prime\prime S}}{\beta^S}$. Both countries consume both the goods at the international prices p_1 and p_2. The global emission level is given by:

$$R'' = \phi^N a_{32}^N \hat{X}_2^N + \phi^S (a_{31}^S \hat{X}_1^{\prime\prime S} + a_{32}^S \hat{X}_2^{\prime\prime S}).$$

The North produces the same amount of commodity 2 as it produced in Case 1. So the emission level in the North remains unchanged (as compared to Case 1). For the South, $\hat{X}_1^{\prime\prime S} < \hat{X}_1^S$ but $\hat{X}_2^{\prime\prime S} > 0 = \hat{X}_2^S$. As compared to Case 1, the emissions in the South due to production of commodity 1 decrease but the emissions arising from the production of commodity 2 increase. Since product 1 is more pollution-intensive than product 2, the South's reduction of emissions due to the decline in its output level of good 1 may be larger than, equal to or less than the increase in emissions due to the rise in the output level of good 2. If the overall emission level in the South is reduced, then we may face a situation where $\overline{R} < R'' < R$. If the overall emission level in the South remains unchanged, then we obtain $R'' = R > \overline{R}$. But if the overall pollution level increases in the South, then we get $R'' > R > \overline{R}$. Regardless of the situation we face, there will be a technology transfer from the North to the South.

After transferring $\theta^* \in \left(\dfrac{\psi^S}{\psi^N}, 1\right)$ from the North to the South, the global emission level becomes:

$$R(\theta^*) = \phi^N a_{32}^N \hat{X}_2^N + (1 - \theta^* \psi^N)(a_{31}^S \hat{X}_1'''^S + a_{32}^S \hat{X}_2'''^S).$$

Similar to the line of reasoning in Case 1, a transfer of abatement technology by the North induces the South to produce more of the two goods. Yet, since abatement per unit of production also increases, it is uncertain whether the global pollution level stabilizes at $\bar{R}$. If the target is not met, then the North will have to reduce its own output of product 2, since it is the commitment of the North to keep the global pollution level at $\bar{R}$. Such action by the North will induce it to substitute the production of commodity 2 by the production of commodity 1. However, the North will never choose such an action as the increase in the production of the pollution-intensive commodity 1 creates even more pollution, which outweighs the reduction of pollution achieved through reduction in the output of commodity 2. In this case, the North will never succeed in keeping its commitment. Rather, the North will prefer to impose much tighter restrictions regarding the output expansion of the South.

If $\theta^* = \dfrac{\psi^S}{\psi^N} m$ then $R\left(\dfrac{\psi^S}{\psi^N}\right) = R'' > \bar{R}$. To make the technology transfer effective in reducing the pollution level, we require $\dfrac{dR}{d\theta} < 0$ for $\theta^* \in \left(\dfrac{\psi^S}{\psi^N}, 1\right)$. $\dfrac{dR}{d\theta} < 0$ holds, if the following condition is satisfied:

$$\varepsilon_1^S < \dfrac{\theta^*}{\left(1 - \theta^* \psi^N\right) \alpha^S (\theta^*) \chi^S \hat{X}_1'''^S} \left[\psi^N \hat{X}_3'''^S + \left(1 - \theta^* \psi^N\right) \dfrac{a_{32}^S}{\beta^S(\theta^*)} \left(\alpha^{S/} \hat{X}_1'''^S + \beta^{S/} \hat{X}_2'''^S\right)\right]. \quad (12.28)$$

As we have already argued earlier $R\left(\dfrac{\psi^S}{\psi^N}\right) > \bar{R}$, if $R(1) < \bar{R}$ as well, there exists a value of $\theta = \theta^* \in \left(\dfrac{\psi^S}{\psi^N}, 1\right)$ such that $R(\theta^*) = \bar{R}$. A partial technology transfer by the North is capable of achieving the global optimum. By a similar argument it follows that if $R(1) = \bar{R}$, then it must hold that $\theta^* = 1$. In this case, only the complete technology transfer by the North achieves the global optimum. If $R(1) > \bar{R}$, no amount of technology transfer is capable of achieving the global optimum.

Next, we look at the conditions under which the technology transfer is accepted by the South.

The South chooses the value of its consumption $\left(\tilde{X}_1^{\prime\prime S}, \tilde{X}_2^{\prime\prime S}\right)$ to maximize its utility subject to its budget constraint $\tilde{X}_1^{\prime\prime S} + p\tilde{X}_2^{\prime\prime S} = X_1^{\prime\prime S} + pX_2^{\prime\prime S}$.

The indirect utility of the South in the post-transfer equilibrium is given by:

$$U^S = U\left(\tilde{X}_1^{\prime\prime S}, \tilde{X}_2^{\prime\prime S}\right) - v\left[R(\theta^*)\right].$$

The South accepts the technology offer of the North only when $\dfrac{dU^S}{d\theta} \geq 0, \forall \theta^* \in \left[\dfrac{\psi^S}{\psi^N}, 1\right]$. Hence, by applying the envelope theorem we obtain the condition for $\dfrac{dU^S}{d\theta} \geq 0$:

$$\varepsilon_1^S \geq \frac{\theta^* \beta^S(\theta^*)}{U_1\{\beta^S(\theta^*) - p\alpha^S(\theta^*)\}\hat{X}_1^{\prime\prime S}} \left[U_1 \left\{ p \frac{\alpha^{S\prime}\hat{X}_1^{\prime\prime S} + \beta^{S\prime}\hat{X}_2^{\prime\prime S}}{\beta^S(\theta^*)} \right. \right.$$
$$\left. \left. - \frac{\left(\hat{X}_2^{\prime\prime S} - \tilde{X}_2^{\prime\prime S}\right)p\eta}{\theta^*} \right\} - \frac{v'R\xi}{\theta^*} \right]. \qquad (12.29)$$

From (12.28) and (12.29), we get the following proposition.

Proposition 4 If the necessary condition given by

$$\frac{\theta^* \beta^S(\theta^*)}{U_1\{\beta^S(\theta^*) - p\alpha^S(\theta^*)\}\hat{X}_1^{\prime\prime S}} \left[U_1 \left\{ p \frac{\alpha^{S\prime}\hat{X}_1^{\prime\prime S} + \beta^{S\prime}\hat{X}_2^{\prime\prime S}}{\beta^S(\theta^*)} \right. \right.$$
$$\left. \left. - \frac{\left(\hat{X}_2^{\prime\prime S} - \tilde{X}_2^{\prime\prime S}\right)p\eta}{\theta^*} \right\} - \frac{v'R\xi}{\theta^*} \right] \leq \varepsilon_1^S < \frac{\theta^*}{\left(1 - \theta^* \psi^N\right)\alpha^S(\theta^*)\chi^S \hat{X}_1^{\prime\prime S}}$$

$$\left[\psi^N \hat{X}_3'''^S + (1-\theta^*\psi^N)\frac{a_{32}^S}{\beta^S(\theta^*)}\left(\alpha^{SI}\hat{X}_1'''^S + \beta^{SI}\hat{X}_2'''^S\right) \right]$$ holds, the North's choice of technology transfer $\theta^* \in \left(\dfrac{\psi^S}{\psi^N}, 1\right)$ is capable of stabilizing the global emission level at the global optimum.

Proof The earlier discussion.

Discussion and Conclusions

Different kinds of transfers from industrialized to developing countries have been addressed in recent international climate negotiations (see the Cancun Accords, for example). They differ, for example, with respect to their purpose (for example, support of adaptation measures or mitigation measures) or their nature (for example, technology transfers or monetary transfers).

In this chapter we focused on the analysis of the scope of transfers of abatement technology from a developed country (North) to an underdeveloped country (South). The objective of the considered transfer is to stabilize GHG emissions at the global optimal level.

Since the main responsibility for combating global warming is largely assigned to industrialized countries, we assumed in our framework that the North is committed to stabilizing the global emission levels while the South faces no GHG abatement obligations. In each country, pollution arises from the production of an intermediate input which, along with labour, produces two final goods. The South has a comparative advantage in the production of commodity 1 which employs the polluting input relatively intensively. In this framework we ascertained the necessary conditions, both under autarky and free trade, for which the transfer of technology successfully stabilizes the global emission level. Furthermore, we investigated under which circumstances the South is willing to accept technology transfers. In the case of free trade we considered all possible configurations of complete and incomplete specialization.

In the autarky situation, after the technology transfer was provided, the South requires less amount of labour for a given level of abatement. So some amount of labour is released from the abatement activity. Since the country always maintains full employment of labour, the extra amount of labour allows for increasing the production of commodities 1 or 2. As commodity 2 was supposed to bring about a low marginal utility, the South decides to increase the production of commodity 1. We defined the increase in output of commodity 1 as the positive scale effect of technology transfer. The increase in output of commodity 1 raises the level of emissions, although the pollution per unit of output is reduced. If the output increases by a very large amount, then the overall level of pollution increases and the North fails to keep its commitment. In order to be successful in attaining climate stabilization, the South's output is allowed to increase by a small amount only. In other words, the output elasticity of commodity 1 must not be very high. Furthermore, the success of the technology transfer also depends on its acceptability by the South. If the South denies accepting the technology transfer, then the North is never going to be capable of keeping its international commitment.

As we have already argued, the technology transfer induces the South to increase the output of commodity 1 and to reduce the output of commodity 2. In this case it gains some utility from increased consumption of commodity 1 but also loses some utility due to reduction in its consumption of commodity 2. The South accepts the technology transfer only when its overall gain in utility is positive. This is not the case, when the output elasticity of commodity 1 is very low.

In case of free trade with complete specialization, the South experiences an adverse terms-of-trade effect which follows from $\frac{dp}{d\theta} > 0$. So, in this situation, the South accepts the technology transfer only when the gain from the positive scale effect dominates the loss from adverse terms-of-trade effects. While in the autarky scenario the North reduces its own output of commodity 1 in response to an increase in South's respective output, under free trade with complete specialization the North does not have any scope to adjust its own output. Hence, it requires a much more stringent condition for the output elasticity of the South to enable the North to keep its commitment. In contrast, when the North incompletely specializes while the South completely specializes, the technology transfer is always accepted by the South as it does not face an adverse terms-of-trade effect and only the positive scale effect persists. Furthermore, it also gains from the reduction in global emission levels.

However, if $\xi \geq \max\left\{\dfrac{U_1 \tilde{X}_2^S \eta p}{v'R}, \dfrac{\theta^* U_1}{v'R}\left[p\dfrac{\alpha^{S'}\hat{X}_1^{\prime\prime S} + \beta^{S'}\hat{X}_2^{\prime\prime S}}{\beta^S(\theta^*)} - \dfrac{\left(\hat{X}_2^{\prime\prime S} - \tilde{X}_2^{\prime\prime S}\right)p\eta}{\theta^*}\right]\right\}$ then in all situations the benefit from reduction in global pollution level outweighs all possible losses and the South accepts the technology offer.

In a related paper, Mukherjee and Rübbelke (2006) consider one of the final consumption goods as a polluting good and obtain the same set of results. Thus, the scope of technology transfer from the North to the South as an instrument to mitigate global pollution is invariant of whether pollution is caused by an intermediate input or directly by a final consumption good.

References

Arrow, K.J. 2007. 'Global Climate Change: A Challenge to Policy', *Economists' Voice*, June, 4(3).

Aslam, M.A. 2001. 'Technology Transfer under the CDM—Materializing the Myth in the Japanese Context?', *Climate Policy*, 1(4): 451–64.

Barrett, S. 2006. 'Climate Treaties and "Breakthrough" Technologies', *American Economic Review*, 96(2): 22–5.

Beladi, H., R.W. Jones, and S. Marjit. 1997. 'Technology for Sale', *Pacific Economic Review*, 2(3): 187–96.

Benedick, R.E. 2001. 'Striking a New Deal on Climate Change', *Issues in Science and Technology Online*, Fall.

Copeland, B., and M.S. Taylor. 1999. 'Trade, Spatial Separation and the Environment', *Journal of International Economics*, 47(1): 137–68.

———. 2004. 'Trade, Growth and Environment', *Journal of Economic Literature*, 42(1): 7–71.

———. 2005. 'Free Trade with Global Warming: A Trade Theory View of Kyoto Protocol', *Journal of Environmental Economics and Management*, 49(2): 205–34.

Cornes, R.C., and T. Sandler. 1996. *The Theory of Externalities, Public Goods and Club Goods*. Cambridge: Cambridge University Press.

Dechezleprêtre, A., M. Glachant, and Y. Ménière. 2008. 'The Clean Development Mechanism and the International Diffusion of Technologies: An Empirical Study', *Energy Policy*, 36(4): 1273–83.

Glachant, M., and Y. Ménière. 2007. *Kyoto Project Mechanism and Technology Diffusion*. Working Paper. Paris: CERNA.

Haites, E., M. Duan, and S. Seres. 2006. 'Technology Transfer by CDM Projects', *Climate Policy*, 6(3): 327–44.

Hoel, M., and A. de Zeeuw. 2008. 'Can a Focus on Breakthrough Technologies Improve the Performance of International Environmental Agreements?', *Environmental and Resource Economics*, 47(3): 395–406.

IPCC. 2000. *Methodological and Technological Issues in Technology Transfer.* Cambridge: Cambridge University Press.

———. 2007. *Climate Change 2007—Mitigation of Climate Change.* Cambridge: Cambridge University Press.

Itoh, A., and M. Tawada. 2003. 'Environment, Trade and the Welfare Gains from the Transfer of Pollution Abatement Technology', *Papers in Regional Science*, 82(4): 519–34.

Jaffe, A.B., R.G. Newell, and R.N. Stavins. 2002. 'Environmental Policy and Technological Change', *Environmental and Resource Economics*, 22(2): 41–69.

Millock, K. 2002. 'Technology Transfers in the Clean Development Mechanism: an Incentive Issue', *Environment and Development Economics*, 7(3): 449–66.

Mukherjee, V., and D.T.G. Rübbelke. 2006. *Global Climate Change, Technology Transfer and Trade with Complete Specialization*, Nota die Lavoro 114.2006. Milan: Fondazione Eni Enrico Mattei.

Neary, J.P. 2006. 'International Trade and the Environment: Theoretical and Policy Linkages', *Environmental and Resource Economics*, 33(1): 95–118.

OECD. 2011. *Financing Climate Change Action and Boosting Technology Change.* Paris: Organisation for Economic Co-operation and Development, flyer update 10 March. Available at: http://www.oecd.org/env/cc/46534686.pdf, last accessed on 22 January 2014.

Rive, N., and D.T.G. Rübbelke. 2010. 'International Environmental Policy and Poverty Alleviation,' *Review of World Economics*, 146(3): 515–43.

Saggi, K. 2002. 'Trade, Foreign Direct Investment, and International Technology Transfer: A Survey', *World Bank Research Observer*, 17(2): 191–235.

Schelling, T.C. 1992. 'Some Economics of Global Warming', *American Economic Review*, 82(1): 1–14.

Stern, N. 2007. *The Economics of Climate Change—The Stern Review*. Cambridge: Cambridge University Press.

Takarada, Y. 2005. 'Transboundary Pollution and the Welfare Effects of Technology Transfers', *Journal of Economics*, 85(3): 251–75.

Yang, Z. 1999. 'Should the North Make Unilateral Technology Transfers to the South? North-South Cooperation and Conflicts in Responses to Global Climate Change', *Resource and Energy Economics*, 21(1): 67–87.

13

Early Withdrawal of Patented Drugs as an Entry-deterring Device

Sugata Marjit, Tarun Kabiraj, and Arijita Dutta

International patent rules came into existence after the Uruguay Round of Multilateral Trade Negotiations under GATT and have been subsequently enforced by the World Trade Organization (WTO). Before the GATT Resolution, the norms and standards of intellectual property protection in the international context were governed by the World Intellectual Property Organization (WIPO). WIPO, as contrary to WTO, had neither enforcing power nor a dispute settlement mechanism; it gave the countries flexibility to design their own patent rules, and choose the coverage of patentability. As a result, there were various products like agricultural machinery, fertilizers, chemical products, food products, and pharmaceutical products, which were excluded from patenting in many developing countries. But the GATT-based patent system called for uniform patent protection for all products including pharmaceuticals, genetically engineered organisms, and plants and animal varieties for 20 years.

This has given rise to an acrimonious debate between the developed and developing countries.[1] In this chapter the issue at hand is the pharmaceutical industry. In fact, the proposal requiring product patents for pharmaceutical innovations has been one of the most sensitive issues. It has evoked a considerable debate and differences of opinion among economists and industrialists. While the developing countries think that medical discoveries should be available free of patents, the developed countries call for a stronger international patent protection so as to ensure high prices and high profits in the pharmaceutical industry, given this industry's uniquely high and risky expenditures on research, development, and introduction of new products.[2]

In the context of the pharmaceutical industry, problems that are usually dealt with in literature reflect concerns over the impact of patent rights on the prices of generic products, rates of innovation, and welfare of the trading nations. For this literature one may look at, for instance, Frank and Salkever (1992), Grabsowski and Vernon (1992), Nogues (1993), Watal (1996) and Lanjouw (1997). However, the present work highlights a different problem. This is motivated from the survey results of Dutta (2003). It is found that some pharmaceutical companies withdraw patented drugs before the expiry of the patent period and simultaneously introduce a new patented drug. Though this seems to be strange as it cuts back the initial period of monopoly for the patent holder, we argue that this type of strategy has a deeper implication. In particular, such a strategy adversely affects the entry of potential firms who wait to introduce the generic drug once the patent period is over, and hence it has implications for drug prices.[3]

---

[1] Already there is large amount of literature focusing on the North–South debate on IPRs. Interested readers may look at Chin and Grossman (1991), Maskus (1990), Diwan and Rodrik (1991), Deardorff (1992), Aoki and Prusa (1993), Helpman (1993), Taylor (1994), Grinols and Lin (1997), Yang (1998), Marjit and Beladi (1998), Kabiraj (2000), Grossman and Lai (2004), etc.

[2] Scherer (2002) discusses the question of whether global welfare is higher under uniform pharmaceutical patent standards or with free riding.

[3] For literature on entry deterrence, see, in particular, Dixit (1980), Milgrom and Roberts (1982), and Salop and Schiefman (1983).

Entry in the drug market depends on the following consideration. The traditional system allowed process patenting and encouraged inventing around. This enabled the firms to develop commercial production capabilities for on-patent drugs before patent expiry and then compete in the world market as soon as the patent elapsed. Market entry by generics was limited only to the extent that they had to take pioneer's tests before gaining market approval. Thus, the originator had to face a tough challenge from the imitators even during the patent period. And after expiry of the patent, its profits dropped substantially due to competition from the generic substitutes. In the new patent system, process patenting as well as compulsory licensing has been almost scrapped. Hence the innovator, the patentee, enjoys almost monopoly for the whole stretch of the patent period.

Theoretically, even under the new patent system, a pioneer's profits should drop to an insignificant amount after the patent expiry with the entry of generics. In practice, this never happens because of the peculiar nature of the pharmaceutical products as a whole. Typically, pharmaceuticals are cited as an example of first-mover advantage. First-movers have natural product differentiation advantages that permit them to charge higher prices and retain substantial market shares (see Conrad [1983], Schmalansee [1982], and Scherer and Ross [1990]). There is a strong brand loyalty in pharmaceuticals for innovative brands over generic competitors. Once physicians gain experience with a new drug during its period of patent exclusively, then even when patents expire and cheaper substitutes become available, many physicians might remain insensitive to the lower-price opportunities, and therefore continue to prescribe the branded product. In the pharmaceutical industry, consumers and consumption decision makers (that is, physicians) are not the same, and sometimes the consumers are not the ultimate contributors due to the existence of third-party reimbursement schemes. The combination of all these factors makes demand for the branded product stronger and less elastic. On the supply side, entry of potential firms is restricted to the extent that they will have to incur costs on getting market access in the post-patent period. There is evidence showing that after patent expiry the price of the branded product has gone up and that there has been only marginal market share gain by generic entrants even several years after patent expiration (see, for instance, Statman

[1981], Frank and Salkever [1992], Grabowski and Vernon [1992], and Hollis [2005]).[4]

This chapter refers to the situation when the patent-holder intends to deter by means of withdrawing the existing-patented product from circulation and then introducing a new patented substitute. The withdrawal date is optimally chosen by the incumbent and is chosen earlier than the expiry date of the patent. The role of the prescribing medical practitioners is very important in this context since their prescriptions in a way determine the marketability of the medicines. The new drug is introduced on the pretext that it has new and interesting characteristics. It gets prescribed before the generic substitutes of the old drug have a chance to appear, since the patent period for the old drug is yet not over. Since doctors are often not fond of prescribing drugs that have gone out of fashion, the potential entrants of the generic drugs find it tough to compete after entry since the original drug itself has been out of circulation for some time. There is no taker for their generic substitute and a newer form of the original drug has already reached the market. This is the case where deliberate withdrawal of a patented drug even before the expiry of the patent period leaves the potential entrants at a disadvantage and acts as an entry-deterring strategy.

Empirical support for our theory is drawn, as mentioned earlier, from the survey reported in Dutta (2003). For a molecule named *Nitrofurantoin*, initially the normal tablet was patented for 20 years. Close to the expiry, a new formulation, named *Vincristine*, was introduced and a patent was again taken. Next, before completing the term of 20 years, a new patent was taken on the solution form of Vincristine, saying that the new form is even more stable. The original drug was withdrawn while the new drug was being marketed. Another example is *Cyclosporin*. Close to the expiry of the patent, the patentee introduced a new micro-emulsion form of the drug. Doctors are usually not interested in prescribing drugs which are not vigorously marketed. The reason behind this is that they derive the knowledge of new drugs from medical representatives,

---

[4] The Indian case shows that in 1998, patented drugs constituted 84.7 per cent market share in anti-hypertensive, 70.3 per cent in Quinolones, and 56.7 per cent in anti-ulcerants.

who constitute the backbone of pharmaceutical marketing. A survey on doctors in Kolkata and Bolpur, a district town in West Bengal, India, revealed that 60 per cent of the doctors surveyed collected information about new drugs from the representatives, though they seldom received any detailing about the chemical and biological characteristics from them. The pharmaceutical companies stress on heavy marketing of new molecules. If they decrease the marketing expenditure in the post patent expiry period, the market share of those drugs falls fast because the memory of the doctors is short. On the other hand, if the firms find that there is no new generation substitute in the pipeline, they increase promotional expenditures on them. This may increase their market share even after expiry of the patents. For example, market shares of *Sulphamides* and antidepressants increased after patent expiry in early 1970s due to the boost in promotional expenditures (Slatter 1977).

We construct a simple dynamic model of an entry game capturing these facts. The key feature of the model is that early withdrawal of the patented drug increases the entry costs of the potential entrants with generic substitutes. Although we do not model the strategy of the prescribing doctor explicitly, early termination implies that the drug is out of circulation and the entrants have to spend more to influence a doctor to prescribe an out-of-circulation drug. But early termination is costly for the incumbent in the sense that it has to forego patent protected profit from the old drug and has to introduce a new drug early. Such a trade-off determines the optimal termination period. The termination date is sensitive to certain basic parameters of the model, such as the cost of introduction and promotion of the new drug and the length of the patent period.

Before we go to the next section, let us summarize the key forces driving our result. First, the existence of patent prevents the imitators to market the product during the patent period. And second, given the behaviour of doctors, the incumbent strategically withdraws its product from the market before its patent expires and simultaneously introduces a new patented product. This behaviour increases entry costs for generic producers and alters market competition in the incumbent's favour.

The chapter is laid out as follows. In the second section we discuss the model and the results. The third section concludes.

Model and Results

In this section we provide a model to show that the incumbent, the originator of a drug, will introduce a new competing drug before the patent of its earlier generation expires. Imitators can enter the market with generics of a drug only after its patent period is over. We focus on the stationary equilibrium where the patent holder withdraws the new patented drug before the old patent expires.

Let T be the length of patent of a drug available from the date it is introduced in the market. Then we are concerned with an equilibrium when the incumbent introduces a new substitute drug t years before the expiry of patent of its earlier generation; $t \in [0, T]$. We further show that introducing the new drug after the expiry of the patent will never be optimum. To make the analysis simple we assume zero discounting rate.

Let $D(0)$ denote the current generation drug. Then $D(-s)$ denotes the s-generation earlier drug and $D(r)$ is the drug to be introduced r generations later. We assume that demand for drugs over time remains unchanged and that the newer version of the drugs will have no market demand effect.[5] However, doctors will be more prone to prescribe the latest generation drug. In other words, the older generation drugs will have a lower market share, as if, older generation drugs become obsolete in the minds of the doctors. To make the structure simple, we further assume that when the latest generation drug (which is presently protected by a patent) competes with the generics of older generations, only the last generation generic will survive and all older generation generics will have zero market shares. The doctors while prescribing the drug do not take into consideration older generation generics except the one in the recent past. Thus, when $D(0)$, $D(-1)$,

---

[5] Here we assume that the patented drug and the generics are perfect substitutes (in their composition and efficiency), but the doctors are more prone to prescribe the latest generation drug, possibly presuming that this is more effective and/or safer. Alternatively, the new drug may have a strong brand loyalty and therefore the physicians may easily prescribe such a drug. We, however, deliberately abstract from the situation when firms produce vertically differentiated products and consumers are willing to pay a higher price for better quality. The assumption of a 'no demand shift effect' facilitates us to focus purely on the entry-deterrence strategy of the incumbent.

and D(–2) compete in the marketplace, D(–2) will have no positive market share, and in competition between D(0) and D(–1), the drug D(0) will have a larger market share.

Think of the period when D(0) is not yet introduced but patent of D(–2) has expired. Then D(–1), which is now under patent protection, will compete with generics of D(–2). Let the flow of gross payoffs of the originator of D(–1) and that of each entrant producing generics D(–2) be $B(n)$ and $G(n)$, respectively, which are decreasing functions of the number of entrants (n); therefore $B'(n) < 0$ and $G'(n) < 0$.

Consider now the period after introduction of D(0). By our assumption, D(0) is introduced t years before the expiry of the patent of D(–1). So these t years the patented D(0) will compete with D(–2) generics. Note that during the first t years after launch of D(0), the drug D(–1) cannot be imitated. Let $A(n)$ and $\tilde{G}(n)$ be the flow of gross payoffs of the patentee of D(0) and each D(–2) generic producer respectively. Given the story underlying our structure, it is then natural to assume that $A(n) > B(n)$ and $G(n) > \tilde{G}(n)$. For our results, however, neither of these conditions is necessary, but these justify why very old generation drugs will not survive competition.

But once t years are over after D(0) is launched, generics of D(–1) will enter (because by this time its patent has expired). Then by assumption, producers of D(–2) generics will cease to operate. Then a next generation drug, D(1), will be launched again t years before the expiry of patent of D(0). Therefore, D(0) and generics of D(–1) will compete for $T - 2t$ years.

This framework suggests that any generic producer will enjoy a flow of gross profit $G(n)$ for $T - 2t$ years before the next generation drug is introduced and $\tilde{G}(n)$ for t years after the new generation drug is introduced. Similarly, for any new innovation, the incumbent will get a flow of gross payoff $A(n)$ for the first t years of the product and $B(n)$ for the next $T - 2t$ years. It is further understood that for $t \geq T/2$, $B(n) = 0$ and $G(n) = 0$.

Since we are assuming away any demand effect of a new drug, the payoff structure of the incumbent and the generic producers will remain the same as mentioned earlier. In other words, the same scenario will repeat every time after a new generation drug is introduced. The sequence of launching new drugs is depicted in Figure 13.1.

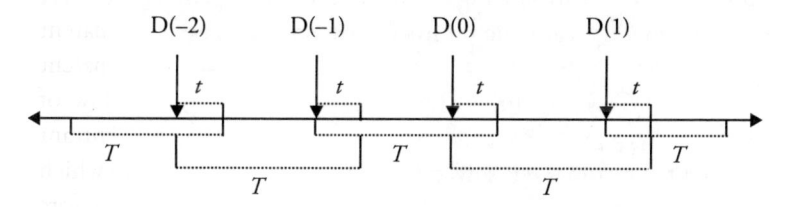

Figure 13.1 Sequence of introducing new drugs before expiry of patents

We now introduce the cost side. Assume that there is a cost to introduce a new drug by withdrawing the existing patented drug from the market before the patent expiry. This may also include the cost of advertising and marketing of the new drug. When the drug is introduced t years before the expiry of patent of its earlier generation, the corresponding cost is given by the function:

$Z(t)$ with (i) $Z(t) = 0$ for $t \leq 0$, (ii) $Z'(t) > 0 \ \forall \ t > 0$ and (iii) $Z'(0) = 0$ \hfill (13.1)

This cost is increasing in t, and is zero if the product is introduced after the expiry of patent of its earlier generation.

Similarly, the generic producers face an entry cost which directly depends on the length of the period that the product goes out of the market before any generics can be introduced. This is given by:

$E(t)$ with (i) $E(t) = \bar{E}$ for $t \leq 0$, and (ii) $E'(t) > 0 \ \forall \ t > 0$ \hfill (13.2)

Since the new product is to be innovated, it involves a R&D cost. Let the cost be given by the function:

$I(t)$ with (i) $I(t) = \bar{I}$ for $t \leq 0$, (ii) $I'(t) > 0 \ \forall \ t > 0$ and (iii) $I'(0) = 0$ \hfill (13.3)

This tells us that the earlier the product is innovated, the larger the cost of innovation.

Given the structure of the model, we are now in a position to find the optimal number of entrants producing generic drugs and the optimal time of introducing a new product. If n generic producers enter the market, each such firm's net payoff becomes:

$$(T - 2t) G(n) + t\tilde{G}(n) - E(t)$$

Then the optimal n is solved from:

$$(T - 2t) G(n) + t\tilde{G}(n) = E(t) \tag{13.4}$$

Equation (13.4) solves $n(.)$ as a function of t. Given the restrictions,[6] we must have $n'(t) < 0 \; \forall \, t > 0$ and $n(0) = n^*$ with $n^* > n(t) \; \forall t > 0$. This is quite intuitive. As t goes up, on the one hand the entry cost goes up, and on the other the period of possible operation of each generic drug is shortened. Therefore, there will be a lower number of entrants.

Now, given $n(t)$, define:

$$\bar{A}(t) = A(n[t]) \text{ and } \bar{B}(t) = B(n[t]) \tag{13.5}$$

Since $\{A', B', n'\} < 0$, we must have $\bar{A}'(t) > 0$ and $\bar{B}'(t) > 0$ for all t. The incumbent's problem is:

$$\max_{t \in [0,T]} V(t) = R(t) - C(t) \tag{13.6}$$

where:

$$R(t) = t\bar{A}(t) + (T - 2t) \bar{B}(t) \text{ and } C(t) = Z(t) + I(t)$$

To see that this problem has an interior solution, note that $R(0) = T\bar{B}(n^*)$, $C(0) = \bar{I}$, $R(T) = 0$ and $C(T) > 0$. Therefore, $V(T) < 0$, and it is reasonable to assume $V(0) > 0$, that is:

$$T\bar{B}(n^*) - \bar{I} > 0 \tag{13.7}$$

---

[6] We have, $n^* = G^{-1}\left(\dfrac{\bar{E}}{T}\right)$ and $n'(t) = \dfrac{2G - \tilde{G} + E'}{(T - 2t)G' + t\tilde{G}'} < 0.$

This tells that the R&D cost associated with an innovation will be fully recovered by the existing patent system. Hence:

$$\exists t < T/V(t) > 0 \tag{13.8}$$

Now to ensure that the optimal t is indeed positive, consider the first order condition of the maximization problem (13.6), that is:

$$V'(t) = R'(t) - C'(t)$$
$$\text{or, } \bar{A} + t\bar{A}' + (T-2t)\bar{B}' - 2\bar{B} = Z' + I' \tag{13.9}$$

If t^* maximizes $V(t)$, then $t^* > 0$ if and only if $V'(0) > 0$, that is:

$$TB'(n^*)\, n'(0) - 2\bar{B}(n^*) > 0 \tag{13.10}$$

Equations (13.7) and (13.10), together ensure that:

$$V(t^*) > V(0) > 0 > V(T) \tag{13.11}$$

Now we show that introducing the new drug at a date after the expiry of the patent of the earlier generation drug will not be optimal. To do so, suppose that the innovation is introduced τ years after the expiry of patent of its earlier generation; $\tau > 0$. The sequence of introduction of new drugs is shown in Figure 13.2.

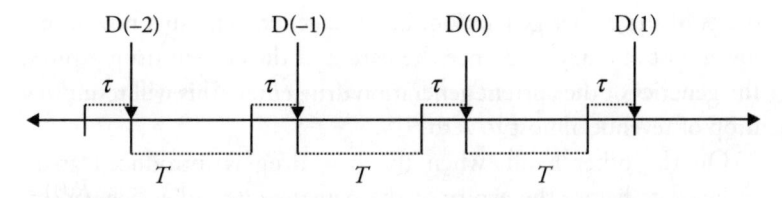

Figure 13.2 Sequence of introducing new drugs after expiry of patents

As Figure 13.2 shows, here the number of generic entrants ($\hat{n}$) will be more than n^*, that is, $\hat{n} > n^*$, because the patent of the existing drug expires before the current generation drug is introduced and hence entrants have low cost of entry. Moreover, these firms compete with the current generation for a period longer than T.

Therefore, the innovator of a drug will derive a flow of gross payoff $B(\hat{n})$ during the patent period; $B(\hat{n}) < B(n^*)$. And once its patent is expired, for the next τ years it will compete with its generics, and hence its payoff may be assumed to drop to zero due to the entry of a large number of generic producers. Hence, the net payoff that the innovator is expecting to derive from introducing a drug τ years after the patent expiry of its earlier generation is:

$$\hat{V}(\tau) = TB(\hat{n}(\tau)) + \tau.0 - \bar{I} = T\hat{B}(\tau) - \bar{I} \qquad (13.12)$$

Comparing Equations (13.7) and (13.12), we have:

$$V(0) > \hat{V}(\tau) \quad \forall \tau > 0 \qquad (13.13)$$

We are now in a position to write the main result of our chapter.

Proposition It is optimal for the originator of a drug to introduce a new competing drug before the expiry of patent of its earlier generation.

Proof Results (13.11) and (13.13) together imply that $V(t^*) > V(0) > \hat{V}(\tau)$, and hence the result.
Q.E.D.

The result can be explained as follows.[7] If the new drug is introduced after the period of patent expiry of the earlier generation, then it will face more competition from the entrants producing generic drugs of the earlier generation, because generic entrants now face a lower cost of entry, and once the patent of the current drug expires, the generics of the current generation drug enter. This will result in a drop of revenue almost to zero.

On the other hand, when the new drug is introduced at an earlier date before the expiry of the patent of its earlier generation, the innovator, by doing so, successfully increases entry costs of the potential generic entrants. Although the innovator itself incurs some

---

[7] The incumbent perhaps has an additional option, namely introducing its own generics. It has, however, two opposing effects: it increases the incumbent's profits to the extent that it saves entry costs for introducing its generics, but it reduces profits to the extent that additional competition dissipates profits.

additional costs of innovating and introducing the product earlier, under some conditions this strategy is profitable. To see the effect of an increase in t on revenue of the innovator, note that as t goes up, the length of the operation of the innovator with this drug is shortened to that extent, and hence there is some loss of revenue. On the other hand, during the period it operates, it faces less competition from generics of earlier generations. These two opposite forces give the necessary tradeoff and determine the optimal $t > 0$.

Before we go to the comparative static results, a number of related issues may be discussed briefly. One such issue is the price caps on drugs. Innovating firms sometimes engage in this kind of practice as a means for extending the patent period with minor improvements. This is also a reason that drugs may be introduced earlier. Since we are considering market-determined outcomes, we are not looking at price caps. Moreover, such a possibility will not hold with the homogeneous good case as in our setup. Second, in our model, both the incumbent and the generic producers play a simultaneous move game at the production stage. One may then think of a scenario where the generic producers have the first mover advantage. However, from the innovator's point of view, less competition (due to rising entry costs induced by early patent termination) is always good and hence our basic result should still hold. Third, our model is entirely deterministic and there is no information problem. In reality, there can be uncertainty regarding the patent termination period. Brand producers may not have perfect knowledge of exactly when the generics will come in. But note that in our model the generic suppliers will never delay their entry beyond the patent period and will enter right after the patent period is over because a delay will not give them an extra payoff. Generic producers can anticipate that there will be a new brand. But they cannot do much about it; they will have to fight armed with the generics of the old brand, given that the new brand is protected by a patent. Finally, we should mention that the present work grows out of empirical evidence in the pharmaceutical industry where the firms are observed to effectively terminate drugs before the patent period is over. We have shown that such an outcome is consistent with the rational strategic action of the innovator. While the empirical evidence generated out of a field-based survey provides the initial motivation for the work, and this appears to be appealing, but the key consideration in this chapter is that the innovator can take some strategic action that makes entry of the generics difficult.[8]

Effects of a change in T

For a comparative static analysis let us assume that t^* is a unique and stable equilibrium within the domain satisfying (13.7) and (13.10). From Equation (13.4) we shall get n as a function of t and T, that is, $n(t, T)$ with $n_t < 0$ and $n_T > 0$. Then Equation (13.9) will solve for $t^* = t(T)$ satisfying $R_t = C'$ and $\Delta \equiv R_{tt} - C'' < 0$. Hence, when T changes, it affects t^* directly (when n and n_t remain unchanged) and indirectly through the change of n and n_t. Therefore, from the condition $R_t = C'$ we shall get:

$$\frac{dt^*}{dT} = \frac{1}{-\Delta}[R_{tT} + R_{tn}n_T + R_{tn_t}n_{tT}] \qquad (13.14)$$

where:

$$\Delta = 2A'n_t + tA'n_{tt} + tA''n_t^2 + (T-2t)B'n_{tt} + (T-2t)B''n_t^2$$
$$-4B'n_t - C''$$
$$R_{tT} = B'n_t$$
$$R_{tn} = A' + tA''n_t + (T-2t)B''n_t - 2B'$$
$$R_{tn_t} = tA' + (T-2t)B'$$

It is clear that $R_{tT} > 0$. Therefore, the direct effect of a change in T is positive, that is, an increase in T will lead to an increase in t^*. Since *a priori* we cannot make any conclusion on the sign of n_{tT}, to make it simple, we may assume that $n_{tT} = 0$, that is, a change of T will lead to a parallel shift of the $n(t, T)$ function. Moreover, it is not

---

[8] For instance, Hollis (2003) and Kong and Selden (2004) have shown that an introduction of a pseudo-generic into the market by the incumbent may act as an entry deterrence or delay the entry of independent generics. And Kamien and Zang (1999) think that pre-emptive pseudo-generics are a form of virtual patent extension.

unreasonable to assume that if n goes up, it leads to a downward shift of the R_t curve,[9] hence assume $R_{tn} < 0$. Under this assumption the indirect effect of a change in T is negative. Hence, the net effect of a change of T on t^* depends on two opposing effects. When the direct effect dominates the indirect effect, t^* will go up as T increases. Then, if further, $n_{tT} < 0$, this will reinforce our conclusion.[10]

If there is a shift of E function, it has only indirect effect—t^* will change through the shift of $n(t,)$. However, if there is a shift of either I function or Z function, to the extent it results in a shift of $C'(t)$ function, t^* will be affected. For instance, if $C'(t)$ shifts up, t^* must fall.

* * *

A strong argument in favour of granting patent rights has to do with encouraging innovations since the monopoly profit of the innovator is protected over the patent period, usually for 20 years. We argue that given a guaranteed patent period, pharmaceutical firms can also engage in further anti-competitive and entry deterring strategies by withdrawing the patented drug before the expiry of the patent period. Our analysis is based on some empirical evidence where early withdrawal of the drug makes future generics less effective as competing products. Although doctors' role is crucial in the analysis, we have not explicitly modelled doctors' behaviour because it is unlikely to alter the qualitative result of the model. We highlight the role of prescribing doctors who are likely to be influenced by the persuasion of the innovating firm. We develop a simple dynamic model to capture the effect of such an interesting entry-deterring strategy.

Our chapter opens up the possibility of an interesting policy question: Should an organization, such as the FDA, allow drug companies to withdraw the patented drug before the expiry of the patented period and to introduce a new drug earlier than what is expected? The generic substitutes which are supposed to come up right after the patent period is over, will be in a disadvantageous

---

[9] We may generally presume that $A'' > 0$, $B'' > 0$. Then the sufficient condition for $R_{tn} < 0$ is $A' - 2B' \leq 0$.

[10] Since a low T means, $t^* = 0$, the strategic mechanism highlighted in the present work is provided by too high a length of the patent.

position if the doctors are somehow convinced of the 'limitations' of the drug the generics are likely to substitute. If the producer of the existing patented drug A, reveals an 'adverse side effect' and uses this as an excuse to prematurely introduce the new drug B, the generic substitute of A will be in a bad shape. We argue that the drug manufacturer/innovator might have all the incentive in the world to use such 'revelations' as a profit-increasing strategy. However, the problem is that there is no obvious way to decipher the fact whether the existing drug should really be replaced, because there is a sudden discovery of an unanticipated side-effect, or something needs to be improved upon immediately. Hence one may think to take up this particular issue, the behaviour of prescribing doctors, 'influence-fee' to induce the doctors to prescribe the new drug, etc., as inputs for further research. But, at the end, our point, that strategic withdrawal of a patented drug can lead to an anti-competitive outcome, is quite a fresh insight, so far as the economics of patents is concerned.

References

Aoki, R., and T.J. Prusa. 1993. 'International Standards of Intellectual Property Protection and R&D Incentives', *Journal of International Economics*, 35: 251–73.

Chin, J.C., and G.M. Grossman. 1991. 'Intellectual Property Rights and North-South Trade', in R.W. Jones and A.O. Krueger (eds), *The Political Economy of International Trade: Essays in Honor of R.E. Baldwin*. Cambridge, Mass.: Basil Blackwell, 90–107.

Conrad, C.A. 1983. 'The Advantages of Being First and Competition between Firms', *International Journal of Industrial Organization*, 1: 353–64.

Deardorff, A.V. 1992. 'Welfare Effects of Global Patent Protection', *Economica*, 59: 35–51.

Diwan, I., and D. Rodrik. 1991. 'Patents, Appropriate Technology and North-South Trade', *Journal of International Economics*, 30: 27–47.

Dixit, A. 1980. 'The Role of Investment in Entry Deterrence', *Economic Journal*, 90: 95–106.

Dutta, A. 2003. 'Economic Reforms and Pharmaceutical Industry in India—A Case Study', PhD thesis, Calcutta University.

Frank, R.G., and D.S. Salkever. 1992. 'Pricing, Patent Loss and the Market for Pharmaceuticals', *Southern Economic Journal*, 59: 165–79.

Grabowski, H.G., and J.M. Vernon. 1992. 'Brand Loyalty, Entry, and Price Competition in Pharmaceuticals after the 1984 Drug Act', *Journal of Law and Economics*, 35: 331–50.

Grinols, E.L., and H.C. Lin. 1997. 'Asymmetric Intellectual Property Rights Protection and North-South Welfare', Office of Research Working Paper No. 98-0106, University of Illinois.

Grossman, G.M., and E. Lai. 2004. 'International Protection of Intellectual Property', *American Economic Review*, 94: 1635–53.

Helpman, E. 1993. 'Innovation, Imitation, and Intellectual Property Rights', *Econometrica*, 61: 1247–80.

Hollis, A. 2003. 'The Anti-Competitive Effects of Brand-Controlled "pseudo-Generics" in the Canadian Pharmaceutical Market', *Canadian Public Policy*, 29: 21–31.

———. 2005. 'How Do Brands' "Own Generics" Affect Pharmaceutical Prices?', *Review of Industrial Organization*, 27: 329–50.

Kabiraj, T. 2000. 'Providing Protection to Foreign-Owned Patents—A Strategic Decision', *Keio Economic Studies*, 37: 9–24.

Kamien, M.I., and I. Zang. 1999. 'Virtual Patent Extension by Cannibalization', *Southern Economic Journal*, 66: 117–31.

Kong, Y., and J. Selden. 2004. 'Pseudo-Generic Products and Barriers to Entry in Pharmaceutical Markets', *Review of Industrial Organization*, 25: 71–86.

Lanjouw, J.O. 1997. 'The Introduction of Pharmaceutical Product Patents in India: "Heartless Exploitation of the Poor and suffering"?', NBER Working Paper No. 6366, National Bureau of Economic Research.

Marjit, S., and H. Beladi 1998. 'Product vs. Process Patents: A Theoretical Approach', *Journal of Policy Modeling*, 20: 193–9.

Maskus, K.E. 1990. 'Normative Concerns in the International Protection of Intellectual Property Rights', *World Economy*, 13: 387–409.

Milgrom, P., and J. Roberts. 1982. 'Limit Pricing and Entry under Incomplete Information: An Equilibrium Analysis', *Econometrica*, 50: 443–59.

Nogues, J.J. 1993. 'Social Costs and Benefits of Introducing Patent Protection for Pharmaceutical Drugs in Developing Countries', *The Developing Economies*, 31: 24–53.

Salop, S., and D. Schiefman. 1983. 'Raising Rival's Costs', *American Economic Review Papers and Proceedings*, 73: 267–71.

Scherer, F.M. 2002. 'A Note on Global Welfare in Pharmaceutical Patenting', Working Paper No. 03-11, Federal Reserve Bank of Philadelphia.

Scherer, F.M., and D. Ross. 1990. *Industrial Market Structure and Economic Performance*. Boston: Houghton Mifflin Co.

Schmalansee, R. 1982. 'Product Differentiation Advantages of Pioneering Brands', *American Economic Review*, 72: 349–65.

Slatter, S.S.P. 1977. *Competitive and Marketing Strategies in the Pharmaceutical Industry*. London: Croom Helm.

Statman, M. 1981. 'The Effect of Patent Expiration on the Market Position of Drugs', *Managerial and Decision Economics*, 2(2): 61–6.

Taylor, M.S. 1994. 'TRIPs, Trade and Growth', *International Economic Review*, 35: 361–81.

Watal, J. 1996. 'Introducing Product Patents in the Indian Pharmaceutical Sector—Implications for Prices and Welfare', *World Competition: Review of Law and Economics*, 20: 5–21.

Yang, Y. 1998. 'Why do Southern Countries Have Little Incentive to Protect Northern Intellectual Property Rights?', *Canadian Journal of Economics*, 31: 800–16.

14

Entry Deterrence in Banking
The Role of Cost Asymmetry and Adverse Selection

Indrajit Mallick, Sugata Marjit, and Hamid Beladi

High barriers to entry have characterized the banking industry throughout history. One reason behind this has been regulatory protection.[1] However, it should be noted that despite the weakening

---

[1] Different legislative barriers like exclusive banking charters (USA), monopoly over the right of note issue (France), or exclusive privileges regarding formation of joint stock banks (England), were in force in the early stages of banking history. While some of these legislations may have been in public interest, there are certainly some exceptions. In many cases, conflict of interests has created regulatory barriers. For example, history is replete with instances where loans to sovereign states have given the incumbent bank, or a cartel of incumbents, the monopoly right in banking in a particular territory and/or in specific products and/or with respect to certain clientele types. Bankers, eager to cultivate profitable relationships with the sovereigns states and to acquire these special privileges, offered loan commitments (one important example of this is the banking practices of the House of the Rothschilds, as documented by Ferguson (1998); also see Kennedy (1989) and his discussion on finance,

of regulatory barriers in different countries in recent times due to financial liberalization and greater competition, entry patterns have not been uniform. In Europe, despite the formation of the European Union, cross-border movements have been relatively small. The national banking markets in most of these countries are still remarkably segmented and well protected with an oligopoly of big banks commanding the major share of assets and a periphery consisting of small banks. In the United States on the other hand, the relaxation of inter-state barriers has led to movements and consolidation across state lines. At the same time, capital has shown an increasing tendency to move through cross-border branching and acquisitions by American and Spanish multinational banks at a global level. Entry seems to be conditional not only on a set of regulatory but natural barriers as well. One clearly needs to develop an industrial organization model of banking that addresses this issue satisfactorily.

There has been a proliferation of work on entry deterrence in industrial organization literature. One factor is increasing returns and literature highlighting that it has primarily focused on the excess capacity creation effect by the incumbent(s) which can directly lead to entry deterrence (see Spence (1977) and Dixit (1980)) who use the Stackelberg model of sequential capacity choices).[2] The presence of increasing returns in the banking industry certainly makes capacity

---

geography, and the winning of wars). Any reasonable model of entry barriers in the banking industry ought to pay attention to this phenomenon. The history of banking in the twentieth century was driven by the political and economic desire of banking regulators to preserve stability of the domestic banking industries through restricted competition and entry (see Caminal and Matutes (1997)). Other reasons behind regulatory barriers could be found in the subsidy requirements for agriculture (leading to protected and nationalized banking as in India or France) or the necessary protection for indigenous industry (creating inter-state barriers in the US) or capital flight that concerns emerging market countries.

[2] Other factors that have been associated empirically with deterrence or entry include product creation and differentiation advantages (with respect to specific markets like retail business, risk customization, and specialized industry), capital requirements, reputation, and the use of contracts as a barrier to entry (see Aghion and Bolton (1987) for a generic model).

creation a natural instrument for deterrence or blockade. However, one can conjecture that in recent times, fixed costs of capacity creation have become less relevant in the banking industry due to the rapid rate of obsolescence in information gathering, processing, and disseminating technology on which banking depends so heavily and the data partially supports this conjecture.[3] Another view of looking at the entry deterrence model is that of the canonical model of limit pricing under incomplete information popularized by Milgrom and Roberts (1982). The limit pricing model shows how even a weak incumbent can discourage entry by developing a reputation for tough play. When cost asymmetry is pronounced in banking and the cost structure of a bank is private information, this model becomes relevant for developing a benchmark model of entry deterrence in the banking industry. In the case of banking, which is highly intensive in the knowledge and human capital industry, cost differentials can be significant. Gehrig and Sheldon (1999) conduct an analysis of scale, scope, and x-efficiency of European banks and find significant cost differentials especially within the national borders. A major part of the cost differential stems from differences in x-efficiency rather than economies of scale or scope.[4] What emerges from all these studies is that, while we are far away from understanding the causes of cost differentials in the banking industry, they are significant and should be given adequate weight in theoretical modelling. Cost structures in banking have two components: the first and the readily observable component is the interest cost of funds generally common to all banks, but there is another component which is the cost of management of the bank which distinguishes a superior from an inferior bank. Another issue regarding cost differences or comparative advantage

---

[3] The evidence on economies of scale in banking is mixed. Using US data from the 1980s in banking, Berger and Humphrey (1991) found that medium sized banks achieve the optimal scale, while Berger et al. (1987) found little evidence on scope and product mix efficiency. On the other hand, using accounting data from the 1990s, Berger and Mester (1997) found significant scale efficiencies for a small sample set of very large banks.

[4] Another factor, which leads to differences in cost structure or comparative advantage, is the difference in the institutional structure of the industry in which the entrant and the incumbent operate (see Berger et al. (2000)).

is that they are often private information.[5] This raises the question on how cost structures are signalled in the process of credit market competition. Do efficient incumbent banks have incentives to fully reveal their costs in order to defend their markets? Can they limit price entrants by cost signalling via forward contracts with their customers? Can entrants enter despite the presence of strong incumbents? Can weak incumbents prevent entry? Answering these questions is certainly a direction of research worth pursuing and is the approach of this chapter. But our analysis of entry deterrence in banking will be incomplete unless one looks at the interaction of cost asymmetry and the classical adverse selection problem.

As Stiglitz and Weiss (1981) pointed out, credit markets are imperfect when banks face a different risk class of borrowers and cannot observe the borrower type directly. Adverse selection can cause different kinds of imperfections and literature has developed to show that entry deterrence is one of them. Broecker (1990) considers a credit market where banks face an adverse selection problem due to the presence of two types of firms (high risk and low risk). Banks use imperfect and independent tests to assess the ability of a potential borrower to repay credit. Each bank competes by announcing interest rates at which it will lend to the applicants who have passed the bank's test. The lowest interest rate of a bank's clientele will be determined by its own creditworthiness test. This is not true for the other banks, their clientele consists of all those firms which are rejected by the lower interest rate bank but accepted by itself (it will therefore contain a high ratio of high-risk firms). This means that banks face externalities caused by interest rates and the rejection decisions of other banks. The average creditworthiness decreases with the increase in the number of active banks, which means that the number of banks in equilibrium will be limited thus limiting entry. In the context of a dynamic strategic entry model, there may also be a similar kind of externality. In addition to the classical asymmetric information problem between banks and borrowers, there is also an asymmetric information problem between entering banks

---

[5] Typically, the cost of managing a bank is private information to the bank, accounting data notwithstanding. Monopoly incumbents initially can pad costs and thus an entrant cannot estimate their true costs from pricing data.

who cannot observe the type of borrowers and incumbents who do observe the types. The most notable paper to explicitly incorporate this idea in the context of entry deterrence is that by Dell'Ariccia et al. (1999). They show that where only incumbent(s) can first screen and make the accept/reject decisions on loan applicants, and entrant(s) can only screen after those accepted have already received credit in the first period, an adverse selection problem develops for the latter and it blockades entry. This is due to the fact that entrants cannot identify those rejected by the incumbents. This raises screening costs and reduces profitability of entrants and creates blockaded entry or deterred entry. Dell'Ariccia (2001) analyses the effects of informational asymmetries on the market structure of the banking industry in a multi-period model of spatial competition. Incumbent banks gather proprietary information about their clients in the process of lending, and acquire an advantage over potential entrants. This informational advantage may act as a barrier to entry unless the growth rate of the new borrowers is sufficiently high. Finally, the chapter shows that even in the absence of fixed costs, there will be a finite number of banks in the steady state. Gehrig (1998) tackles the issue of sequential competition by using a dynamic framework. He shows that when such an adverse selection problem exists for entrants, and, to reinforce that, incumbents can offer contracts that meets the lowest interest rate offered by entrants (competition meeting clauses), barriers to entry remain very high. However, to the extent that screening costs are increased due to greater competition, both entrants as well as incumbents will have the incentive to reduce screening intensity. As a result, there will be some entry but the asset qualities of banks may worsen severely due to negative effects on screening incentives. Hauswald and Marquez (2000) focus on the interaction of the adverse selection effect which curtails competition and the effect of competition on informational rent erosion. In their model, banks tend to shift more resources in their core sector as competition can be more effectively tackled in the core sector where they have closer relationships with clients rather than at the periphery where they give transactions loans. Marquez (2002) argues that with increased competition in the banking industry, information about borrower quality becomes more dispersed, reducing screening ability of banks and lowering efficiency. The incumbency information advantage is shown to deter entry unless there is a high borrower turnover and entrants have expertise in dealing with specific credit risks. Since information under adverse selection and moral hazard is a valuable good, banks may have an incentive to strategically display and share information. A pertinent question is the effect of information sharing on banking competition. Padilla and Pagano (1997) argue that banks may try to release information in order to raise the effort levels of borrowers but this increases the degree of competition also so that information sharing will be limited. Gehrig and Stenbacka (2001) show that information sharing may act as a collusive device, because a reduction in future informational rents reduces current competition. Another paper worth mentioning in this context is that by Bouckaert and Degryse (2006). They argue that incumbent lenders' releasing information about their profitable borrowers through private credit registries are motivated by strategic reasons. The pool of unreleased borrowers creates a severe adverse selection problem and prevents or restricts entry for high type but unsuccessful borrowers.

In all these mentioned papers (and others in this specific literature), there is an externality problem between banks. This externality takes the form of adverse selection between banks in addition to that between banks and their borrowers. In other words, incumbent banks know more about the market of borrowers than the entrant(s). As long as the adverse selection problem is not uniform, the externality remains, creates, and sustains an oligopolistic structure in the banking industry with emphasis on diversity of outcomes like differential credit, information, and entry blockade or deterrence.

In this chapter, we attempt to make a contribution to existing literature and derive some general conditions for entry deterrence in banking. First, we have a model without the adverse selection problem between banks and borrowers, but in terms of information asymmetry about cost differentials. We show that adverse selection between banks and borrowers is not necessary for entry deterrence and develop an alternative externality generating model in terms of cost asymmetry. Next, we incorporate the classical adverse selection problem of the credit market. We show that a differential adverse selection may not be sufficient to deter entry in this model.

The Model with Cost Asymmetry and without Adverse Selection

In this section, we highlight the role that cost asymmetry can play in entry deterrence in banking. We assume that the borrower type is uniform and well known so that there is no adverse selection problem in the credit market. Generating entry deterrence in this setup has two implications. Firstly, if cost differentials in banking are significant (as is documented in the empirical literature so far), then relative cost efficiency can create the externality needed for entry deterrence. Incumbents charge an interest rate for forward contracts and the interest rate charged can signal the type of the incumbent to the entrant and cause entry deterrence at when the signal is that the incumbent is of the strong/low cost type. Thus, this model asks us to take cost differentials in banking seriously. Secondly, the fact that we generate entry deterrence without an adverse selection problem implies that adverse selection is not strictly necessary for entry deterrence.

There are two dates $t = 0$ and $t = 1$ which mark the beginning and the end of a contractual period respectively. At $t = 0$ a forward market for loan opens where the incumbent bank can promise a loan to a borrower at a specified interest rate. If the borrower accepts the contract then the contract is executed at $t = 1$ and there is no entry. Otherwise, if the forward contracts offered by the bank are rejected at $t = 0$ then at $t = 1$, the spot market for credit opens and the entrant takes the decision to enter or not, and a limit pricing game ensues in the spot market.

There is a single borrower who has no funds of its own and needs one unit of credit at $t = 1$. Its project has a return denoted by V. Also, there exists a single incumbent bank. It can be of one of the two types, distinguished by its cost of funds, r_i, where i denotes type of fund cost, and the type can be strong ($i = s$) or weak ($i = w$) with probability p and $1 - p$ respectively.

Let us assume that $r_w > r_s$ and the incumbent knows its type but others do not. Also, the entrant appears at $t = 1$. Its cost of funds is r_e. Next we assume that, $V > r_w > r_e > r_s$. This is an interesting and non-trivial case. Assuming the entrant's cost is higher than either type ($r_e > r_w > r_s$) rules out entry trivially and similarly assuming a cost advantage over both ($r_w > r_s > r_e$) generates entry with probability of one in all states of nature.

In order to ascertain the sequence of moves, we construct Table 14.1.

Table 14.1 Sequence of Moves

Date	Event
$t = 0$	Nature determines type 'i'
$t = 0$	Incumbent offers forward contract $r(i)$
$t = 0$	Borrower accepts or rejects
$t = 1$	Entrant decides on entry
$t = 1$	Bertrand competition if entry

The incumbent can offer any rate of interest belonging to the real line R. Note that given the forward contract offer, the entrant can make an inference about the type of the incumbent. Thus, we have a posterior probability function $q_i(r[i])$ which gives the probability that a signal is coming from a strong type given the signal is $r(i)$. The entrant can either enter or decide not to. We have the entrant's decision function as $d_e(r[i])$ which takes the value E (enter) or D (do not enter). Given the posterior beliefs of the entrant about the incumbent type, there is an optimal decision function of the entrant which maps each possible belief to a unique point in the binary action space of the entrant (enter, do not enter).

Assumption I(i) The borrower is strategic and updates priors by Bayes' Rule. The borrower accepts the forward contract only when it believes that the incumbent is of a strong type and the participation constraint of the borrower is satisfied.

Assumption I(ii) We assume that no bank will offer a contract that gives it a zero profit.

As described earlier, we have a dynamic game of incomplete information. The relevant equilibrium concept for this type of game is Perfect Bayesian equilibrium. Therefore, the equilibrium of this signalling game G is a strategy profile $[r(i), d_e\{r(i)\}]$ and posterior beliefs $q_i[r(i)]$ such that:

$$\forall i, r(i) \in \arg\max \Pi_i[q_i\{r[i]\}, d_e(q_i)] \qquad \text{(i)}$$
$$\forall r(i), d_e(q_i) \in \arg\max \Pi_e[r(i), q_i\{r(i)\}]. \qquad \text{(ii)}$$

For the information sets belonging to the equilibrium path of game G, the posterior probabilities are related to the priors in the following way:

$$q_i\{r(i)\} = [p(i)\,p\{r(i)/i\}] / \Sigma[p(i)\,p\{r(i)/i\}] \text{ (Bayes' Rule)}. \qquad \text{(iii)}$$

Proposition 1 There exists a unique separating equilibrium (in pure strategies) where the strong incumbent deters entry and entry takes place if the incumbent is weak.

Proof Consider the case when the incumbent is of a strong type. The borrower will compare between the expected spot market contract (if it rejects the forward contract) and the forward contract. If the incumbent is strong, then there is no entry since when the strong incumbent successfully signals its type, the entrant will not enter as limit pricing under Bertrand competition will imply zero profit for the entrant. Given Assumption I(ii), the entrant will not enter. Thus, the participation constraint of the borrower will be determined by the forward contract given the signal that the incumbent is of the strong type. The strong type of incumbent has to also offer a contract that ensures that a weak type of incumbent cannot mimic the contract given Assumption I(ii). So the strong type incumbent solves the following maximization problem:

$$\max_{r(s)} [r(s) - r_s]$$

subject to:

$$V - r(s) \geq 0 \qquad (14.1)$$

$$r(s) - r_w \leq 0. \qquad (14.2)$$

The inequality (1) is the participation constraint of the borrower(s) and the inequality (2) is the incentive compatibility or no mimicking condition.

Given that $r_w < V$, the optimal solution is $r(s) = r_w$. Note that this satisfies the participation constraint and that the weak type of incumbent cannot mimic this contract with positive profit. When the entrant observes the contract $E(r)$ it correctly infers that—with probability of one—the incumbent is of a strong type. Hence, it results in deterrence. For all other contracts $r \neq E(r)$, the entrant infers, with probability of one, that the incumbent is of a weak type. Therefore, in such cases, it enters. Further, since the pure strategy solution to the strong type's and the weak type's problem is unique, the equilibrium of the game is unique as well.

Q.E.D

The Model with Asymmetric Costs and Differential Adverse Selection

Our benchmark model can now be easily modified to accommodate the adverse selection problem in the credit market. Now we introduce two kinds of borrowers ('high return, low risk', and 'low return, high risk'). In this section, we introduce a differential adverse selection by assuming that the incumbent has an information advantage over the entrant. We allow the advantage to be maximum in the sense that the incumbent is assumed to have complete and perfect information about the type of borrowers, while the entrant knows only the distribution of the borrower types.

To formally introduce adverse selection, we modify the benchmark model in the following way:

Assumption II(i) There are two types of borrowers: the high type incumbent bank (denoted by h), which has a marginal revenue f_h from borrowing with probability p_h, and the low type (denoted by l), which has a marginal revenue ϕ_l from borrowing with probability p_l, where:

(a) $p_l \phi_l < p_h \phi_l < r_w < p_h \phi_h$, and,

(b) $\{(\phi_h - (r_w / p_h)\} / (\phi_h - \phi_l) \geq (\lambda)/(1-\lambda)$.

The type of the borrower is private information to the entrant but known to the incumbent.

Assumption II(ii) Resource constraint of the bank is given by:
$B_1 \lambda N + B_2 (1-\lambda) N = L$

where L is total loanable funds, λ is the proportion of high type of borrowers, N is the total number of borrowers, B_1 is the amount lent to high type in exchange for promised return R_1, and B_2 is the amount lent to low type of borrowers who are supposed to pay back R_2.

Assumption II(iii) The borrowers are strategic and update priors by the Bayes Rule. They accept a forward contract only when they believe that the incumbent is of a strong type.

The sequence of moves and the definition of equilibrium is as discussed earlier. In order to show that differential adverse selection is not a sufficient condition for entry deterrence, we have to basically show that for a strong incumbent, there will exist some parameter values which generate entry. The following proposition shows this.

Proposition 2 The strong incumbent will offer contract for the high type of borrower only. When the incumbent is strong the entrant will enter only if $\phi_l p_l > r_e$ (in this case the entrant will target the low type of borrower) and the entrant will not enter if $r_e \geq \phi_l p_l$.

Proof Since the project returns are linear, the strong incumbent will target the high type only. The decision problem of the strong incumbent is as follows:

Choose (R_1, B_1) to solve $\max[R_1 p_j - r_s B_1]\lambda N$, subject to:

$$p_h(\phi_h B_1 - R_1) \geq 0 \tag{14.3}$$

$$0 \geq \{R_1 p_h - r_w B_1\}\lambda N, \tag{14.4}$$

where Equation (14.3) is the participation constraint of the high type of borrower and the inequality given by Equation (14.4) is the no mimicking condition that ensures effective signalling about the (strong) incumbent type. The no mimicking condition is binding from Assumption II(i)(a), so that:

$$\{R_1 p_h - r_w B_1\}\lambda N = 0.$$

Then we have,

$$R_1 = r_w[B_1/p_h]$$

or,

$$(R_1/B_1) = (r_w/p_h), \tag{14.5}$$

where $(r_w/p_h) < \phi_h$.

Note that the other given constraint is also satisfied.

With this strategy we can state the following:

Whenever $(R_1/B_1) = (r_w/p_h)$, the entrant believes the incumbent is strong and targets the low type and we have:

$$\max \{R_2 p_l - r_e B_2\} (1 - \lambda)N$$

subject to

$$(\phi_l B_2 - R_2) \geq 0 \text{ (participation constraint)} \tag{14.6}$$

Since the low return borrowers form a captive market of the entrant, there is no incentive constraint to satisfy. $(R_2/B_2) = \phi_l$.

From Assumption II(i)(b) we have $\{\phi_h - (r_w/p_h)\}/(\phi_h - \phi_l) \geq (\lambda)/(1-\lambda)$.

or $\{\phi_h - (r_w/p_h)\} L/(\lambda N) \geq (\phi_h - \phi_l) L/[(1-\lambda)N])$

Note that this implies that incentive constraint for the high type is also satisfied, since:

$$(\phi_h B_1 - R_1) = \{\phi_h - (r_w/p_h)\}L/(\lambda N) \geq (\phi_h - \phi_l)L/[(1-\lambda)N] = (\phi_h B_2 - R_2).$$

It is easy to verify that the condition for entry is $\phi_l p_l > r_e$.
Q.E.D.

When the incumbent bank is of a strong type, the market essentially becomes segmented and there is room for everybody under certain parameter values. The efficient incumbent takes the market of the high return, low risk client by threatening the entrant with the signal of the limit price while the entrant may find that entering the market for the low return, high risk borrowers might still be better than not entering at all when credit market segmentation offsets the externality effect between banks. Our market segmentation result has the same flavour as that of Marquez (2002) who shows that increased competition under adverse selection increases information dispersion and causes segmentation in the credit market. Hauswald and Marquez (2000) show that with increasing competition, banks shift their focus on their core sectors (where they have a comparative advantage) and the resulting market structure is segmented. In our model segmentation results from signalling given linearity of returns for borrower types.

* * *

In this chapter we reviewed and explored the strategic mechanisms that deter entry to the banking industry. The existing models of entry deterrence in banking primarily highlight adverse selection as the main driving force behind deterrence and ignore the role of cost differences or comparative advantage in banking. This chapter attempted to contribute to emerging literature on the subject and to clarify certain issues. There are two basic premises of this chapter. The first is arguing that cost asymmetry and private information about costs can be important in the context and then building upon the premise of cost differences to show that pre-emptive forward contracts which signal cost differences play a vital role in entry deterrence in banking. The second point of the chapter was illustrating that adverse selection in the credit market between a bank and its borrowers is neither a necessary nor a sufficient condition for entry deterrence.

To show that adverse selection is not a necessary factor for entry deterrence in banking, we constructed a game where there is cost asymmetry between incumbent banks and private information about the incumbent type. This allowed us to use a signalling game approach to entry deterrence in banking. The insight generated is that pre-emptive forward contracts are sufficient to convey incumbent strength and discourage entry when the incumbent is strong. Thus, even without adverse selection one can have entry deterrence though it should be noted that there must exist some kind of asymmetry between the banks which creates an externality as mentioned in the literature studied. The asymmetry in cost structure is thus a complementary way of looking at entry deterrence in banking with respect to existing literature.

Incorporating the adverse selection problem of the credit market in our model shows that entry becomes possible even if the incumbent is of a strong type. This is because the incumbent does not find it optimal to monopolize the market faced with the problem of signalling under linear project returns of borrowers. The information advantage of the incumbent in the latter model cannot deter entry for some parameter constellations.

One must note that we focused on adverse selection between banks and borrowers and we did not label the externality between banks as 'adverse selection'. However, our approach relying on cost asymmetry and incomplete information with signalling of cost, can be viewed as a model of externality or 'adverse selection' between banks. While adverse selection between banks and borrowers has been shown to be neither necessary nor sufficient for entry deterrence, adverse selection or externality between banks is clearly necessary for entry deterrence. The spirit of the chapter should be taken in the sense of enriching the literature by means of developing a complementary approach.

Another point should be clarified here: adverse selection does ensure that the strong incumbent prevents entry in the market for high return borrowers, but cannot (and does not want to) prevent entry for low-return borrowers. Thus, there is entry deterrence for a class of borrowers while there is also entry for another class of borrowers. Thus, while one concurs with literature that the adverse selection problem usually acts in the favour of the incumbent bank and may restrict entry, adverse selection can also cause effective segmentation of the credit market and ease entry.

In reality, competition for markets and entry games in banking takes place under a variety of institutional settings. In industrial organization models, mergers are usually anti-competitive and deter entry in an industry in most cases though there are exceptions to this general rule. Berger et al. (1999) find that mergers among incumbents increase entry by de novo lenders. On the other hand Seelig and Critchfield (1999) find that local market entry by acquisition deters concurrent entry by de novo banks and thrifts. Two aspects are highlighted in these studies: first, mergers between big banks can cause a gap in small business lending which de novo banks are can fill up. Second, entry can take place by acquisition rather than branching. These indicate that the strategy choices for both incumbents as well as entrants can be quite rich. Further, the types of incumbents (strong or weak, big or small) and entrants (established in other markets versus de novo lenders) do matter and can arise endogenously in equilibrium as a result of investment strategies or mergers. Exploring these issues remains another challenge for future research.

References

Aghion, P., and P. Bolton. 1987. 'Entry Prevention Through Contracts with Customers', *American Economic Review*, 77: 388–401.

Berger, A., S. Bonime, L. Goldberg, and L. White. 1999. 'The Dynamics of Market Entry: The Effects of Mergers and Acquisitions on De Novo Entry and Small Business Lending in the Banking Industry', Working Paper, Board of Governors of the Federal Reserve System.

Berger, A., G. Hanweck, and D. Humphrey. 1987. 'Competitive Viability in Banking: Scale, Scope and Product Mix Economies', *Journal of Monetary Economics*. 20: 501–20.

Berger, A., and D. Humphrey. 1991. 'The Dominance of Inefficiencies over Scale and Product Mix Economies in Banking', *Journal of Monetary Economics*, 28: 117–48.

Berger, A., and L. Mester. 1997. 'Inside the Black Box: What Explains the Differences in the Efficiencies of the Financial Institutions', *Journal of Banking Finance*. 21: 895–947.

Berger, A., G. Udell, R. DeYoung, and H. Gunay. 2000. 'Globalization of Financial Institutions: Evidence from Cross Border Banking Performance', Brookings-Wharton Papers on Financial Services Vol. 3.

Broecker, T. 1990. 'Credit-Worthiness Tests and Interbank Competition', *Econometrica*, 58(2): 429–52.

Bouckaert, J., and H. Degryse. 2006. 'Entry and Strategic Information Display in Credit Markets', *The Economic Journal*, 116: 702–20.

Caminal, R., and C. Matutes. 1997. 'Can Competition in the Credit Market be Excessive?', CEPR Discussion Paper No. 1725, London.

Dell'Ariccia, G. 2001. 'Asymmetric Information and the Structure of the Banking Industry', *European Economic Review*, 45: 1957–80.

Dell'Ariccia, G., E. Friedman, R. Marquez. 1999. 'Adverse Selection as a Barrier to Entry in the Banking Industry', *RAND Journal of Economics*, 30: 515–34.

Dixit, A. 1980. 'The Role of Investment in Entry Deterrence', *The Economic Journal*, 90(357): 95–106.

Ferguson, Niall. 1998. *The House of Rothschild—Money's Prophets 1798–1848*. Cambridge: Penguin Books.

Gehrig, T. 1998. 'Screening, Cross-border Banking, and the Allocation of Credit', *Research in Economics*, 52: 387–407.

Gehrig, T., and G. Sheldon. 1999. 'Costs, Competitiveness and the Changing Structure of European Banking', Working Paper, Report to Fondation Banque de France.

Gehrig, T., and R. Stenbacka. 2001. 'Information Sharing in Banking: A Collusive Device?', Discussion Paper 2911, Centre for Economic Policy Research.

Hauswald, R., and R. Marquez. 2000. 'Relationship Banking, Loan Specialization and Competition', Working Paper, University of Maryland.

Kennedy, P. 1989. *The Rise and Fall of Great Powers: Economic Change and Military Conflict from 1500 to 2000*. Oxford: Fontana Press.

Marquez, R. 2002. 'Competition, Adverse Selection and Information Dispersion in the Banking Industry', *Review of Financial Studies*, 15: 901–26.

Milgrom, P., and J. Roberts. 1982. 'Limit Pricing and Entry under Incomplete Information: An Equilibrium Analysis', *Econometrica*, 50: 443–60.

Padilla, J.A., and M. Pagano. 1997. 'Endogenous Communication among Lenders and Entrepreneurial Incentives', *Review of Financial Studies*, 10: 205–36.

Seelig, S., and T. Critchfield. 1999. 'Determinants of De Novo Entry in Banking', *FDIC Banking Review*, 12(2): 1–14.

Spence, A. 1977. 'Entry, Capacity, Investment and Oligopolistic Pricing', *Bell Journal of Economics*, 8: 534–44.

Stiglitz, J., and A. Weiss. 1981. 'Credit Rationing in Credit Markets with Imperfect Information', *American Economic Review*, 71: 393–410.

About the Editors and Contributors

Editors

SUGATA MARJIT is the RBI Professor of Industrial Economics at, and former Director of, the Centre for Studies in Social Sciences, Calcutta; Member of the State Planning Board, Government of West Bengal; and the former Chairman of the West Bengal State Council of Higher Education. He is a recipient of the Mahalanobis Medal of the Indian Econometric Society (2002) and the VKRV Rao National Prize in Social Science (2003). He has held visiting teaching and research positions at the Universities of Bonn, Cornell, Queensland, Rochester, among others and at the International Monetary Fund. He has published widely in international journals and edited volumes.

MEENAKSHI RAJEEV is the RBI Chair Professor at the Centre for Economic Studies and Policy in the Institute for Social and Economic Change, Bangalore. She has graduated from the Indian Institute of Technology, Kanpur and thereafter obtained her PhD degree in Economics from the Indian Statistical Institute, Kolkata, under the supervision of Professor Dipankar Dasgupta. She has extensive teaching experience in both India and abroad. Her current research interests include issues related to monetary theory and financial sector and industrial economics. She has wide-ranging publications in both theoretical and empirical aspects of economics.

Contributors

ASIS KUMAR BANERJEE is a former Vice-Chancellor and a former Professor of Economics, University of Calcutta. He has held visiting positions at the Centre for Economic Studies, Presidency College (now Presidency University), Kolkata, Indian Statistical Institute, New Delhi, and the University of California, Riverside, California. He is presently an Honorary Professor of Economics at the Institute of Development Studies, Kolkata. His present research interests include game theory, the microeconomics of developing economies and the measurement of multidimensional inequality and poverty.

HAMID BELADI is Professor of Economics and IBC Bank Senior faculty Fellow at the University of Texas at San Antonio. He is the Editor of *International Review of Economics and Finance*, Series Editor of *Frontiers of Economics and Globalization*, Associate Editor of *Review of International Economics*, and Managing Editor of the *North American Journal of Economics and Finance*. Beladi has published in a wide spectrum of scholarly journals including *Journal of International Economics*, *European Economic Review*, *Review of International Economics*, *Journal of Economic Theory*, *Journal of Mathematical Economics*, and *Mathematical Social Science*.

KALYAN CHATTERJEE is Distinguished Professor of Economics and Management Science at the Pennsylvania State University. His research interests include game theory, bargaining, networks and research, and development, especially diffusion.

SARBAJIT CHAUDHURI is Professor, Department of Economics at the Calcutta University. He mainly performs policy-oriented theoretical research. His areas of interest include development economics, labour economics, international economics, and micro-economics.

PRABAL ROY CHOWDHURY is Professor of Economics at the Delhi Centre of the Indian Statistical Institute. His research interests include game theory, industrial organization, bargaining theory, development economics and political economy. Some of his recent works deal with issues in micro-finance, land acquisition, and terrorism.

ROMAR CORREA is the RBI Professor of Monetary Economics at the University of Mumbai. He works on the interface between micro-funded and structural macroeconomics.

About the Editors and Contributors

KRISHNENDU GHOSH DASTIDAR is a Professor of Economics, at the Jawaharlal Nehru University, New Delhi. His research interests are oligopoly theory, auction theory, and game theory.

BHASKAR DUTTA is Professor of Economics, University of Warwick. His main research interests are in Cooperative Game Theory, Mechanism Design, Strategic Formation of Social Networks, and Social Choice Theory.

ARIJITA DUTTA is Associate Professor of Economics at Calcutta University. She completed her master's degree from Jawaharlal Nehru University, New Delhi and PhD from University of Calcutta. Her research interest lies in Health Economics, Development Economics, and Econometrics. Arijita has a number of publications in national and international journals to her credit and has completed a number of research projects.

TARUN KABIRAJ is Professor of Economics and a faculty member of the Indian Statistical Institute, Kolkata. He is an economic theorist. His current research is related to the issues of joint venture, merger, technology transfer, R&D, and patent protection.

MUKUL MAJUMDAR is H.T. and R.I. Warshow Professor of Economics and a faculty member of the Center for Applied Mathematics, Cornell University. He is an economic theorist. His current research is related to models of corruption, insurance theory, and management of resources under uncertainty.

INDRAJIT MALLICK received his PhD from Jadavpur University. He has worked for Boston University, PricewaterhouseCoopers, as well as Centre for Studies in Social Sciences, Calcutta. Mallick has published in areas of finance, game theory, and legal philosophy.

TAPAN MITRA is Goldwin Smith Professor of Economics at Cornell University. He is an Alfred P. Sloan Fellow and a Fellow of the Econometric Society. His research interests are economic dynamics, social choice, and natural resource economics.

VIVEKANANDA MUKHERJEE is an Associate Professor at Department of Economics, Jadavpur University, Kolkata. His area of research is public economics.

ANJAN MUKHERJI is Professor Emeritus at Jawaharlal Nehru University and Honorary Visiting Professor at the National Institute of Public Finance and Policy. He is also the Country Director of the International Growth Centre's India–Bihar programme.

GORDON MYERS is Professor of Economics at Simon Fraser University (SFU) who works in the areas of Urban Economics and Public Economics. He is currently working as Associate Vice-President Academic at SFU.

DEBRAJ RAY is Julius Silver Professor of Economics, Faculty of Arts and Science, and Professor of Economics, at New York University. He is Co-editor of the *American Economic Review* and Research Associate at the National Bureau of Economic Research (USA). His research interests are microeconomics, game theory, and development economics.

DIRK T.G. RÜBBELKE is Professor of Economics at Freiberg University of Mining and Technology in Germany. Before he joined Freiberg University, he was Ikerbasque Research Professor at the Basque Centre for Climate Change (BC3), Bilbao in Spain (2010–14), Senior Research Fellow at the Center for International Climate and Environmental Research, Oslo (CICERO) in Norway (2008–10) and Junior Professor of European Economics at Chemnitz University of Technology in Germany (2002–8). His main fields of research are environmental and resource economics.

TILAK SANYAL did his MA in Economics from Jadavpur University in 2005 and PhD in Public Economics from Jadavpur University in 2011. Sanyal currently teaches Economics at Shibpur Dinobundhoo Institution (College). His areas of interest lie in private provision of public goods, its application in different fields and economics of corruption.

ABHIRUP SARKAR is Professor of Economics at the Indian Statistical Institute, Kolkata. He is also the current Chairman of the State Finance Commission of West Bengal, Chairman of West Bengal Infrastructure Development Finance Corporation, and a member of West Bengal State Planning Board. His research interests are in international trade, economic development, and political economy.

ABHIJIT SENGUPTA is a senior lecturer at the University of Sydney. His research interests are in game theory and its applications to fields such as coalition formation, political competition, and auction theory.

SEUNG HAN YOO is an Assistant Professor of Economics, Korea University. His current research interests include models of corruption, signalling theory with investment, discrimination, and learning under incomplete information.

Index

absolute power 24
admissible strategy profile 31
adverse selection xxvi–xxvii, 271–4
   differential 274–7
   problems 148, 268–70
agents
   indirect exchange of goods 82
   looking for trading
      opportunities 85
   searching for trading partners
      82–3
   specialized in production 84
   types of 84
   welfare derived by 92
aggregate payoffs 144–5, 168, 170–3, 177, 181, 184
Arthashastra 18, 21
asset securitization 110
assortative matching xx, 137–9, 144–7
asymmetric information xxvi–xxvii

bad governance 153
bank/banking system 110
   credit 119
   financing of inventory
      accumulation 110
   loans 109

market segmentation 276
money 108
monitoring of lending 138
officers's/official(s) 118, 120
   behavioural patterns of 119
   maximization exercise 130
   second stage 122–4
   profits 108, 110
   resource constraint of 274–5
   superstructure for profits 112
banking industry
   classical asymmetric information
      problem between borrowers
      and 268–9
   compete by announcing interest
      rates 268
   cost asymmetry 267–8, 270–4
   cost structure in, components of
      267–8
   credit markets impact on 268
   entry deterrence model in
      banking sector (*see* entry
      deterrence model in banking
      sector)
   high barriers 265
   impact of competition on 277
   increased competition impact
      on 269

increasing returns presence in 266–7
informational asymmetries on market structure on, effects of 269
lowest interest rate of bank's clientele 268
releasing of information to raise levels of borrowers 270
banking sector in India xviii
bargaining
and competition, relationship between xxiv
with incomplete information 194
Bayesian equilibria xxiv
Bayes' rule 35, 201, 212, 272–3, 275
Bertrand competition 33, 36, 272–3
bilateral bargaining under incomplete information 194
four-player game with incomplete information (*see* four-player game with incomplete information)
two-player bargaining game with incomplete information (*see* two-player bargaining game with incomplete information)
binding contracts 8
borrowed funds xx
borrower(s) xviii, xx, 133, 136–8, 140–2, 147, 268–70, 272–3, 278
bad 139, 144–5
classical asymmetric information problem between bank and 268–9
cross-reporting by 148
failure to repay 143
good 144–6
increased competition in banking industry 269, 276
informal interest rates to paid by final xix
loan recoveries from 118
marginal 118
participation constraint of 273
positive assortative matching impact on 138–9
private 112
single 271
small 118
strategic and update priors by Bayes Rule 275
suicides committed by xix
types of 274–7
Bose, Amitava xii–xiv, 3–4, 57, 81
bribes xix, 25–32, 119–21, 131
bureaucracy in Indian subcontinent, inherited from British Raj 25
bureaucrats (BUs)
demand for bribe for each approval 25, 27
interaction between investor and 27–32
L-M-R model interpreted as 25
rotation of xv
buyers' xxiv, 195
common 196
many 210–11
movement in sequence 197–8
payoffs 198–9
capital
gains 111
inflow xxi, 156–7, 159

Index

mobility 156
stock xvi, 44–7, 55, 108
Capital 107
capital accumulation xv–xvi
capital (government investment) budget
   Keynes' recommendation to separate budget into 113
   policy of public works accounted in 113
capitalist economy xviii
capital over-accumulation 44
central bank 110–11
   funding of economic activity and its impact xviii
   purchase of long-term debt 113
   purchases of short-term riskless paper 112–13
   purchase to affect long-term interest rates 112
characteristic function of coalition 180
Chaudhuri and Dastidar (CD) model 118–19
   bank official (*see* bank official)
   dominant moneylenders (*see* dominant moneylenders)
   fringe moneylenders (*see* fringe moneylenders)
circuit approach 108
citizens 22, 24
clean development mechanism (CDM) of Kyoto scheme 219–20
ψ-coalitional form 180–4
coalition concept
   formal analysis of 169
   formation 169
   function 180
   -proof equilibrium xxiii, xxiii
   structure 178–9

coalition formation model 169
coalition proof Nash equilibrium (CPNE) 174, 178, 182–3, 186, 189
collusion building 26
columns first approach 69
combined market 95–9
commercial banks 110, 113
commodity markets xvi
comonotonic poverty matrices 65, 68
competition with incomplete information
   among buyers to equalize equilibrium 195
   among sellers 194
competitive behaviour 8, 19
   options to restore 16–18
competitive economy 81
competitive equilibrium xvii, xiv–xv, 19
   configuration 4
   and Nash equilibrium 8–10
   rationale for interest in 5–8
   trades at and possible deviations 12–13
      general results of deviations 14–16
competitive market forces 5–6
competitive market framework 5
competitive strategy for agents xiv
competitive transactions xiv, 16–17
   incentive for 10–12
complementary trading partner xvii, 89–91, 97, 100
complete information game 198–200, 207–8
Congress regime xxii
consistent stock-flow modelling strategy 108
consumption(s) 43, 95–9

agents specialization in
  production 84
associated 47
of commodity/goods xxv, 83,
  85, 89, 109, 224, 245
credit 107
government 113
level in each country,
  determination of 234
South country chooses value of
  its 242
contingent renewal 139
cooperative games 180
core equivalence theorem 180n6
correlation increasing majorization
  (CIM) 58–9, 64–5, 67–8, 72–3
correlation increasing transfers
  (CITs) 58, 64
corruption xiv–xv
  in distribution of formal credit
    118
  interest in 21
  primary ingredients/
    environments of 23
  public debates on 22
  role in discouraging foreign
    investment in developing
    countries 25
  types of 22–3
cost asymmetry role in banking
  industry xxvii, 267–8, 270–4
cost of participating concept 83
costs in banking sector,
  components of xxvi–xxvii
credit 107
  formal (*see* formal credit)
  informal (*see* informal credit)
  markets xx, 118, 268, 271, 276
  subsidy policy 118–19, 130
current (government
  consumption) budget, Keynes'
  recommendation to separate
    budget into 113
current prices 108

Dasgupta, Dipankar xii–xiv, 3–4,
  57, 81
decentralized exchange process
  xvii
decentralized process of exchange
  82
deficit financing
  of capital spending 113
  of current spending 113
democracy
  effect on growth xxi
  elected officials favour to specific
    group 26
  functioning in less-developed
    countries 154–5
  relationship between
    and economic development
      153–4
    and economic performance
      xx–xxi
  with universal franchise xxi
de novo lenders 278–9
deprivation 58, 66
developed (North) country(ies)
  advantage in production of
    relatively less pollution-
    intensive good 2 xxiv, 233
  choice of technology transfer
    237, 240
  consumption of goods at
    international prices 233–4,
    240
  equilibrium consumption levels
    of 234
  global welfare function
    maximization 228
  goods production in 222–4

Index

partial technology transfer by 239
specialization in goods production 240
technology transfer to South 230, 240–1
tighter restrictions on output expansion 241
transfer of abatement technology by 241
utility function for consumption of goods 224–5
developing countries/economy
multiple forms of markets, existence of xvi–xvii
trying to adopt market-driven institutional systems xi
development economists 133, 156
direct barter trade 86, 88–9, 94, 96–101
diversified consumption 98–9
dominant moneylenders 121, 125
double-entry book keeping 108
drug market, conditions for entry in 250
drug prices 249
dynamic game-theoretic framework xvii
dynamic joint liability 143

early withdrawal of patented drugs (*see* patented drugs, early withdrawal of)
economic agents xix, 193
behaviour and payoff functions of 119–20
economic development 153
economic freedom xx–xxi, 153
economic growth, aggregative model of 47
economic institution xx

economic performance xx–xxi, xxii
economic reforms xi
efficiency 43–5, 178–82
efficient allocation 15
endogenous group formation, analyses of problem 138
entrepreneurial profits 106, 108–9
entry deterrence model in banking sector 266–8
by acquisition 278
with asymmetric costs and differential adverse selection 274–7
conditions for 270
with cost asymmetry and without adverse selection 271–4
equilibrium/equilibria concept 178–82
federation structures 173–4
four-player game with incomplete information 209
of one-stage game 31–2
payoffs 171, 198–200, 205–8, 212
regulation profile 37
subgame perfect equilibrium (*see* subgame perfect equilibrium)
types of 86
in undominated strategies 29–31
without commitment 225–7
equilibrium for the economy 15
equilibrium framework 220
equity
fixed at issue price 108
valued at current prices 108
Equivalence Theorem 5–8
European banks 267
European Union (EU) 185
cross-border movements in 266

excess demand 14
  functions of 17
exchange process of goods 82
expenditure of workers 108

FDA 261
Federal Convention of 1787, Philadelphia 167
Federal Reserve (Fed) 106, 112–13
federation
  aggregate payoff of 170
  assignment of shares of 171
  definition of 169–70
  economic motive for 167
  externalities across 171
  formation xx, xxii, 180, 183
    equilibrium structures 173–4
    partnership plans and federation structure rules 172–3
    restrictions on structure rules 175–7
  grand (*see* grand federation)
  sharing rules for each 177–9
  smallest (*see* smallest federation)
  states coordinate actions within 172
  structure of 168–70, 176
    conjecture 175
    determination of 171
    rule 181, 183–4, 186–7
    stages in 171
    strict consensus rule 185
  transfers of resources made within 170
final consumption goods 245
financial crises in US xviii
financial entities, challenge to bank spread through asset securitization 110

financial institutions, activities of xvi
financial scandals xiv–xv
foreign direct investment (FDI) xviii
formal credit 117
formal sector xxi, 156
  agents preference for infrastructure 163
  capital inflow and employment in xxi, 159
  credit to poor 135–6
  impact of size increase in probability of re-election of ruling party 162
  interest rate in xix, 119, 132
  as non-political sector 157
  production carried on without political patronage 157
  production of output in 156
  ruling party's preference for expanding 163
  voters preference for infrastructural investment xxii
  wage rate in 156
Foster, Greer, and Thorbecke (FGT) class of unidimensional, poverty indices 58–9, 70, 76–7
founders' game 178
four-player game with incomplete information 201–10
free trade equilibrium 233
frequent repayments 147
fringe moneylenders
  credit in equilibrium 127
  decision on formal credit amount 120
  first and second order conditions for maximization 121–2

income of 120
fundamental equilibrium 86

game, stages of 119
game-theoretic analyses 31
game-theoretic model of
  interaction xv
game theory 169, 180
GATT-based patent system
  xxv–xxvi, 248, xxv–xxvi
Glass-Steagall Act 110
global climate change 219
global emission level xxiii, 231,
  238
  level of value in new
    equilibrium 230
  North commitment to stabilize
    xxv, 229, 233, 240
  in post technology transfer
    equilibrium 236
  transfer from North to South
    238
global environmental protection
  221
global warming xxiv–xxv, xxiv, xxv,
  219
Godley and Lavoie (G&L) model
  108–13
golden rule capital stock 44–5,
  56
government
  bonds 108
    return on 111
  budget constraint 111
  main function of 18
government deficit, financed by
  freshly-issued bills 111
Government money 110–13
gradual repayment 137, 146–7
Grameen Bank, Bangladesh
  Grameen I programme 136

  success in repayment rates
    135–6
grand corruption 22–4
grand federation xxiii, 168, 175,
  178–9, 181–2
  as equilibrium structures 182–4
'great moderation' era 106
greenhouse gas (GHG) emissions
  218–19, 221, 225, 243
gross payoff function of state 169
group lending/group lending
  schemes 135–6, 138
  encourage assortative matching
    144
  dynamic aspects of 139
  with joint liability xviii

Heckscher-Ohlin framework 221
heterogeneous buyers 194
high return, low risk borrowers
  274–5
high type incumbent bank
  borrowers 274–6
high values of privately informed
  seller 195
'holding together federation' xx
household budget, constraints in
  109–10
human capital transfer 26

illegal transactions 19
income 111
  of dominant moneylender 121
  of fringe moneylender 120
India Drug Manufacturing
  Association (IDMA) xxvi
indirect trade 86, 88–9, 91, 94,
  96–7
Individual Deprivation Gaps
  Function (IDGF) 60–1, 66–8,
  70, 76–7

individuals
  classification into groups 22
  lending 144
industrial organization xi
inflation xi
influence peddling xiv, 23, 26
informal credit market 117, 119
  credit flow to lenders in 118
  entry of new lenders in 118
informal mutual insurance schemes 138
informal sector 156
  equilibrium level of 163
  formal credit supplied to lenders in 117
  interest rate in xix, 118–19, 133
  lenders asymmetric information regarding borrowers' ability to repay loans 118, 133
  people earning their bread, features of 157
  political patronage importance in 157–8
  as political sector 157
  proportion of workers joining ruling party 159–60
  ruling government advantage in xx, 155–6
  voters 160
infrastructure xxi
  increase in output per unit of capital 156–7
  sub-optimal investment in xxii
interior equilibrium 11, 123
interlinked markets 138, 142
international patent rules 248
inter-state barriers relaxation in United States 266
intertemporal efficiency xvi
investment banks 110

investor(s) 25–32, 112, 220
'invisible hand' 6, 16
involuntary unemployment 109
IPCC 219
issue price 108

joint liability lending under micro-finance xix–xx, 137–8, 144
  positive assortative matching 145
  in presence of collusion 142–3
  with simultaneous loans 141

Kautilya 21
Kyoto Protocol 218

laissez-faire economy 110
Lange-Lerner tradition 38
lending
  group lending schemes (*see* group lending schemes)
  individual 144
  joint liability xix–xx, 137, 145
  lending xviii, 112, 118, 143
  profit-maximizing agency xx
  sequential xix, xx, 137, 143, 146–7
large-scale asset purchases (LSAPs) 112
less-developed economies/region 154
  people earning from informal sector in 155
  people politics in 155
  universal franchise in 155–6
less-privileged informal sector, ruling government advantage to keep people in xx
limited-commodity local shop xviii
limit pricing model 267
L-M-R model 24–5, 32

Index

loans xix, xx, xxv, 23, 108–9, 121, 138, 140, 145–7, 269, 271
   under Grameen Bank 136
   group lending 136
   joint liability lending with simultaneous 141–3
   mortgage 107
   recoveries from borrowers 118
local market entry by acquisition 278
Lok Sabha elections in India, voting pattern in 2009 xxii
long-term government bonds xviii, 111, 113
long-term interest rates 112
low return, high risk borrowers 274–6
low type incumbent bank borrowers 274
low values of privately informed seller 195

marginal borrowers 118
market(s)
   demands 14, 253
   entry by generics 250
   housing 196
   -less trading arrangements process 82, 87, 93–5
   matched pairs leaving 197
   microstructure of 193
   role in exchange process 82
   with small numbers of buyers and sellers 193–4
market manager (MM) 8–9
market setup
   advantages of 82–3
   trade through 83
McKenzie, Lionel 4
medical practitioners 251
mergers 278–9

micro-finance institutions (MFIs) xi, xix–xx, 143, 146
   access capital at gross interest 140
   interest rate charged by 139
   maximize borrowers' welfare 140
micro-finance schemes
   innovative schemes role in 137–8
   unusual features of 136
moneylender 118–21, 124–5, 127, 129–30, 147
moral hazard, problem of xxvi, 138, 140, 147, 270
moribund banks 112
mortgage loans 107
multi-commodity market xviii, 84
multi-dimensional poverty index (MPI) xvi, xvi–xvii, 58–9, 68–9, 72
   definition of 73
   mapping of 63
   nature of 76
   rows approach to problem of constructing 78
Multi-dimensional Watts Index 72
multiple verifications problem 24–5
M-Y model 24, 26–7, 38

Nash equilibrium/equilibria xxiii, 8–10, 84, 88, 91–3, 95, 98, 173, 225–6, 230
   federation structure 170
   founders' game 178
   global pollution level at 227
   trading strategies 85–6
Nash pollution level, globally desired level and overshooting of 228–9
national banking markets 266

national income accounts 108
near-zero short-term rate 112
new equilibrium 17, 127, 229–30
non-colluding firm 38
non-elected members of the judiciary 22
non-elected officials (bureaucrats/civil servants) 22
non-income attributes 65–6
non-negative indecomposable square matrices 73
non-trivial equilibrium 123–4
North-South technology transfer 220
null strategy profile (NSP) 30–1

OECD report (1994) xxv
old equilibrium 17
old generation 158, 254
one-stage game 24, 26–7, 31–2, 34–5, 37–8
one-time cost of participating in combined market 96
out-of-circulation drug xxvi, 252
out-of-equilibrium 207
over-accumulation of capital xv–xvi, xviii, 44, 46, 55–6

pair-wise commodity markets xvii–xviii, 86
pair-wise trading post setup xviii, 83, 88
  vs. combined market
    specialized production and diversified consumption 98–9
    specialized production as well as consumption 95–7
Pareto Optimal 15, 142
partial technology transfer 230, 239

partition function 170, 180, 182
partnership plans and federation structure rules 172–3
patented drugs, early withdrawal of xxvi, 249, 251–61
patent rights 261
  demand effect of new drug 254
  drug availability from date it introduced in market 253
  extension of patent period with minor improvements in drugs 259–60
  impact of expiry 250
  introducing new drugs before expiry of needed increases entry costs by innovator 258–9
  sequence of 255
  problems faced by pharmaceutical industry 249–50
peer monitoring by borrowers 139–40
  joint liability lending in presence of collusion 142–3
  joint liability lending with simultaneous loans 141
  sequential lending schemes 143
people politics in less developed region 155
perfect Bayes equilibrium concept 195, 197, 201, 272
Perron-Frobenius theorem for positive square matrices 73, 79
petty corruption 23–4
pharmaceutical industry
  (*see also* patented drugs, early withdrawal of)
  consumers and consumption decision makers in 250

entry on restriction of potential firms 250
first-mover advantage 250
older generation drugs 253
out-of-circulation drug 262
patented drug increases cost of potential entrants 252
patent rights impact on generic products prices 249
Phelps–Koopmans property 46, 48–53, 55
Phelps–Koopmans theorem xvi, 44–7
neoclassical functions 53–5
Pigou-Dalton principle of transfer among the poor 61–2
policy change, detrimental to development of Indian generic industry xxvi
policy prescriptions
designing of 23
types of 32
political freedom xxi, 153–4
political party(ies) 157, 164
political society 155
pollution xxiv, xxv, 221–9, 234–5, 238, 240–1, 243–5
pooling equilibrium 35–6
poor, strategic policy of xxii
population size of workers, in old and young generations 158
positive assortative matching xx, 137–9
post-government employment opportunities (PGEO) 26–7, 34, 36
in one-stage game 37
post-Kyoto agreement/plan 218–19
poverty 66
alleviation xviii
construction for individuals

standard of living 60
in less-developed economies 154
measurement in multidimensional context 57
unidimensional indices of 58
premature democracy, dysfunctional consequences of 154
Prioritization of Attributes under Comonotonicity (PAC) xvi–xvii, 58–9, 66–8, 70–3
private banking 109–10
private equity 108
private information 195–6, 210, 216, 277
about cost structure of bank xxvii, 267–8
borrower 274
privately-known reservation price 194–5
production of goods by developed and underdeveloped country 222–4
production possibility frontier (PPF) 223, 225
productive credit 107
productive state investment 113
profit-maximizing lending agency xx
profits
aggregate 113
in capitalist economy, emergence of 106
entrepreneurial (*see* entrepreneurial profits)
extinguished in equilibrium 110
superstructure of 112
project approval processes after liberalization 24
property rights for ordinary citizens 155

in formal sector 157
  stress on importance of 154
public resources xvii
public space xxii
pure random search process xvii–xviii, 82, 82–3, 88–95

qualified projects, demand of bribe by bureaucrats for 27
qualified regulator 27, 32–8

re-elections xxii, 161–4
regulation rate for each firm 33
relative price discovery 111
relending xix
repayment rates 135, 138
reservation
  income of moneylender 120
  price xxiv, 195
  value xxiv, 196, 198–200, 210
resource constraint of bank 274–5
restrictions on federation structure rules 175–7
revolving doors xv, 26, 32–8
Ricardian model of trade 221, 233
rotation policy 32
ruling government/party
  cares for re-elections xxii
  objective of 163
  probability of re-election due to increase in formal sector size 162
  probability of winning for 160
  wish in democracy with universal franchise xxi
rural credit market 119

scale effect 221, 236, 244–5
scams xiv–xv, 16, 19
Schuman Declaration of 1950 168
second World War 43
sellers xxiv, 87, 95, 102, 195–6, 202–4, 206–7
  equilibrium payoffs in bargaining game 199
  knows reservation prices xxiv
  many 210–11
  markets with small numbers of 193–4
  non-bank 113
  reservation values 198
  single 194
  two privately-informed 196, 211–16
  valuations 198–9
senior public servants, favour to firms during their tenures xv
separating equilibrium 35–6
separation principle (SEP) 182–3, 186
sequence of events in economy 158–9
sequential lending/financing schemes 137, 146–7
  incentivizes peer monitoring 138–43
Shapley value 181
sharing rules 171, 177–8
simultaneous loans 141
single window clearance of policies xv, 32
small/smaller borrowers xix, 109, 118
smallest federation 188
small incumbents 278
social capital 138–9, 147
social choice correspondence (SCC) 9
South country(ies) (*see* underdeveloped (South) country(ies))

specialized production
and diversified consumption
98–9
as well as consumption 95–7
speculative equilibrium 86
Stackelberg leader xix, 118, 125
Stackelberg model of sequential
capacity choices 266
state treasury 21
depletion by officials for
personal gains 22
static joint liability 137, 143
stationary strategies to sustain
equilibrium payoffs 206–8
strategic repayment game 138
strict consensus rule 176–7 (*see also*
federation, structure of)
strong incumbents 268, 273, 275,
278
strong Nash equilibrium (SNE)
174, 178, 186
criticism against 182–3
subgame perfect equilibrium
125–33
superadditivity property (SUP)
182, 187, 189
super market xviii
supply 109, 112, 250
inherent in 107
of institutional credit xix, 119
matching of demand in market
4
surplus of wage earners and rentiers
111

technology transfer xxiv, xxv, 245
under Autarky 230–3, 243
CDM role North-South
technology transfer 220
effective in reducing pollution
level 241

feature of 219
under free trade 233–43
international trade plays to
effects of 220–1
issue and its interaction with
pollution differs 221
in large projects 220
pollution-mitigating effect of
221
probability of 220
Ricardian model causes
mitigation of GHG
emissions 221
three-stage game, solving for
121–33
trading equilibrium. 233–8, 240,
xxv
trading partner 81, 83–4
agents search for 82
complementary xvii
trading post setup xviii, 83, 87
and random search 88–95
trading through and its impact
87–8
vs. market-less trading
arrangements 93–5
trading process 83, 85
Transparency International (TI) 22
Treatise 107
'T-transformation' matrix 62
two-player bargaining game 196–7,
200–1, 204

underdeveloped (South)
country(ies)
acceptance of technology
transfer of North, conditions
for 237
advantage in production of
relatively less pollution-
intensive good 1 xxiv–xxv

conditions to accept technology transfer by 242–3
consumption of goods at international prices 233–4, 240
equilibrium consumption levels of 234
global welfare function maximization 228–9
goods production in 222–4
indirect welfare in post transfer equilibrium 236–7
technology transfer impact on xxv
terms-of-trade effect 244
trading equilibrium 233
utility function for consumption of goods 224–5
undersupply/undersupplying 12, 15, 19
UNDP human poverty indices 69
UN Framework Convention on Climate Change (UNFCCC) 218–19, 221
Article 4 of 222
unanimous principle 173–7, 182, 186
unidimensional poverty index (UPI) 69
Uniform Pigou-Dalton Majorization (UPDM) 61–3
unique equilibrium 37, 161, 170, 199–201
universal franchise xxi, 155–6
universal voting rights 155
unproductive credit 107
unqualified projects, demand of bribe by bureaucrats for 27
unqualified regulator 33, 35, 37
Uruguay Round of Multilateral Trade Negotiations 248

vertical linkage between formal and informal credit markets 117
Chaudhuri and Dastidar (CD) model (*see* Chaudhuri and Dastidar (CD) model)
development economists concern regarding efficacy of policy 133
effects on borrowing terms 118
subgame perfect equilibrium (*see* subgame perfect equilibrium)
violation of property rights xxii

wage bill (WB) 108–9
Walrasian auctioneer, notion of 178
Walrasian economy 82
weak consensus rule 176 (*see also* federation, structure of)
weak incumbents 278
welfare comparisons
of agents 92–3
trading post *vs* market-less trading arrangements 93–5
welfare economics 5–8
welfare state, strategic policy of xxii
without loss of generality (WLOG) 84, 96, 202, 211
World Intellectual Property Organization (WIPO) 248
World Trade Organization (WTO) 248

young generation 158

zero-bound interest rate problem 112
zero market shares of older generation drugs 253
zero-trade equilibrium 15